THE FIRST ENGLISH TRANSLATIONS OF MOLIÈRE
DRAMA IN FLUX 1663-1732

LEGENDA

LEGENDA is the Modern Humanities Research Association's book imprint for new research in the Humanities. Founded in 1995 by Malcolm Bowie and others within the University of Oxford, Legenda has always been a collaborative publishing enterprise, directly governed by scholars. The Modern Humanities Research Association (MHRA) joined this collaboration in 1998, became half-owner in 2004, in partnership with Maney Publishing and then Routledge, and has since 2016 been sole owner. Titles range from medieval texts to contemporary cinema and form a widely comparative view of the modern humanities, including works on Arabic, Catalan, English, French, German, Greek, Italian, Portuguese, Russian, Spanish, and Yiddish literature. Editorial boards and committees of more than 60 leading academic specialists work in collaboration with bodies such as the Society for French Studies, the British Comparative Literature Association and the Association of Hispanists of Great Britain & Ireland.

The MHRA encourages and promotes advanced study and research in the field of the modern humanities, especially modern European languages and literature, including English, and also cinema. It aims to break down the barriers between scholars working in different disciplines and to maintain the unity of humanistic scholarship. The Association fulfils this purpose through the publication of journals, bibliographies, monographs, critical editions, and the MHRA Style Guide, and by making grants in support of research. Membership is open to all who work in the Humanities, whether independent or in a University post, and the participation of younger colleagues entering the field is especially welcomed.

ALSO PUBLISHED BY THE ASSOCIATION

Critical Texts
Tudor and Stuart Translations • *New Translations* • *European Translations*
MHRA Library of Medieval Welsh Literature

MHRA Bibliographies
Publications of the Modern Humanities Research Association

The Annual Bibliography of English Language & Literature
Austrian Studies
Modern Language Review
Portuguese Studies
The Slavonic and East European Review
Working Papers in the Humanities
The Yearbook of English Studies

www.mhra.org.uk
www.legendabooks.com

TRANSCRIPT

Transcript publishes books about all kinds of imagining across languages, media and cultures: translations and versions, inter-cultural and multi-lingual writing, illustrations and musical settings, adaptation for theatre, film, TV and new media, creative and critical responses. We are open to studies of any combination of languages and media, in any historical moments, and are keen to reach beyond Legenda's traditional focus on modern European languages to embrace anglophone and world cultures and the classics. We are interested in innovative critical approaches: we welcome not only the most rigorous scholarship and sharpest theory, but also modes of writing that stretch or cross the boundaries of those discourses.

Editorial Committee
Chair: Matthew Reynolds (Oxford)
Robin Kirkpatrick (Cambridge)
Laura Marcus (Oxford)
Patrick McGuinness (Oxford)
Ben Morgan (Oxford)
Mohamed-Salah Omri (Oxford)
Tanya Pollard (CUNY)
Yopie Prins (Michigan)

Advisory Board
Jason Gaiger (Oxford)
Alessandro Grilli (Pisa)
Marina Grishakova (Tartu)
Martyn Harry (Oxford)
Linda Hutcheon (Toronto)
Calin-Andrei Mihailescu (London, Ontario)
Wen-Chin Ouyang (SOAS)
Clive Scott (UEA)
Ali Smith
Marina Warner (Birkbeck)
Shane Weller (Kent)
Stefan Willer (Berlin)

Managing Editor
Dr Graham Nelson
41 Wellington Square, Oxford OX1 2JF, UK

www.legendabooks.com/series/transcript

TRANSCRIPT

1. *Adapting the Canon: Mediation, Visualisation, Interpretation*, edited by Ann Lewis and Silke Arnold-de Simine
2. *Adapted Voices: Transpositions of Céline's Voyage au bout de la nuit and Queneau's Zazie dans le métro*, by Armelle Blin-Rolland
3. *Zola and the Art of Television: Adaptation, Recreation, Translation*, by Kate Griffiths
4. *Comparative Encounters between Artaud, Michaux and the Zhuangzi: Rationality, Cosmology and Ethics*, by Xiaofan Amy Li
5. *Minding Borders: Resilient Divisions in Literature, the Body and the Academy*, edited by Nicola Gardini, Adriana Jacobs, Ben Morgan, Mohamed-Salah Omri and Matthew Reynolds
6. *Memory Across Borders: Nabokov, Perec, Chamoiseau*, by Sara-Louise Cooper
7. *Erotic Literature in Adaptation and Translation*, edited by Johannes D. Kaminski
8. *Translating Petrarch's Poetry: L'Aura del Petrarca from the Quattrocento to the 21st Century*, edited by Carole Birkan-Berz, Guillaume Coatalen and Thomas Vuong
9. *Making Masud Khan: Psychoanalysis, Empire and Modernist Culture*, by Benjamin Poore
10. *Prismatic Translation*, edited by Matthew Reynolds
11. *The Patient, the Impostor and the Seducer: Medieval European Literature in Hebrew*, by Tovi Bibring
12. *Reading Dante and Proust by Analogy*, by Julia Caterina Hartley
13. *The First English Translations of Molière: Drama in Flux 1663-1732*, by Suzanne Jones
14. *After Clarice: Reading Lispector's Legacy in the Twenty-First Century*, edited by Adriana X. Jacobs and Claire Williams
15. *Uruguayan Theatre in Translation: Theory and Practice*, by Sophie Stevens
16. *Hamlet Translations: Prisms of Cultural Encounters across the Globe*, edited by Márta Minier and Lily Kahn
17. *The Foreign Connection: Writings on Poetry, Art and Translation*, by Jamie McKendrick
18. *Poetics, Performance and Politics in French and Italian Renaissance Comedy*, by Lucy Rayfield

The First English Translations of Molière

Drama in Flux 1663-1732

Suzanne Jones

LEGENDA

Transcript 13
Modern Humanities Research Association
2020

Published by Legenda
an imprint of the Modern Humanities Research Association
Salisbury House, Station Road, Cambridge CB1 2LA

ISBN 978-1-78188-839-1 (HB)
ISBN 978-1-78188-840-7 (PB)

First published 2020

All rights reserved. No part of this publication may be reproduced or disseminated or transmitted in any form or by any means, electronic, mechanical, photocopying, recording or otherwise, or stored in any retrieval system, or otherwise used in any manner whatsoever without written permission of the copyright owner, except in accordance with the provisions of the Copyright, Designs and Patents Act 1988, or under the terms of a licence permitting restricted copying issued in the UK by the Copyright Licensing Agency Ltd, Saffron House, 6–10 Kirby Street, London EC1N 8TS, England, or in the USA by the Copyright Clearance Center, 222 Rosewood Drive, Danvers MA 01923. Application for the written permission of the copyright owner to reproduce any part of this publication must be made by email to legenda@mhra.org.uk.

Disclaimer: Statements of fact and opinion contained in this book are those of the author and not of the editors or the Modern Humanities Research Association. The publisher makes no representation, express or implied, in respect of the accuracy of the material in this book and cannot accept any legal responsibility or liability for any errors or omissions that may be made.

Trademark notice: Product or corporate names may be trademarks or registered trademarks, and are used only for identification and explanation without intent to infringe.

© Modern Humanities Research Association 2020

Copy-Editor: Charlotte Brown

CONTENTS

Acknowledgements		ix
Note on Presentation		xi
Introduction		1

PART I: EARLY ENGLISH TRANSLATIONS OF MOLIÈRE: THEORY AND FORM

1	Dramatic Theory and Plotting	17
2	Translation Theory and Paratext	41
3	Rhythm, Rhyme, and Song	59

PART II: LEXICAL CHOICES AND RECONTEXTUALIZATIONS

4	Cuckoldry and Gallantry	85
5	Zealotry and Hypocrisy	105
6	Malady and Quackery	127
7	Bourgeoisie and Urbanity	157
	Conclusion	175
	Appendix	183
	Bibliography	191
	Index	201

For my parents

ACKNOWLEDGEMENTS

In developing this book from my doctoral thesis I owe a debt of gratitude to many people.

I would especially like to thank my mentor, Michael Hawcroft; his unerring guidance and generosity have been invaluable in my academic life. I am also grateful to Tiffany Stern for her supervisorial advice during my doctoral research, and to my DPhil examiners, Marie-Claude Canova-Green and Richard Parish, who recommended I publish the thesis in book form.

The early stages of research were enriched by interaction with the group attending the Oxford Early Modern French Research Seminar; during later stages of book editing I was thankful for the encouragement of colleagues in the School of Modern Languages and Cultures at Durham University. I would like to record my appreciation of such nurturing academic environments, including an acknowledgement to Tom Wynn for the career support he has offered me.

My sincere thanks go to the editorial board of Legenda, particularly to the Managing Editor, Graham Nelson, whose patience and assistance have allowed me to follow my own, often uneven, rhythm of publication preparation. Many thanks to Charlotte Wathey for her close attention to detail in the copy-editing process, and to the manuscript reader for a comprehensive and insightful report.

My family and friends have, as ever, been a tremendous source of support. My heartfelt gratitude is due to Alejandro, whose optimism and faith in me bridged a long distance, to my sister Diane, and to my long-suffering parents.

s.J., Oxford, August 2020

Frontispiece to Molière's *Sganarelle ou le Cocu imaginaire* (*The Imaginary Cuckold*), in *The Select Comedies of Mr. de Molière* (1732), after William Hogarth, etched by John Vandergucht (photo: Metropolitan Museum of Art)

NOTE ON PRESENTATION

Most references to Molière's plays in French and several references to the first performances and variant texts in French are to the Pléiade edition, *Œuvres complètes*, ed. by Georges Forestier and Claude Bourqui, 2 vols (Paris: Gallimard, 2010). References to plays in verse take the form, for example, 'II.4.815; *OC*, II, 157' (meaning Act 2, sc. 4, l. 815; vol. 2, p. 157). In the case of single-act plays the references take the form '6.190; *OC*, I, 50' (meaning sc. 6, l. 190; vol. 1, p. 50). References to plays in prose take the form 'II.4; *OC*, II, 283' (meaning Act 2, sc. 4; vol. 2, p. 283).

In most cases it has not been possible to trace the specific French editions of Molière from which the early modern translators worked. The 2010 Pléiade edition prioritizes the first authorized single print editions of Molière's works in French, so they correlate with the first English translations. One exception is the source-text for a late seventeenth-century manuscript translation of *Le Malade imaginaire* by James Wright (Folger Shakespeare Library MS V.b.220); Wright translated from an unauthorized early edition, either *Le Malade imaginaire, comédie en trois actes meslés de danses et de musique, Suivant la Copie imprimée a Paris* ([Amsterdam : Daniel Elzevir], 1674) or *Le Malade imaginaire, comédie en trois actes mélez de danses et de musique* (Amsterdam: Daniel Elzevir [but France], 1674).

Select Comedies of Mr. de Molière, in French and English, trans. by Henry Baker, James Miller and Martin Clare, 8 vols (London: printed for J. Watts, 1732) reproduces the French of *Les Œuvres de Monsieur de Molière*, 8 vols (Paris: printed by Denys Thierry, Claude Barbin, and Pierre Trabouillet, 1682).

All references to the English translations of Molière's plays under analysis are to the earliest printed editions. I give a full footnote reference to a translation the first time it is quoted and further references are given in the text.

Some references from the paratextual material of early modern plays are to modern edited works because they include helpful glosses.

Seventeenth- and early eighteenth-century English spelling is erratic. I have retained the original spellings in all quotations from early modern editions. I correct only missing accents from play-titles in the text. Thus the title *The Damoiselles a la mode* is spelled *The Damoiselles à la mode*. It should be noted that Molière's name is spelled without a grave accent in all the translators' prefaces quoted. The spellings of the names of other authors and the punctuation of titles follow the editions to which I refer.

Titles to plays in both French and English are frequently followed by dates of first performance (or publication in the case of print translations). This is to remind the reader of the time between first appearance and translation. Some dates of first performance for English translations are in the form, for example, '1704/5' to acknowledge the Julian calendar system that was used in Britain until 1752 and to avoid confusion with publication dates.

INTRODUCTION

In the mid-seventeenth century civil wars raged in both England and France and beyond the seismic effects on the political and social stability of the respective nations, the strife also had an impact, albeit to differing degrees, on English and French theatre. On 9 February 1648, as the second phase of the English Civil War between Parliamentarians and Royalists broke out, an ordinance was passed demanding the demolition of theatres, the arrest of any players found to be flouting the ban on public performance that had been in place since 1642, and severe fines for any spectators; although political pamphlets were read aloud in illicit gatherings, the climate in Britain was not conducive to theatrical invention. Later in 1648, across the channel in France, the first phase of the Fronde, a series of revolts against the policies of the Queen Regent Anne of Austria and Cardinal Mazarin was underway and causing rippling effects emanating from the Paris *parlement*. An itinerant group of French actors who had stayed in towns as far away from the capital as Bordeaux and Toulouse the previous year now dipped out of records as their patron, the duc d'Épernon, was facing rebellion in Bordeaux owing to his allegiance to Mazarin. In 1649 the actors resumed regular performances in south-western France but in 1650 the second phase of the Fronde saw the revolt of several nobles and civil unrest intensified around Bordeaux, leading the actors to seek new patronage from Languedoc officials. The actors' survival courted controversy from disaffected provincial communities who saw expenditure on theatre as a frivolous waste. Nevertheless by the end of the Fronde in 1653 the troupe was supported by the pardoned prince de Conti and one of the actors, Jean-Baptiste Poquelin, known as Molière (1622–73), became the new head of the group.

Although the second phase of the Fronde in France had led to a temporary closure of Paris theatre and significantly reduced production, the hiatus was relatively short-lived. It was a period in which Molière was cutting his teeth as a comic playwright in the provinces, not only creating his own farces but also improving his managerial skills (his early attempt at leading the Parisian Illustre Théâtre between 1643 and 1645 had quickly met with financial problems). Meanwhile the English Civil War had come to an end in 1651, but the theatres remained shut during the Commonwealth period under Oliver Cromwell. Towards the end of the interregnum, however, some made tentative steps towards reintroducing theatrical performances to Britain. In the mid-1650s, for example, Sir William D'Avenant, former Emissary to France, started holding entertainments at Rutland House and, having curried favour with Cromwell, he put on the anti-Spanish musical propagandist piece *The Cruelty of the Spaniards in Peru* (1658) in the Cockpit Theatre near Drury Lane. So by the late 1650s theatre was gradually making a come-back in England and once it became clear that the monarchy was to be restored in 1660 there was a rush to re-establish the drama scene.

A month after Oliver Cromwell's death in September 1658, Molière made his return to Paris and performed before Louis XIV at the Louvre. His troupe, which had secured the patronage of the King's younger brother, Philippe d'Orléans (known as 'Monsieur'), performed Pierre Corneille's *Nicomède* followed by one of Molière's farces that had proved popular in the provinces, *Le Docteur amoureux*. Louis XIV allowed the actors to use the Théâtre du Petit-Bourbon, alternating their performance days with the Italian *commedia dell'arte* group which was already installed. Given that the Troupe de Monsieur had arrived in Paris part-way through the theatrical year, the rest of the 1658–59 season included only two Molière provincial farces, *L'Étourdi* and *Le Dépit amoureux*, but the following season the repertoire was significantly expanded and included Molière's first satirical comedy, *Les Précieuses ridicules*. The 1660–61 season saw the successful one-act comedy *Sganarelle ou le Cocu imaginaire*, as well as a big move; in October 1660 the Petit Bourbon theatre was demolished to make way for a new wing of the Louvre palace, so Louis XIV granted the troupe the use of the Palais-Royal theatre complete with renovations. This was the home of Molière's actors for the rest of his life as he became the most prolific seventeenth-century French comic playwright within the short expanse of just fifteen years. His works, however, were to live on not only within, but also beyond, France.

The Troupe de Monsieur went from strength to strength as public performances were supplemented by court entertainments for which Molière collaborated with composers such as Lully and later Charpentier to create the *comédie-ballet* genre. Owing to this swift success and the competitive environment of the Paris theatre world, rival companies set out to criticize; condemnation was especially intense from the Troupe royale based at the Hôtel de Bourgogne, though the Théâtre du Marais was also threatened by the competition. Molière's creation of *L'École des femmes* (1662) caused a backlash for its supposed impiety and suggestive comedy, prompting a fierce literary quarrel led initially by the writer Jean Donneau de Visé. Molière responded in the most penetrating way he could; by staging further plays: *La Critique de L'École des femmes*, in which fictional spectators of the play discuss their opinions of it, and *L'Impromptu de Versailles* in which the actors, playing themselves, satirize detractors of the play as well as the acting style of the rival Troupe royale.

It seemed, however, that the more controversy Molière inspired the more readily the King supported him; in 1663 the dramatist received one of the first royal *gratifications*, a financial reward which was renewed annually. In addition to public performances at the Palais-Royal theatre, Molière's troupe frequently played at court for special occasions. One of the most well-known of these events was *Les Plaisirs de l'île enchantée* (May 1664), the first spectacular entertainment held at Versailles. Amongst the plays performed was a three-act version of the controversial *Le Tartuffe*. This comedy centring on religious hypocrisy led to a five-year battle between the playwright and various Church figures before the play was finally authorized for regular public performance. Though the King's hands were tied to some degree in the *Tartuffe* controversy, Molière forged on and presented another contentious play in the form of *Dom Juan* in 1665, though this piece was censored. Nevertheless the same year the King transferred the patronage of Molière's troupe from his brother to himself, the company became known as the Troupe du Roi, and they received an annual subsidy of 6,000 *livres* in return for rapidly commissioned performances at court. Soon after this development Molière created the successful *comédie-ballet*, *L'Amour médecin*, and kept up a steady stream of new plays throughout the 1660s and early 1670s, including *Le Misanthrope* (1666), *Le Médecin malgré lui* (1666), *Amphitryon* (1668), *Monsieur de Pourceaugnac* (1669), *Le Bourgeois gentilhomme* (1670), and *Les Femmes savantes* (1672). Molière was such a tireless writer and actor that illness caught up with him and he died after the fourth performance of *Le Malade imaginaire* on 17 February 1673.

While at first glance it might seem that the mid-seventeenth-century theatrical worlds of Britain and France were travelling on different courses and rotating at different speeds, their orbits did intersect. Ten years prior to Molière's death one of his early plays from the Petit Bourbon theatre appeared on the English stage in translation. William D'Avenant, the first impresario to have tested the Cromwellian waters with musical theatrical pieces in the 1650s, came to combine them into a strange hybrid called *The Playhouse to be Let* (1663), in which a translation of Molière's *Sganarelle ou le Cocu imaginaire* features as Act II. The preceding upheaval of the Civil War was not an incidental backdrop to the influx of French plays into English theatre during the Restoration. The people who were dispersed and in flux as a result of the wars were those who drew on their experience abroad in reshaping the theatre. The Restoration court, for example, was heavily influenced by French court fashions; Charles II had joined his exiled French mother in Paris for two years during the English Civil War, and for almost three years during Cromwell's rule. Charles's sister Henrietta, who had been in exile in France from a young age, married Louis XIV's brother in 1661. Furthermore, English dramatists such as William D'Avenant and probably George Etherege had spent some time in France during the Civil War period and a young William Wycherley had been there during the interregnum. Given the need for new dramatic material to be pumped into the restored theatre, it is unsurprising that dramatists looked across the Channel for inspiration as well as source texts.

With the Restoration came the opportunity to see French troupes act in London. There was a group of French actors at the Cockpit Theatre, Drury Lane, as early as 1661, and one company of actors who performed at court was given permission to bring over scenery, costumes, and stage properties from France.[1] Unfortunately, records do not show which plays were performed, but John Dryden was sceptical about whether English audiences were aware of what they were watching. In the prologue to *Arviragus Reviv'd* he describes the popular frenzy occasioned by the visit of French actors in late 1672 and early 1673:

> And therefore, *Messieurs*, if you'll do us grace,
> Send Lacquies early to preserve your Place

> We dare not on your Priviledge intrench,
> Or ask you why you like 'em, they are *French*.
> Therefore some go with Courtesie exceeding,
> Neither to Hear nor See, but show their Breeding,
> Each Lady striving to outlaugh the rest,
> To make it seem they understood the Jest:
> Their Countrymen come in, and nothing pay,
> To teach us *English* where to clap the play.[2]

For all that Dryden's tone is cynical, there seems to have been a gap in the market for English translations of French plays.

This book focuses on the first English translations of Molière, but it is important to identify that the drive to make use of the French comic playwright's works was part of a wider and varied burst of what could be called 'adaptive energy'.[3] Not only did dramatists translate and adapt French works, but they also looked further into Europe to Spain and Italy.[4] Nor did their gaze settle solely on contemporary or near-contemporary foreign works; the period witnessed several reworkings not only of Greco-Roman classics but also of Shakespeare in acted and operatic forms.[5] Some popular Jacobean plays were also revived for performance at topical historical junctures.[6] The reappropriation of existing plays was not merely an expedient way to revivify the theatre; the politics of adaptation was fundamental to drama of the period. As Michael Dobson notes:

> It is perhaps most useful to examine the period's revivals and adaptations alike as experiments in negotiating the political position of the restored theatres, and attempts to find new genres which might flourish within them. Publicly reviving pre-war drama at all, and with it by implication the Royalist culture of the Caroline court, made a conspicuous comment about the defeat of the Commonwealth in 1660.[7]

Even translations could act as revivals with political implications. In 1663, for example, Katherine Philips completed a translation of *La Mort de Pompée* (1642) by Molière's elder contemporary Pierre Corneille. The Roman subject is the civil war between Caesar and Pompey which ended with the victory of Caesar and a period of peace. It was no coincidence that Philips chose to present the play in English soon after the restoration of the monarchy, and, given Cromwell's controversial policies in Ireland, it was even more resonant that it was performed at the Smock Alley Theatre in Dublin. Philips also went on to translate Corneille's *Horace* (1640) but this had to be completed by Sir John Denham following her death from smallpox in 1664. The works of Pierre Corneille's tragedian contemporary, Jean Racine, appeared in English from the 1670s onwards, though the peak translating period for Racine was the early eighteenth century.

Despite the range of authors undergoing intensive adaptation and reworking from the 1660s onwards, Molière's works appear more frequently than those of any other dramatist in English translation throughout the period following the reopening of the theatres. The concentration of Molière translations was partly due to the famous satirical impact of plays such as *L'École des femmes* and *Le Tartuffe* (1669) and partly due to the playwright's prolific dramatic output. The King's Company, founded by

Thomas Killigrew in 1660, was initially granted rights to a greater number of pre-Civil War plays for their repertory than Sir William D'Avenant's troupe, the Duke's Company. A royal warrant suggests that D'Avenant's request to match the rival company by reviving pre-war plays was connected to his proposition that he should 'reform' them and 'make them fit for the Company of actors under his Command'.[8] Thus a certain spirit of adaptation was associated with the Duke's Company from its inception, and D'Avenant soon employed John Dryden to help him in his endeavour. Owing to this adapting vein, between 1663 and 1682 more translations of Molière's plays were performed by the Duke's Company than by the King's. A cross-section of Duke's Company plays shows the breadth of interest shown in the French playwright. Dryden reworked a translation of *L'Étourdi* (1653) into *Sir Martin Mar-all* (1667), Thomas Shadwell translated elements of *Les Fâcheux* (1661) and *Le Misanthrope* in *The Sullen Lovers* (1668), John Caryl translated sections of *L'École des femmes* in *Sir Salomon; or, The Cautious Coxcomb* (1670), Thomas Betterton converted *George Dandin* (1668) into *The Amorous Widow; or, Wanton Wife* (1670?), and Edward Ravenscroft blended *Monsieur de Pourceaugnac* (1669) and *Le Bourgeois gentilhomme* (1670) in *The Citizen Turn'd Gentleman* (1672), reusing elements of his translations in *The Careless Lovers* (1673) and *Scaramouch a Philosopher, Harlequin a School-Boy, Bravo, Merchand and Magician* (1677). The King's Company, however, was not immune to Molière's influence; they offered Charles Sidley's loose adaptation of *L'École des femmes*, *The Mulberry-garden* (1668), John Lacy's *The Dumb Lady; or, The Farriar Made Physician* (1669), and Matthew Medbourne's *Tartuffe; or, The French Puritan* (1670).

When the companies were forced to merge in 1682, the so-called United Company, performing at the Theatre Royal, Drury Lane, under the actor-dramatist Thomas Betterton, presented several translations of Molière's plays, though the reduced level of competition led to a limited number of plays overall. Christopher Rich took over in 1693 but caused a rift that impelled Betterton and other actors to form a new group at Lincoln's Inn Fields. Rivalry once again triggered the production of several translations, including a version of *Monsieur de Pourceaugnac* entitled *Squire Trelooby* put on at Lincoln's Inn Fields in 1704, and translations of Molière's medical satires at Rich's theatre at Drury Lane. The renewed competition between the companies goes some way towards explaining why there were several repeated translations of the same Molière play as translators sought to show that their approach had diverged from those of their rivals.

Disquiet amongst managers of the Drury Lane theatre contributed to a dip in production around 1710, but interest in printing Molière translations grew and the first collected works in English appeared in 1714. Following this, numerous adaptations of Molière appeared at the Theatre Royal, Drury Lane, now under the management of Colley Cibber. Though the sometimes volatile conditions of Restoration theatre occasionally threatened the production of Molière translations in English, these same conditions helped to promote experimentation in translation for the stage and a simultaneous drive to preserve the texts in print. The present study marks the shift from a focus on using the French plays to boost the reopened theatres to a dual approach where evolving translation practices were supplemented by the publication of print editions of Molière in English. This move in the early eighteenth century mirrored Molière's own ambitions to publish a complete works edition of his plays; in 1671 he had taken out a *privilège* ostensibly for an illustrated edition of all of his plays, but also allowing him rights to publications of single as well as collective works. The *privilège*, however, was invalidated by the Communauté des librairies, which refused to register it and so the illustrated complete works did not appear until 1682, nearly ten years after the author's death. It was this edition that was emulated fifty years later in the 1732 *Select Comedies of Monsieur de Molière*.

Over the seven decades covered in this book, it was not only changes in the dramatic taste of the audiences that determined the translation methods adopted. There is also a correlation between the professional status of the translator and his or her translation style. Actor-dramatists such as Matthew Medbourne tend towards translation mixed with conspicuous adaptation that showcases several acting roles. Prolific writers such as John Dryden tend towards freer adaptations with small sections of close translation. The collected translated works of the early eighteenth century were more literal translations because they were produced by professionals who considered themselves men of letters. The dramatist's career-stage also has a bearing on translation method. Writers such as Dryden, Thomas Shadwell, and Edward Ravenscroft relied on inspiration from Molière earlier in their careers, as they were still making their names, though Dryden returned to Molière at a late stage when he produced *Amphitryon* (1690). In order to remind the reader of the relationship between translation style and contextual factors I include a footnote of biographical information each time I first analyse the approach of a translator within the following chapters.

The wealth of Molière translations outlined above has not gone unnoticed by literary critics, but their studies have limitations. The first survey work that recorded the translations of Molière's plays into English did so in reference to plagiarism, even where the translator or adaptor acknowledges a 'debt' to Molière. Gerard Langbaine's 1691 *Account of the English Dramatic Poets* helped to establish the prevailing idea that throughout the Restoration the French works were simply stolen and disguised.[9] A glut of studies at the beginning of the twentieth century looked for the presence or the absence of Molière in English dramatists' contributions to a genre known as 'Restoration Comedy'.[10] The *OED*'s earliest record of the usage of the term 'Restoration Comedy' dates from 1866, and the general definition is loose: 'a style of drama which flourished in London after the Restoration in 1660, typically having a complicated plot marked by wit, cynicism and licentiousness'. The classification of comedy written after the Restoration can be helpful in terms of tracking changes in theatrical taste, but it can also be limiting, particularly when assessing the English reception of French drama. The problem with the label 'Restoration Comedy' is that it can be used without making a clear distinction between its definition as satirical comedy of manners and its definition as comedy written during the Restoration period (a time span which is difficult to demarcate).[11]

The treatment of Restoration Comedy as one homogenous genre is problematic because it leads to conclusions that do not take into account the great variety of ways in which existing plays were translated or adapted during the years following the reopening of the theatres. Louis Charlanne presents the idea that there was one dominant type of comedy in Restoration England that remained impervious to the influence of Molière:

> Par la variéte et vérité des caractères, Molière aurait pû empêcher les Anglais de tomber dans la peinture uniforme et exclusive des défauts, des mœurs, des folies, des hommes de ce temps-là [...] jamais peut-être, en aucun temps et en aucun pays, on ne vit défiler sur la scène, plus fidèlement reproduits, les débauchés, les viveurs, les courtisanes qui formaient surtout le monde de la Restauration [...] ce n'étaient pas les types, c'étaient des portraits dont, à tout instant, on pouvait coudoyer les originaux. Et c'est à cette peinture que les comiques de la Restauration ont surtout excellé.[12]

The use of the word 'surtout' in this assessment, however, points to the idea that there were types of comedy beyond the 'peinture uniforme' of Restoration Comedy and suggests some small acknowledgement of theatrical variety. Nevertheless, Restoration Comedy was treated as a fixed genre in several other early twentieth-century studies of Molière in England. Dudley H. Miles for example, argued that 'Restoration Comedy, taken as a type, owed its inception and found its development in an imitation of the comedy of manners of Molière'.[13] His bold statement was bound to provoke strong critical reaction. John Wilcox argued against the influence of Molière in *The Relation of Molière to Restoration Comedy*, stating that 'an investigation' was required to give 'accurate information regarding the exact nature and extent of each borrowing from Molière in Restoration comedy' that could 'appraise these borrowings judiciously as contributions to the development of each author using him, and show clearly the extent and limits of his influence on the English comedy of manners'.[14] Wilcox duly obliged and concluded that 'there is [...] no contradiction in the final decision that, though [Molière's] plays were often used, he made no significant contribution to the type of comedy we associate with the Restoration' (p. 200). A broader examination of the type, or rather types, of comedy that existed following the Restoration, accommodates an assessment and analysis of the ways that Molière's plays were first anglicized.

My work is inspired by the changing tide of criticism in the later twentieth century, which moved away from the sweeping assessments of influence studies. Frank J. Kearful offers a detailed summary of the earlier critical works of Molière in Restoration England, observing that:

> Their findings are predetermined not only by their methods but their conceptions of what is 'essentially' the form, tone, and spirit of Molière's comedy, as well as the form, tone, and spirit of Restoration comedy. As there is even less agreement on this question concerning his English contemporaries than there is concerning Molière, a definitive study of Molière's influence on Restoration comedy is hardly to be expected.[15]

Kearful posits the idea of reframing inquiries about the presence of Molière on the Restoration English stage, but does make 'tentative' accounts of Molière's 'creative influence' on William Wycherley (p. 207). Harold C. Knutson takes an original comparative approach in *The Triumph of Wit*, in which he analyses 'the common traits' of Molière's comedy and Restoration comedy to show 'that the two comic traditions share much more than had hitherto been assumed'.[16] But both Molière's corpus and comedy from the Restoration period were characterized by experimentation, sometimes responding to convention and sometimes innovating, so neither can be described as a tradition with certain traits. How, then, can the relationship between Molière's comedies in French and contemporaneous and near-contemporaneous comedies in English be approached from an analytical perspective?

With the advent of translation studies in the late twentieth century came the view that the act of translating was a type of literary practice in itself. Alongside theoretical works, several bibliographies devoted to translated works have been published. Early translations and adaptations of Molière are recorded in *The Oxford History of Literary Translation in English* and *The Oxford Guide to Literary Translation in English*.[17] In *The Encyclopedia of Literary Translation into English* Noël Peacock acknowledges that Molière was translated for the English stage, but emphasizes that adaptation of his plays was central. The observation that 'only four renderings of Molière's plays by Restoration dramatists are generally accepted as translations' is distinctly conservative, and Peacock points out that 'even in the so-called translations, liberties were taken in Molière's texts'.[18] It could be argued, however, that liberties are necessarily taken in any act of translation: the boundaries between translation and adaptation are blurred. This is likely to be the reason why earlier twentieth-century critics avoided assessing translations of Molière and instead focused on the French playwright's 'influence', though this approach led to biased conclusions that pigeonholed plays too inflexibly and consequently misrepresented an inventive process in which theatre production, translation, and adaptation coincided. Critics have regarded dramatic translation with unease because it is prone to looser, more spontaneous alteration than monumental editions of classical works. But to categorize the first translations of Molière too rigidly is to disregard the frequency with which — and variety of ways in which — the French playwright was absorbed into English. A flexible notion of translation can instead offer new insights into the way Molière's works gained new audiences in England in the late seventeenth and early eighteenth centuries.

In recent years some critics have acknowledged the multidisciplinary nature of translation by creating new labels for the practice. The French-Canadian theatre director Michel Garneau, for example, coined the term 'tradaptation' to refer to his translations of Shakespeare in Québécois produced from 1978.[19] One way in which the English- and French-compatible portmanteau is helpful when considering the first translations of Molière is that it is intended to enact a blurring of the distinction between the processes of translation and adaptation. The term, however, has since been most commonly associated with postcolonialism. Denis Salter, for example, writes that

> Tradaptations should be exercises in radical contingency, responsible only for the particular historical moment in which they attempt to decolonize and reinterrogate the Shakespearean text. They should vanish once their particular historical moment has passed and new tradaptations should take their place.[20]

This observation correlates with the ephemeral nature of some repeated translations of the same Molière play in the late seventeenth and early eighteenth centuries, as translators navigated the radical changes in British politics following the Restoration, including the Popish Plot, the Exclusion Crisis, the Glorious Revolution, the Acts of Union, and the start of Hanoverian rule. But owing to its neological origin in the postcolonial context of Quebec the term *tradaptation* has assumed a politicized connotation which does not gel with the varied and often organically developed or expedient techniques of Molière's first translators. Furthermore, *tradaptation* is frequently associated with radical re-perceptions of so-called 'classics'. Writing about Jatinder Verma's self-defined *tradaptations* of Molière's *Tartuffe* (Tara Arts, 1990) and *Le Bourgeois gentilhomme* (Tara Arts, 1996) set in Mughal India, Derrick Cameron claims that *tradaptation* 'is a wholesale re-working and re-thinking of the original text, as well as its translation and/or translocation into a new, non-European, aesthetic context'.[21] But the gulf between Molière's works and the social environment of the first audiences of their English translations was not so great and in fact many translators aimed to keep the French source in sight as a recognizable and close parallel to contemporaneous non-translated plays. It was only towards the end of the period covered by this book that Molière's plays were presented as classics in English translation, but this was achieved within the knowledge that translations, especially translations of drama, always have the potential to be mutable and so are always in flux. Although the term *tradaptation* represents an attempt to diversify the definition of translation, its application to the 'the annexing of old texts to new cultural contexts' actually creates a new confining category that does not fit the diverse range of interdisciplinary approaches of theatre translation in the early modern period.[22] I therefore aim to avoid rigid categorizations of translation in my analyses of the early English versions of Molière's plays in English.[23]

Translation, according to its simplest definition, means a 'carrying across', a 'transportation'. The term can therefore accommodate a wide range of literary transformations that might all be considered adaptations. A broad conceptualization of translation has informed the methodological approaches of the present study. Translation of drama requires a range of considerations in addition to the evidently necessary linguistic alterations, so I shall interrogate a variety of early English translations of Molière from several different angles, including analysis of the mechanics and aims of dramatic plotting, an investigation of prosody in relation to dramatic convention, and close readings that chart changes in the translation of terms that are central to the satirical impact of drama, thereby offering a comprehensive analytical framework for the first English translations of Molière.

It is important to consider that the component parts of this book do not represent clearly demarcated translation processes — early modern translation of drama provides the opportunity to explore intersections not only between languages in close contact, as one might expect, but also between various literary and cultural areas. The chapters in Part 1, 'Early English Translations of Molière: Theory and Form', focus explicitly on the overlap and negotiation between the theory and practice of both drama and translation. Chapter 1, 'Dramatic Theory and Plotting', centres on an assessment of the macrostructural elements of plot-formation with reference to the precepts of dramatic theory in both France and England. Dramatic theory and conventions in France and England respectively affected how plots were constructed, or reconstructed in translation, and the drive to satisfy audiences in turn informed the reception of the plays in translation. In the printed translations, paratextual material was often included to justify particular approaches in such a way that it represents an early form of translation theory; Chapter 2, 'Translation Theory and Paratext', explores this overlap between theory and practice. Some of the paratextual material touches on the challenges of translating verse; many of Molière's first translators found ways to circumvent the problem by simply translating into prose, but as I show in Chapter 3, 'Rhythm, Rhyme, and Song', several experimented with different forms of sound patterning.

The fundamental multi-directional influences of dramatic theory and plotting, translation theory and paratextual material, and verse and prose are all explored in the first part of the book, but a Venn diagram representing the literary and cultural factors involved in the first translations of Molière could include multiple overlapping circles which offer substantial scope for further research. Another intersection that has a bearing on the present work, for example, is the relationship between performance, print, and translation. In analysing the approaches of Molière's first translators I largely rely on the printed text as evidence; detailed discussion of the reception of Molière's translations in the seventeenth and early eighteenth centuries is scarce, not least because some plays were presented as new works rather than translations. Yet the printed text is not merely a straightforward record of terms rendered in another language, but another means of engaging with and representing the translation process. A printed play is itself an intermedial translation of a performance (or an imagined performance) on stage, and the first translators of Molière employed print to show the relationships between the performed context of the source text and its transition to both the performed and printed context of its translation. While a printed preface or dedication offered a space to articulate translation choices, in some cases typographical choices and print format offered visual clues to the parallels and contrasts between source text and translated text. Furthermore, when Molière's Œuvres were emulated in English translation some new illustrations were commissioned by artists including William Hogarth, and these illustrations in turn presented Molière's plays in the context of early eighteenth-century theatre.[24] A full exploration of early modern intermedial translations of Molière's plays in English is beyond the scope of the present work, but the interplay between performance and print remains an undercurrent.

The aim of the second part of the book, 'Lexical Choices and Recontextualizations', is to trace the lexical choices of Molière's first English translators in order to demonstrate how the satirical drive of key social themes in the source texts were carried across the Channel. The theories and practices explored in the first part inform the texts analysed in the second part, but close reading of the uses of lexical terms broadens into discussion of the cultural themes they describe: 'Cuckoldry and Gallantry' (Chapter 4), 'Zealotry and Hypocrisy' (Chapter 5), 'Malady and Quackery' (Chapter 6), and 'Bourgeoisie and Urbanity' (Chapter 7). The social topics covered emerge from the prevalence of translations or re-translations of certain plays in the period, and are therefore not exhaustive. One of the most striking aspects of the first English translations of Molière is that the plays that are now considered most well-known were not necessarily the ones that were translated most frequently. Molière's farces, for example, appeared in English in various versions and in combination with other works because their brevity made them easy to fit into new forms. So the chapters in the second part of the book present themes that recur in translation from the late seventeenth and early eighteenth centuries. As the Appendix shows, however, there were also outlying translations of Molière's best-known plays; there is potential for comparative study of themes such as misanthropy and avarice in translation by focusing on the relatively small number of English versions of *Le Misanthrope* and *L'Avare* (1668) amongst the earliest translations of Molière. Owing to the focus on drama in flux during the period covered in the book, I concentrate instead on the themes that are in regularly repeated translation.

An intersection between translation and gender also presents itself in the first translations of Molière. With the Restoration and the accompanying French influence on theatre came the inclusion of women on stage in England, and some female playwrights emerged. Only two women produced texts based on Molière plays in the period covered by this book. Aphra Behn made use of a manuscript translation of *Le Malade imaginaire* 'by a Gentleman' to produce *Sir Patient Fancy* and Susanna Centlivre (born Susanna Freeman and known professionally before her second marriage as Susanna Carrol) translated *Le Médecin malgré lui*. The question arises as to whether these female translators treat the male-authored source text differently from male translators, but rather than annex gender questions to a separate chapter, I address intersections of translation and gender studies where they arise within the literary and cultural contexts presented in the two parts of the book. Thus, the possible interplay between grammatical gender, gendered rhymes, and characters' gender lends itself to the discussion of masculine and feminine rhymes in Chapter 3, 'Rhythm, Rhyme and Song'. In terms of the cultural and social resonance of gender, the ways in which Behn and Centlivre accentuate or reconfigure elements of the medical satires to present female agency over the body are discussed in the subsection 'Milady Malady: Gender and Translation' in Chapter 5. The reason why gender issues are better subsumed in these chapters is that there was not a straightforward 'female' or proto-feminist translating vein on display in the first translations of Molière; the interactions between gender, authorship, and translation were more complex than a case of a female writer choosing to reconfigure a male writer's work; Behn for one did not translate directly from Molière, but through the conduit of a male translator's work, and both Behn and Centlivre were negotiating the prejudices of the male-centred literary world by embedding presentations of agency-bearing female characters within the well-known theatrical contexts of the medical satires.

Owing to the heterogeneous nature of the first translations of Molière, little work has hitherto been done on the way that Molière's texts, or parts of Molière's texts, were rendered out of French vocabulary into English vocabulary. This is an important omission because with the rise in interest in French literature and fashion came an increased usage of French-derived terminology that could be tested out in the translations. The ambiguous provenance of a translated play, being in a sense part-French, part-English, allowed for an exploration of the cultural influence of late seventeenth-century urban France upon urban England, and a comparison of translations can show how that influence evolved over time. Thus each chapter in Part II is underpinned by close readings both of the core Molière texts identified at the head of each chapter, and their translations. All English translations of the core texts published within the period 1663 to 1732 are compared and contrasted with the source-text and with each other. This includes material from the translations published as collected works in 1714 and 1732. Though these publications were intended to preserve Molière in print for generations to come, it can be seen that they too were the products of their time and the translators created the texts with a mind to the way readers could imagine performances on stage.

Reliance on the printed editions of the first translations of Molière is necessary but it represents only one means amongst many by which the French playwright's works were absorbed into English theatrical history. Many of the printed plays had been performed on the London stage, as the oft-repeated subtitles 'As it is acted at the Theatre Royal' or 'As it is acted at the Duke's Theatre' attest. Molière's work also became a focus of much critical thought on the writing of comedy within printed prefatory material, theoretical writings on drama, and in newspapers.[25] Though the main focus of this book is the dramatic and literary forms of the translations and the translators' exercise of specific linguistic choices in regard to theatrical form and satirical content, it is important to bear in mind that these points of detail contributed to a wide and varied anglicizing system that transmitted the French dramatic imports to new audiences.

Notes to the Introduction

1. See Kenneth Richards, 'The French Actors in London', *Restoration and Eighteenth-century Theatre Research* 14.2 (1 November, 1975), 48–52.
2. John Dryden, *Poems, 1649–1680*, ed. by Edward Niles Hooker and H. T. Swedenberg, Jr., The Works of John Dryden, 1 (Berkeley, Los Angeles, & London: University of California Press, 1956), p. 145.
3. Some key works on the historical background and conditions of English theatre after the Restoration are: Richard W. Bevis, *English Drama: Restoration and Eighteenth Century 1660–1789* (London: Longman, 1988); Peter Holland, *The Ornament of Action: Text and Performance in Restoration Comedy* (Cambridge: Cambridge University Press, 1979); Robert D. Hume, *The Development of English Drama in the Late Seventeenth Century* (Oxford: Oxford University Press, 1976); Allardyce Nicoll, *A History of Restoration Drama, 1660–1700*, 4th edn (Cambridge: Cambridge University Press, 1952); *The Cambridge Companion to English Restoration Theatre*,

ed. by Deborah Payne Fisk (Cambridge: Cambridge University Press, 2000); David Roberts, *Restoration Plays and Players: An Introduction* (Cambridge: Cambridge University Press, 2004); and *Restoration and Georgian England, 1660–1788: A Documentary History*, ed. by David Thomas and Arnold Hare (Cambridge: Cambridge University Press, 1989).
4. See Jorge Braga Riera, *Classical Spanish Drama in Restoration England (1660–1700)* (Madrid: Complutense University of Madrid, 2009)
5. D'Avenant and Dryden adapted Shakespeare's *The Tempest* into the comedy *The Tempest; or, The Enchanted Isle*, first performed at the Duke's Theatre, Lincoln's Inn Fields, in 1667. This was in turn adapted into operatic form by Thomas Shadwell in 1674.
6. The King's Company repeatedly performed Ben Jonson's *Bartholomew Fair* (1614), an anti-Puritan play which in the context of the Restoration would have been viewed as an affirmation of the downfall of the Commonwealth.
7. Michael Dobson, 'Adaptations and Revivals', in *The Cambridge Companion to English Restoration Theatre*, ed. by Payne Fisk, pp. 40–51 (p. 48).
8. Lord Chamberlain's warrant to William D'Avenant, 12 December 1660 (The National Archives, Kew, L C 5/137, p. 343). See Nicoll, *A History of Restoration Drama, 1660–1700*, pp. 352–53.
9. Gerard Langbaine, *An Account of the English Dramatick Poets* (Oxford: printed by L.L. for George West and Henry Clements, 1691). A helpful list of following histories which build on Langbaine's overview is outlined by Frank J. Kearful in his essay 'Molière among the English', in *Molière and the Commonwealth of Letters: Patrimony and Posterity*, ed. by Roger Johnson, Guy T. Trail, and Editha Neumann (Jackson: University Press of Mississippi, 1975), pp. 199–217 (p. 201).
10. Max Besing, *Molières Einfluss auf das englische Lustspiel bis 1700* (Borna-Lepizig: Buchdruckerei Robert Noske, 1913); Dudley H. Miles, *The Influence of Molière on Restoration Comedy*, (New York: Columbia University Press, 1910).
11. The term 'Restoration Comedy' became particularly prevalent in influence studies of the early twentieth century. See, for example, W. Moseley Kerby, 'Molière and the Restoration Comedy in England' (unpublished doctoral thesis, Université de Rennes, 1907).
12. Louis Charlanne, *L'Influence française en Angleterre au XVIIe siècle* (Paris: Société Française d'Imprimerie et de Librairie, 1906), p. 300.
13. Miles, *The Influence of Molière on Restoration Comedy*, p. 221.
14. John Wilcox, *The Relation of Molière to Restoration Comedy* (New York: Benjamin Blom, 1938), p. 17.
15. Kearful, 'Molière among the English', p. 127.
16. Harold C. Knutson, *The Triumph of Wit: Molière and Restoration Comedy* (Columbus: Ohio State University Press, 1988), p. 207.
17. *The Oxford History of Literary Translation in English: Volume 3, 1660–1790*, ed. by David Hopkins and Stuart Gillespie (Oxford: Oxford University Press, 2005); Peter France, *The Oxford Guide to Literature in English Translation* (Oxford: Oxford University Press, 2001).
18. Noël Peacock, 'Molière', in *The Encyclopedia of Literary Translation into English*, ed. by Olive Classe, 2 vols (London, Chicago: Fitzroy Dearborn, 2000), II, 956–61.
19. See *Routledge Encyclopedia of Translation Studies*, ed. by Mona Baker (London & New York: Routledge, 2019), p. 8.
20. Denis Salter, 'Acting Shakespeare in Postcolonial Space', in *Shakespeare: Theory and Performance*, ed. by James C. Bulman (London & New York: Routledge, 1996), pp. 113–32 (p. 126).
21. Derrick Cameron, 'Tradaptation: Cultural Exchange and Black British Theatre', in *Moving Target: Theatre Translation and Cultural Relocation*, ed. by Carole-Anne Upton (London & New York: Routledge, 2000), pp. 17–24 (p. 17).
22. Ibid.
23. I have made some use of labelling in the Appendix, 'Table of English Translations and Adaptations of Molière, 1663–1732', to indicate where linguistic translations lie in relation to the many looser adaptations of Molière's plots in the period.
24. See Suzanne Jones, 'Printing Stage: Relationships between Performance, Print and Translation in Early English Editions of Molière', *Early Modern French Studies*, 40.2 (2018), 146–65. See also the front cover image of the present work showing a detail from an engraving designed by William Hogarth as the frontispiece to *Sganarelle ou le Cocu imaginaire / The Cuckold in Conceit*

(in Molière, *Select Comedies of Mr. de Molière, in French and English*, trans. by Henry Baker, James Miller, and Martin Clare, 8 vols (London: printed for J. Watts, 1732), I, A^v; further references are given after quotations in the text).

25. See H. M. Klein, 'Molière in English Critical Thought on Comedy to 1800', in *Molière and the Commonwealth of Letters*, pp. 218–31.

PART I

Early English Translations of Molière: Theory and Form

CHAPTER 1

Dramatic Theory and Plotting

In his *Poetics* Aristotle likens plot to the soul of tragedy.¹ Plot is also the core of comedy. Late seventeenth- and early eighteenth-century dramatists who translated the work of Molière took varying approaches, but all had to consider primarily whether to retain or adapt the plots of the original works. There were marked differences in approaches to plotting in seventeenth-century French plays and in English plays of the same period. So some English adaptors, taking raw dramatic material from across the Channel, found ways to rearrange it for new audiences, the expectations of whom were based on English plot conventions. This chapter provides an overview and an analysis of the changes that English translators made to Molière's plots.

Theorizing Plot: Unity of Action

To understand the work of Molière's adaptors, it is useful to be aware of theoretical discussions of plot construction in seventeenth-century France and England. From the 1630s onwards French dramatic plots had been increasingly formed in relation to the three so-called unities of time, place, and action, though the exact definitions of these terms were debated in theoretical works of the period. Since then theorists have come to identify the core significance of the unities of time and place: unity of time is the requirement that the action not exceed the time-span of twenty-four hours, and unity of place is the circumscription of the onstage action within one single stage set. The complexities of unity of action, however, are not so easily summarized.

The action of a play, or its plot, consists of the measures that the dramatist makes the characters take when they are confronted with a particular problem to be overcome. This problem is known as a *nœud*, or 'knot', in French drama, hence the term *dénouement* which signifies the resolution to the problem.² It is worth noting that *nœud* was synonymous with *intrigue*, the term that comes from the Latin *intrigare* meaning to 'entangle' or 'entrap' and that is now used in French to signify plot. The English word 'intrigue' was commonly used alongside *plot* in seventeenth-century discourse (*OED*). So dramatic plotting consisted of fashioning and resolving an entanglement. In French drama, there could be more than one factor that contributes to the forming of the *nœud*, and more than one consequence resulting from it. Dramatic theorists, from ancient to early modern times, were not really referring to unity in terms of its fundamental meaning of 'oneness' but in terms that are closer to the sense of unification, the process of making a whole from multiple component elements.

Yet dramatic theorists did seek to define how unity was to be achieved in the ordering of the action. This is why the concept of unity of action is fundamental to the plotting process. Both ancient and seventeenth-century French dramatists and theorists stated that a play must have a main action. If there is one main action, there can also be one or more secondary actions. Until unity of action was adopted almost unanimously in France from the 1640s onwards, many plays included multiple exciting and surprising secondary actions that were not always linked to the main action. In his *Pratique du théâtre* (1657) the dramatic theorist François Hédelin, abbé d'Aubignac, criticizes this approach to plotting and offers an alternative by stating:

> Que la seconde histoire ne doit pas être égale en son sujet non plus qu'en sa nécessité, à celle qui sert de fondement à tout le poème; mais bien lui être subordonnée et en dépendre de telle sorte, que les événements du principal Sujet fassent naître les passions de l'Épisode, et que la Catastrophe du premier, produise naturellement et de soi-même celle du second; autrement l'Action qui doit principalement fonder le Poème, serait sujette à une autre, et deviendrait comme étrangère.[3]

D'Aubignac's reference to 'l'Épisode' could be misleading because the term was originally applied to portions of an epic, and could signify episodic actions that were loosely linked; it later came to refer more generally to literary actions, including plot events in drama.[4] D'Aubignac is arguing against episodic actions; secondary actions that relate to each other and are linked to the main action are preferable to events that merely follow on from each other.[5]

Seventeenth-century French dramatists found ways to nuance the definition of unity of action so that they had greater freedom when creating plays. Pierre Corneille writes in his *Discours des trois unités* (1660) that:

> L'unité d'action consiste, dans la comédie, en l'unité d'intrigue, ou d'obstacle aux desseins des principaux acteurs, et en l'unité de péril dans la tragédie, soit que son héros y succombe soit qu'il en sorte. Ce n'est pas que je prétende qu'on ne puisse admettre plusieurs périls dans l'une, et plusieurs intrigues, ou obstacles dans l'autre, pourvu que de l'un on tombe nécessairement dans l'autre; car alors la sortie du premier péril ne rend point l'action complète, puisqu'elle en attire un second; et l'éclaircissement d'un intrigue ne met point les acteurs en repos, puisqu'il les embarrasse dans un nouveau.[6]

Corneille allows for numerous actions within one play without emphasizing that some must be subordinate to others, as d'Aubignac states. Corneille does maintain that there should be a principal *sujet*, a complete action, but that for this to be fulfilled there must be a progression of 'imperfect' actions that keep audiences in anticipation of it: 'il est nécessaire que chaque acte laisse une attente de quelque chose, qui se doive faire dans celui qui le suit' (p. 175). Corneille also points out that a dramatist need not explain what characters have been doing in the intervals between acts or when they are absent from acts, unless their actions are pertinent to the on-stage action. He also condones the inclusion of more events in the later acts than in the earlier, provided that the acts are of similar length in terms of performance-time (p. 181). Corneille's definition of the unity of action allows the dramatist a certain amount of liberty in balancing the actions that lead to the dénouement.

Yet like d'Aubignac, Corneille emphasizes the advantage of avoiding episodic plots where there is little or no relation between different events. In the third *Discours* Corneille discusses *liaison des scènes*. This is a dramatic practice in which all scenes are made to follow on directly from one another and in which the reasons for entrances and exits of characters are made clear:

> La liaison des scènes qui unit toutes les actions particulières de chaque acte l'une avec l'autre [...] est un grand ornement dans un poème, et qui sert beaucoup à former une continuité d'action, par la continuité de la représentation; mais enfin ce n'est qu'un ornement, et non pas une règle. (p. 177)

Corneille goes on to give examples of instances in which ancient dramatists had not practised *liaison*. Corneille's examples of exceptions to the 'rule', however, only demonstrate singular instances; he actually acknowledges that the 'rule' should be a general practice. It is worth noting here that there is a key difference between French and English scene division. In French drama the transition from one scene to another indicates the continuity of action; the stage is never left empty, hence the term *liaison*. In English drama, scene division often signifies scene *breaks,* interruptions to the dramatic action. The very structural hinges of seventeenth-century French and English drama are distinct; one system is geared towards unity while the other is geared towards variety.

Just as plot construction was debated in France, so too was it examined in England. The conflict surrounding unity of action in English seventeenth-century dramatic theory is demonstrated in *Essay of Dramatick Poesie* (1668) by John Dryden.[7] The essay was probably written during the plague year of 1665–66 and is presented as a dramatic dialogue between four characters: Crites, Eugenius, Lisideius, and Neander. They take up Corneille's *Discours* to aid their discussion of the merits and demerits of French and English drama of the time. Neander addresses the issue of unity of action thus:

> *Crites* has already shown us, from the confession of the *French* Poets, that the Unity of Action is sufficiently preserv'd if all the imperfect actions of the Play are conducing to the main design: but when those petty intrigues of a Play are so ill order'd that they have no coherence with the other, I must grant that *Lisideius* has reason to tax that want of due connexion; for Co-ordination in a Play is as dangerous and unnatural as in a State. In the mean time he must acknowledge our variety, if well order'd, will afford a greater pleasure to the audience.[8]

By 'Co-ordination' Neander means that the equality of more than one plot would be as harmful as the equality of more than one ruler in a state. The comment that the unity of action might be 'sufficiently' preserved indicates that in the practice of drama the unity of action is not a science. Instead of seeking to define it more and more prescriptively some theorists tried to simplify its meaning to allow dramatists more flexibility in plotting.

It is evident that the unity of action was not unanimously defined in either English or French dramatic theory. In fact, the term was rarely used by dramatists in the prefaces to their works. Jean Racine, the seventeenth-century dramatist who observed the unities most thoroughly, for example, writes of his play's 'simplicité d'Action' in the preface to *Bérénice* (1671), not of the unity of action.[9] Yet however loosely and varyingly defined it may be in dramatic theory, d'Aubignac, Corneille, and Dryden all emphasize that the unity of action centres on the practice of choosing *one main action* and working towards that by presenting other actions that relate to it.

Given this fundamental point about the unity of action, it might seem surprising that the first English dramatists to adapt Molière chose more than one source when composing their material. Adaptations of the 1660s were typically combinations, or 'hybridizations' of two or more plots. The late 1660s onwards saw looser 'hybridized imitations' in which plot elements from more than one Molière play were mixed with invented material and structure was often subordinated to comic dialogue. From the 1670s onwards dramatists often preserved single Molière plots but expanded or added character-roles to suit English dramatic taste or to emphasize the new satirical slant of the adaptations. The early 1700s saw a clear shift towards the preservation of Molière plots in their original form. From 1663 to 1732 the plots were broken up, rearranged, combined, enlarged, contracted, and finally put back together again and packaged for posterity. The aim of this chapter is to illustrate this taxonomy of plot adaptation and to analyse the ways in which the process of plot adaptation was also a double exercise in anglicization and intensification of comic effect. It will therefore be composed of three main sections that address a range of texts in chronological order. The first section on 'hybridization' will include a close analysis of Richard Flecknoe's *The Damoiselles à la mode*, paying particular attention to the anglicized plot structure. The second section will explore the plotting effects derived from adaptors' addition of characters or enhancement of existing roles, focusing on Matthew Medbourne's *Tartuffe* and Dryden's *Amphitryon*. The final section will address the ways in which Molière's original plots were retained and presented as models that English writers were encouraged to emulate.

Hybridization

In John Dryden's *Essay of Dramatick Poesie* Neander presents a lengthy defence of English drama:

> The reason is perspicuous, why no French Playes, when translated, have, or ever can succeed upon the English Stage. For, if you consider the Plots, our own are fuller of variety [...]. We have borrow'd nothing of them [the French]; our Plots are weav'd in English Loomes: we endeavour therein to follow the variety and greatness of characters which are deriv'd to us from *Shakespeare* and *Fletcher*: the copiousness and well-knitting of the intrigues we have from *Johnson* [Ben Jonson]. (pp. 53–54)

Neander's main argument against English writers' translating from French drama is the unsuitability of the concentrated French plot-form for the English stage. The need for 'copiousness' and 'variety' in the plotting of a play for an English audience is paramount. He is, however, being self-consciously perverse in the comment 'we have borrow'd nothing of them', because by 1668 several French plays had already been translated and reworked for the English stage.

The first English play that included material from Molière was *A Playhouse to be Let*, performed around 1663 and attributed to William D'Avenant.[10] It is really a collection of five short plays presented in five acts, the first of which sets the scene: a playhouse in which the chief player is hoping to rent out the theatre during the quiet vacation. The first 'audition', performed in the second act, is a condensed version of Molière's one-act play, *Sganarelle ou le Cocu imaginaire* (1660).[11] D'Avenant does not extend the influence of the French drama to the overall plot, and, on the contrary, describes his play as a 'monster' whose limbs have no correspondence.[12] He does not anglicize Molière's play by adapting the original, but by embedding it in a framing plot. Subsequent adaptors, however, not only took bolder approaches to reworking Molière plots but also referred to the theoretical principles by which the original plots had been formed.

Flecknoe's The Damoiselles à la mode (1667)

Several seventeenth-century adaptors of Molière decided to formulate new plays by combining different plots. Of course, the process of using elements from various existing plays was nothing new in theatre, but the combination of whole plots by the same, near-contemporaneous dramatist was symptomatic of the urgency with which late seventeenth-century English dramatists sought to adapt from French. The first dramatist to adopt this hybridization approach was Richard Flecknoe, in *The Damoiselles à la mode* of 1667. The title page states that the play is 'compos'd' as well as written' by Flecknoe, and thereby draws attention to the idea that it is a piece made from different components.[13] This is also suggested in the mixture of English and French words and spellings in the title itself. The prefatory material indicates that the play was printed before performance; there are in fact no firm records to indicate that it was performed after publication.[14]

Any reader wanting to understand the hybridization process is done a disservice by Flecknoe's own explanation of it. His comments in the preface are confused and confusing. For example, he acknowledges the plays which he blends together in the text, but either he or someone involved in the printing of the play makes the error of muddling Molière's *L'École des maris* (1661) with *L'École des femmes* (1662): 'The main plot of the *Damoiselles* [is] out of *Precieusee's Ridiculee's* [sic]; the Counterplot of *Sganarelle*, [is] out of his *Escole des Femmes*, and out of the *Escole des Marys*, the two *Naturals*'.[15] The term 'Naturals' refers to the so-called 'natural fools' which are taken from *L'École des femmes*, not from *L'École des maris*. These characters, based on Alain and Georgette, Arnolphe's servants in *L'École des femmes*, provide a farcical enhancement to the English version. Readers should also be aware that when Flecknoe mentions '*Sganarelle*' he is referring to the main character in *L'École des maris*, not Molière's other play *Sganarelle, ou Le Cocu imaginaire*. The italicization of the character's name is used for emphasis rather than to indicate the title of a play. The reference to the 'Counterplot' is misleading, because it does not work in opposition to the main plot, but rather in parallel to it, as strands from both sources are woven together. The suggestion in the preface that the three plays have served equally is also deceptive. In total, eighteen scenes are translated more or less loosely into prose from *L'École des maris*, sixteen scenes from *Les Précieuses ridicules*, and three scenes are based on events in *L'École des femmes*. These scenes were arranged and linked by Flecknoe to form a hybrid plot that was intended to satisfy the expectations of an English audience.

Despite the claim made in the preface, the largest contribution in Flecknoe's work comes from Molière's *L'École des maris*, in which the morally conservative Sganarelle aims to marry his ward Isabelle whom he keeps on a tight leash while his liberal-minded brother Ariste aims to marry his ward Léonor to whom he grants a relatively large amount of freedom. The comic focus is in part Isabelle's scheme to escape with her young admirer Valère, and in part the manoeuvres that Sganarelle unwittingly makes to help her to this end. Into this comic situation Flecknoe weaves the plot of *Les Précieuses ridicules*. This Molière play centres on a trick that two rejected suitors play upon two sisters whose lives are dominated by preciosity. The gentlemen's lackeys disguise themselves as fine gallants and try to woo the young women, but their true identities are comically laid bare at the end of the play. In Flecknoe's play some elements from a third Molière play, *L'École des femmes*, are largely incidental to the main plot, though the themes bear much comparison with those of *L'École des maris*. Arnolphe, not unlike Sganarelle, keeps his young ward Agnès under lock and key, intending her to become his faithful bride. Her head, however, is turned by the young Horace, and despite her naivety and virtual imprisonment she manages to pursue a relationship with him. The ineptitude of Arnolphe's servants, charged with keeping the suitor away, provides several farcical episodes which Flecknoe inserts at various points in his combination of the other two plots.

Flecknoe's starting point for melding the plots of *L'École des maris* and *Les Précieuses ridicules* is a comparison of the approaches that 'Monsieur Bonhomme' and his cousin Sganarelle take in bringing up the young women in their care. Monsieur Bonhomme takes a fairly liberal approach, allowing his daughters to attend balls and receive male suitors, whereas Sganarelle seeks to keep his niece Isabella away from society, intending to marry her himself. The first scene of Flecknoe's play, then, is part-translation, part-adaptation of the opening scene of Molière's *L'École des maris*, in which Sganarelle argues with his brother Ariste over the question of whether one should conform to society and fashion. The focus of the first scene of the French text is the fundamental difference between the two men in their attitudes towards societal conformity, whereas in the English text the focus is on some added lines in which Sganarelle actively engages his cousin in a challenge: 'Well then since y'ar so resolv'd, take you your course, and I'll take mine, and see who'll have the better of it at the end' (p. 5). The results of Bonhomme's liberal attitude towards his daughters will later be contrasted with the results of Sganarelle's attempted subjugation of Isabella. By setting up the challenge Flecknoe orientates his readers at the beginning of what will be a complex plot.

Flecknoe maintains a focus on guiding his reader-audience in Act I, scene 2. This scene is based on the second scene of Molière's *L'École des maris* in which Isabelle describes her solitary life. Flecknoe follows Molière closely, but again adds some explanatory material at the end of the scene to indicate the course that his revised plot will follow and to accentuate Sganarelle's tyranny and Isabella's defiance:

SGAN.	So — make your curtsie, and be gone, —— — very good —— and look to your business, d'ye hear!	
ISAB.	Which is only to be rid of you, which till I am, I will be nothing but Plot and Stratagem.[16]	*Aside* *Exit*
SGAN.	Now let me think a little. (p. 10)	

The end of this scene, like the preceding scene, acts as an indicator of plot progression. Isabella's reference to plot is in relation to her scheme to escape the ties of her guardian, but the comment also focuses attention on the character's actions as fundamental to the whole plot of the play.

Having established the main instigators of action in the play, Flecknoe introduces more minor characters that will contribute to the variety of the plot. Act I continues with scenes from *L'École des maris*, in which Isabelle's suitor Valère becomes acquainted with Sganarelle. Act I, scene 5 of *The Damoiselles*, however, is inspired by *L'École des femmes* by including the two so-called 'natural fools' based on the servants Alain and Georgette. Sganarelle gives them strict instructions to guard Isabella from any visitors, and the servants reply facetiously and repetitively. Such scenes satisfy the English taste for a variety of comedic characters and styles promoted by Neander in Dryden's *Essay of Dramatick Poesie*: 'Ours [our plots], besides the main design, have under plots or by-concernments, of less considerable Persons, and Intrigues, which are carried on with the motion of the main Plot' (p. 47). Neander's reference to 'less considerable Persons' is related to his complaint that French drama tends to focus only on the concerns of a small number of 'great' characters, particularly in tragedies. Flecknoe's inclusion of the farcical characters in a comedy, however, functions likewise as a means of providing entertaining 'by-concernments'. These are essentially farcical interludes rather than subplots, but they serve to provide the diversity that was expected of English drama.

Variety of tone is sustained as Act I of *The Damoiselles* concludes with a return to the plot of *L'École des maris* in which Sganarelle tells Valerio that he plans to marry Isabella. The only deviation in content is a soliloquy at the end of the act, in which Sganarelle lauds the modesty and innocence of his niece in comparison with his cousin's flighty daughters. Sganarelle's thoughts serve to reintroduce the *Précieuses ridicules* plot-thread which is to become dominant in Act II. Their inclusion also provides a reminder of the overarching premise of the plot: which of the cousins will be more satisfied by their approach to guardianship? The comic drive lies in the sense that Sganarelle has been destined to fail from the start.

It is not only Sganarelle's style of custodianship that is tested in the play. Monsieur Bonhomme's more liberal attitude is explored in Act II. It begins with his daughters' two rejected suitors, Du Buisson and La Fleur, bemoaning their lot and coming up with a plan to seek revenge. The plan is formulated quickly so that plot momentum is maintained in the hybridized form.

> DU BUIS   [...] now will I cloath my Laquey like one of your Gallants, whom they admire so much, all Fool and Feather, and send him thither, and see how they'll entertain him.
> LA FL.   Content, and I've another as foolish and fantastical as he, who can imitate all their Cringes and Complements [sic], talk bilk as loud and confidently as any of them, and throw himself like a Tumbler after the Ladies, and he shall along with him.
> DU BUIS   The more the merryer. (pp. 23–24)

Although in the French text there are likewise two valets that take part in the trick, the comment 'the more the merryer' seems to point to the English theatrical ideal in which the more characters are embroiled in a plot the more comic the play is said to be. Flecknoe achieves a proliferation of characters by combining the plots of several Molière plays, but does not invent any entirely new characters. This is not only an expedient way of adapting Molière, but allows Flecknoe to claim that he has preserved the essential components of the French sources.

Flecknoe uses his wide range of characters to break up and redirect the plot. His inclusion of a slapstick interlude featuring the 'Two Natural Fools' and Sganarelle refocuses attention on his plan to guard Isabella. Thereafter the plot of *L'École des maris* is taken up again and occupies the last scenes of the act. Isabella claims that Valerio has thrown a box containing a letter into her bedroom, and she wants Sganarelle to return it unopened. This is a ruse which allows her to communicate with her suitor. Valerio's delight at reading the letter is contracted in the English text, but Sganarelle's misguided joy at Isabella's behaviour and his gloating over his rival are accentuated in order to set him up for a fall.

Though Flecknoe does not invent new characters he does extend certain roles to suit English dramatic taste. Act III opens with the beginning of Mascarillo's trick on the *damoiselles*, taken from *Les Précieuses ridicules*. But Act III, scene 2, a scene featuring Mascarillo and Lysette, is extended in the English text so that Mascarillo can describe his sudden 'gallant Itch' upon seeing her. The two exchange some witty remarks as Mascarillo propositions her. The interaction of male and female servant-figures is a common feature of the English comedy of manners and recurs in many adaptations of Molière's plays. Not only do many adaptations of Molière's plays increase the number of character-interactions, they also turn them into actual or potential unions. The hint of a liaison between Mascarillo and Lysette allows for some bawdy English humour, but more significantly provides another means of uniting two plots.

Lysette's function as a bridge between plots becomes more significant as Mascarillo and Jodelet's trick becomes increasingly elaborate. In Act III, scene 4, the first scene that is invented by Flecknoe, she visits Sganarelle in order to invite Isabella to the ball that the *damoiselles* and the 'gallants' are holding. Lysette is dismissed with a refusal:

LYS.   And so I humbly take my leave, and rest your most humble servant
                                                                Exit Lysette
SGAN.   She's at her Complements agen! this woman is a compound of all
         women together, and has more ingredients in her then *Mithridate* or
         Treacle, but the main is *Mercury* and *Quick-silver*. (p. 72)

Sganarelle's comment relates primarily to Lysette's sprightly temperament, but given the frequency of other metatheatrical remarks about Flecknoe's plot adaptation it seems likely that the reference also points towards the dramatist's combination of the characters of Marotte and Lisette from *Les Précieuses ridicules* and *L'École des maris* respectively. Lysette's impertinence also triggers Sganarelle's next interaction with his 'natural fools' whom he berates for having granted access to a waiting woman. In quick succession, two different kinds of Molière-inspired servant characters are contrasted while the plot is driven forward. At the end of Act III the plot of *L'École des maris* is neatly reintroduced when Isabella enters to announce that she has heard that Valerio plans to abduct her. This allows Flecknoe to complete the act with an adaptation of the clowning Act IV, scene 5 of *L'École des femmes*, in which the overprotective guardian encourages his servants to rehearse what they would do if there were an intruder, but consequently gets beaten himself. This scene is representative of the main thrust of the plot; over-assurance can lead to results that are opposite to the intended effect.

Flecknoe includes more invented scenes as the two plots become more closely entwined. Lysette's comic role, for example, is amplified in Act IV. She comments on the large food consumption of the gallants at dinner, thereby creating dramatic irony for a reader who knows that they are servants in disguise. The act then centres on the denouement of *Les Précieuses ridicules*, in which the servants' trickery is discovered. A few changes, however, work towards blending the different plot-threads. Lysette, for example, berates Mascarillo for his attempt to seduce her earlier in the play. This has a bawdy comic effect because she had initially been willing when she thought he was a gentleman. Contrary to the ending of Molière's *Les Précieuses ridicules*, the unveiling of the disguises in the English play leads to attempts to resolve the situation by pairing off the characters. This is so that Flecknoe can maintain interest in the two combined plots to the very end.

Flecknoe has to introduce some new scenes that work towards the conclusion of the *damoiselles*' plot-thread. He intersperses scenes in which the gentlemen suitors return with contracted, punchy versions of late scenes from Act II of *L'École des maris*, in which Sganarelle confronts his rival. In part, these scenes are shortened so that the hybridized plot does not become too unwieldy, but there is also an element of anglicization. In Dryden's *Essay of Dramatick Poesie* Lisideius expresses admiration for the elaborate speeches to be found in French drama. Neander argues against this with the comment that:

> Short Speeches and Replies are more apt to move the passions, and beget concernment in us [...] for it is unnatural for any one in a gust of passion to speak long together, or for another in the same condition, to suffer him, without interruption. (p. 48)

There are several instances in Flecknoe's play where longer speeches are cut or interrupted by a comment or aside by another character, thereby giving an English flavour to the rhythm of the dialogue while quickening the progress of the plot.

The final act includes many incidents that happen in quick succession. The beginning of Act v is based on the third act of *L'École des maris*, though Sganarelle's clowning servants are also thrown into the mix. Isabella's plan to flee to Valerio's house is more firmly established in the English text, thereby emphasizing her defiance but diminishing some of the dramatic impact. She pretends that her cousin Mary is in love with Valerio and has arrived to replace her in the abduction (in the French text Isabelle pretends that her sister Léonor is his beloved). Sganarelle therefore gloats over Bonhomme, Mary's father. They all agree that Valerio should marry Mary, just as Isabella unveils herself. Owing to the need to tie up the loose ends of the other plot-thread, these episodes occur much more quickly in the English text than in the French. Sganarelle bemoans women's wiles, says that he will vent his frustration on his servants, and still criticizes the behaviour of Bonhomme's daughters. In this English version, however, Bonhomme's daughters are to be married to the rich gentlemen, thereby rendering Sganarelle comically erroneous.

The latter half of the final act is entirely invented by Flecknoe, as the plot is rounded into a coherent whole. The *damoiselles* finally agree to marry the gentlemen, Valerio and Isabella are welcomed, and the couples arrange to be married the next day. This reference points to the observation of the unity of time, which Flecknoe is keen to emphasize as a means of acknowledging the French origins of the play. Flecknoe claims that the play observes three unities, but the unities to which he refers are the 'Unities of Persons, Time, and Place' (A7ᵛ). He carefully avoids claiming that it observes unity of action and instead refers to an invented 'Unity of Persons'. This is because there are two main actions in Flecknoe's play, not one. The ending of the play, therefore, is not a denouement in the seventeenth-century French theoretical sense but rather an invented resolution that satisfies English dramatic taste.

Hybridization as a Method of Anglicization

It is worth returning to Dryden's *Essay of Dramatick Poesie* in order to summarize the ways in which Flecknoe's hybridization of several Molière plays was an expedient method not only of forming a semi-original play, but also of anglicizing the French originals. Lisideius criticizes the English tendency for:

> Two actions, that is, two Plays carried on together, to the confounding of the Audience [...] From hence likewise it arises that the one half of our Actors are not known to the other [...] and seldom begin an acquaintance till the last Scene of the Fifth Act, when they are all to meet upon the Stage. (p. 39)

Flecknoe contrives a meeting of the characters from the two main base-plots in the fifth act of his play, with the prospect of marriage as the common ground for the paired couples. A throng of characters is considered an advantage by Dryden's

Neander, who argues that

> 'Tis evident that the more the persons there are, the greater will be the variety of the Plot. If then the parts are manag'd so regularly that the beauty of the whole be kept intire, and that the variety become not a perplex'd and confus'd mass of accidents, you will find it infinitely pleasing to be led in a labyrinth of design, where you see some way before you, yet discern not the end till you arrive at it. (p. 49)

Flecknoe's mixing of the different plots creates a more labyrinthine plot than the separate original French plays, but he often draws attention to what will happen next through additional lines uttered by Sganarelle or Isabelle, thereby allowing prolepsis.

Flecknoe's hybrid approach to adapting Molière provides him with a swift way to increase the number of characters, the variety of interactions between characters, and the comic influence of servant-figures, and to contract lengthier exchanges into fast-moving repartee. Most of the base elements are to be found in Molière, but it is through plot reformulation that Flecknoe 'Englished' French drama. In the preface to *The Damoiselles à la mode* Flecknoe justifies his work thus:

> I have not only done like one who makes a posie out of divers flowers in which he has nothing of his own, (besides the collection, and ordering of them) but like the *Bee,* have extracted the spirit of them into a certain Quintessence of mine own. (A3ʳ)

There is irony in the fact that Flecknoe borrows a metaphor from Plato: 'For they [the lyric poets] tell us that they bring songs from honeyed fountains, culling them out of the gardens and dells of the Muses; they, like the bees, winging their ways from flower to flower'.[17] Flecknoe's reference to the posie-maker's collection and ordering is an apt metaphor for his method of plot formation. Yet the claim that he has created a quintessence, by definition the purest or most highly concentrated essence of something, is stretching his justification too far; *The Damoiselles à la mode* is an entirely composite work.

Looser Hybridizations

Apart from the final act, Flecknoe's play is largely true to the original plots from which it is formed. Other adaptors of Molière in the 1660s, however, took more liberal approaches to combining plots. Despite engaging closely with French dramatic theory in his *Essay of Dramatick Poesie,* Dryden took a flexible approach to hybridization in *Sir Martin Mar-all; or, The Feign'd Innocence* (1668). This play is a combination of the plots of Molière's *L'Étourdi* (1655) and Quinault's *L'Amant indiscret* (1653). Dryden worked from a translation of *L'Étourdi* by the Duke of Newcastle, adding the subplot from Quinault. The choice of sources is hardly surprising given that the two French plays had a common Italian source, Nicolò Barbieri's *Il inavvertito* (1630). The essential premise of the Italian play, the two French plays, and the English play is that the eponymous character is so lacking in discretion that he unwittingly gives important information to his rivals, thereby exasperating the cleverer companion who tries to help him. This companion is a cunning servant-figure in Barbieri, Quinault, and Molière. The English version deviates from the other plays in pairing off the equivalent servant-figure 'Warner' with his master's love interest; it transpires, conveniently, that Warner is actually a gentleman in disguise. This altered ending is due to Dryden's reconfiguration of the eponymous character, Sir Martin, as an outright fool. Sir Martin is vain and stupid whereas the main characters in the other versions are largely victims of their own generosity of spirit and slowness in comparison with their more cunning companions. The adapted outcome in the English version is indicative of the increasingly flexible approach that dramatists took when adapting from Molière.

Dryden and Newcastle also take a different approach to overall plot-construction. The editors of *Sir Martin Mar-all* in *The Works of John Dryden* explain the adaptors' process thus:

> Largely ignoring considerations of neoclassical theory, they addressed themselves pragmatically to the construction of a series of entertaining scenes, joining them loosely together on two strands of plot, and endowing them with a unity of tone rather than of theme. Close attention to dramatic construction is scarcely to be expected in a farcical comedy of situation.[18]

This assessment demonstrates the discrepancy between theory and practice when dramatists adapt Molière plots. When more than one plot is combined the unity of action is called into question. Thus Dryden's editors use the vague term 'unity of tone' to describe the rationale behind the linking of scenes. In other loose hybridizations of the period, dramatists justify their approach by claiming that the unities have been observed.

Thomas Shadwell makes the spurious argument for dramatic unity in *The Sullen Lovers* (1668), a combination of *Les Fâcheux* (1661) and elements of *Le Misanthrope* (1666):

> The time of the Drama does not exceed six hours; the place is in a very narrow Compass; and the Main-Action of the Play, upon which all the rest depend, is the Sullen-love betwixt *Stanford* and *Emilia*, which kind of love is onely proper to their Characters.[19]

Shadwell demonstrates knowledge of the idea that there should be a main action towards which all other actions tend. His reference to the sullen love as being proper to the characters, however, is suggestive of unity of interest or theme rather than unity of action.[20] Some of the subplots that Shadwell includes, which serve to exasperate the misanthropic eponymous lovers, also serve to highlight the character trait rather than to work towards a denouement. In his preface, however, Shadwell goes on to dismiss dramatic regularity, because he claims his play has been criticized for having 'too thin an intrigue'. Ironically, he claims that being slave to the unities leads to poor dramatic design.

Perhaps owing to the difficulty of reconciling French theoretical principles with the practice of combining multiple plots, dramatists from the late 1660s onwards started to adapt single Molière plays. That is not to state that there were no further hybrid adaptations, but rather that they tended to include only plot elements from multiple plays rather than the closely woven plot-threads seen in Flecknoe's play. When adapting single plays dramatists found new ways to anglicize the plots.

Plot Adaptation: Addition or Enhancement of Character Roles

Some adaptors added characters to Molière plots in order to complicate the intrigue and to intensify the satirical focus in the new English context. This approach became dominant from the 1670s onwards. Dryden, addressing the topic of adaptation yet again, notes in his preface to *An Evening's Love* (1668), that since no foreign text, ancient or contemporary, can 'afford characters enough for the variety of the English stage, it follows that it is to be altered, and enlarged, with new persons, accidents, and designs, which will almost make it new'.[21] Dryden's language betrays a desire to lay claim to some originality simply by the execution of the process of plot adaptation, but his reference to making it new could also be read as a need for recontextualization in a new era and environment.[22] The addition or enhancement of character-roles was an expedient way for adaptors to achieve this.

Considerable Additionals: Medbourne's 'Tartuffe' (1670)

Tartuffe; or, The French Puritan, written by the actor-dramatist Matthew Medbourne, is part blank-verse translation, part adaptation of Molière.[23] The play presents the reactions of characters to a religious hypocrite who cunningly ingratiates himself into Orgon's household in order to enjoy the master's worldly goods, chattels, and wife. Molière's first version, consisting of three acts, was performed at Versailles in 1664. It is not definitively clear whether this play was initially composed fully of three acts, or if they were the first three acts of a potential but incomplete five-act play.[24] Either way, the play was banned from public performance almost immediately, because the Church authorities deemed it offensive.[25] Molière subsequently protested in three *placets au Roi*, and rewrote it as a five-act play for public performance in 1667, this time entitling it *L'Imposteur* and changing the name of the protagonist to Panulphe. This version was also immediately banned. He modified it once more and he was finally allowed to have it performed in 1669. The third version, entitled *Le Tartuffe, ou L'Imposteur* is the only extant text, though an anonymous audience member's account of the 1667 performance also survives.[26]

Any reader familiar with Molière's 1669 play will see obvious additions in Medbourne's version. There are eight considerable additions in total, six of which are highlighted on the page by 'pointing hands', or manicules. Most of these sections relate to diversification of the plot through the addition of the character of Laurence, Tartuffe's servant. In Molière's text 'Laurent' is a non-speaking part, and he is not even listed as a character in many of today's productions, because Tartuffe needs only to address an offstage Laurent. The addition of the speaking role of Laurence in the English text gives a wider range of characters more agency in defeating Tartuffe and in making Orgon see how foolish he has been. The changes to the plot and structure of the source-text are triggered by the need to suit the dramatic, social, and political environment of late seventeenth-century England.[27]

Medbourne appears to set out a simple reason for the changes. In his preface to the 1670 edition he states that:

> What considerable Additionals I have made thereto [to the play], in order to its more plausible Appearance on the English Theatre, I leave to be observed by those who shall give themselves the Trouble of Comparing the several Editions of this Comedy. How successful it has prov'd in the Action, the Advantages made by the Actors, and the Satisfaction received by so many Audiences, have sufficiently proclaim'd.[28]

It is not clear that the play was especially successful on stage; it does not seem to have had a long run of performances.[29] Medbourne's suggestion that his text and Molière's could be compared perhaps reads as an over-compensatory assertion that he has created something original. Anne Barbeau Gardiner argues that Medbourne's references to the French original were meant to veil his anti-Puritan satire rather than to encourage parallel readings.[30] A comparison of the texts now, however, offers insights into the means and motives of a dramatist who adapted Molière plots for an English audience of the time.

The addition of the speaking role of Laurence in Medbourne's version is significant not only because it allows for a corresponding character to the clever Dorina (as well as an amorous interest for her), but also because the scenes in which he appears add a satirical edge to the play. Laurence takes part in the dramatic action in Acts I, scenes 4 & 5, Act II, scene 5, Act III, scene 8, Act IV, scenes 2 & 8, Act V, scenes 6 & 8. The character first appears and speaks on stage at the end of Act I, scene 4; this is one of several instances when Laurence enters at the end of a scene or act. This structuring is due in part to expediency, but it also serves to increase expectation and a certain dramatic tension because at the end of several scenes Laurence hints that he will help Dorina by implicating Tartuffe:

> LAUR.   Now art thou far more beautiful and glorious
> Then are those Saints and Angels my Master so much
> Talks of, and thou shalt be the Load-star of all my Actions,
> And the Saint to whom my best of Services shall
> Be devoted. (p. 13)

The satirical comic focus of this section from the final scene of the first act is largely linguistic, as Laurence mixes Puritan language relating to the 'Elect' with pagan reference to astrology and idolatry. Crucially though, Dorina's salvation is fundamental to the progression and resolution of the plot. It is Laurence who tells Dorina to contrive a meeting between Elmire and Tartuffe, with Orgon concealed but within earshot. It is Laurence who advises that Cleanthes, Damis, and Valere should defend Orgon before the king. Laurence's scheming diminishes the ingenuity and skill of Orgon's wife Elmire who concocts the trick in Molière's original. But his suggestion that the family apply to the king points to an awareness that the king (then Charles II in England) would be in favour of anti-Puritan action. This may be why Laurence, seemingly counter-intuitively, encourages Tartuffe in his acquisitive exploits at the end of Act III; he encourages his master to incriminate himself. He also serves to add dramatic tension as neither Dorina nor the audience have yet fathomed whether Laurence is a trustworthy character or Tartuffe's accomplice.

Laurence's frequent hinting and concoction of the plan to bring down Tartuffe also work to remove the *deus ex machina* element of Molière's plot, when Louis XIV intervenes, via a royal officer, to save the day. Surprisingly, in this example of an English dramatist's plot adaptation, the addition of a character serves to enhance unity of action, not to diminish or undermine it. All of Laurence's actions may be guided by his 'load-star' Dorina, but they also serve as secondary actions to one main exploit: the exposure of Tartuffe. The plot structure of Medbourne's *Tartuffe* allows for additional satirical content, but also satisfies the expectation of variety from an English audience while abiding by the French ideal of unity of action which was becoming increasingly influential in England. Medbourne's adaptation represents a sort of negotiation with the French original. He turns plot-driven characters taken from Molière into a character-driven plot in the sense that his addition of the speaking role of Laurence becomes a catalyst in the events that lead to Tartuffe's downfall. It is by means of this modification that something 'almost new', to reuse Dryden's phrase, is formulated.

The Perquisite of My Place: Dryden's 'Amphitryon' (1690)

Dryden himself made use of character addition in his 1690 adaptation of Molière's *Amphitryon* (1668), which in turn had drawn on the classical source-text of Plautus's *Amphitruo* (190–185 BC) in a two-fold translating and adapting process. The core plot in all the versions centres on a trick of assumed identity; Jupiter's desire for Alcmena, the wife of the Theban general, Amphitryon, leads him to take on the bodily form of her husband in order to bed her. This plot-thread is complemented by Mercury's assumption of the identity of Sosia, Amphitryon's servant. In Molière's version there is the additional character of Cléanthis, Alcmena's maid and Sosia's neglected wife (in Plautus Alcmena's maid Bromia is a peripheral character). Comedy ensues in Molière's version in the different reactions of the husbands to the behaviour of their imitators. Amphitryon is outraged and distressed when he finds out that Jupiter has had relations with his wife. Sosia is principally relieved that Mercury has not bedded his spouse, not because he has avoided being cuckolded, but because he will not be expected to follow suit. Dryden follows the same principle, with a view to the variety of English comedy, in complicating the pairings even further. In Dryden's *Amphitryon* Sosia is married to Bromia. But Mercury seeks to seduce the additional character of Phædra, Alcmena's mercenary maid.[31] Sosia is therefore in trouble with two women and bawdiness saturates their exchanges; Phædra demands a substantial material gift before lying with Mercury/Sosia, and Bromia is horrified at her husband's neglect. Sosia's relative unconcern is contrasted with Amphitryon's despair, and Mercury's complicated bargaining with Phædra is contrasted with Jupiter's comparatively easy execution of his plan. The increase in doubled situations serves not only to intensify the dramatic action, but also to explore and satirize the imitative behaviour of human or human-like characters.

The addition of Phædra also brings about the enhancement of another character. In Molière's play, Naucratès the judge is called in to help discern the real Amphitryon.

Dryden turns this character into the grasping and corrupt Judge Gripus, who starts off as Phædra's paramour until he is persuaded by her and Mercury to give up his claims to her. This is achieved by Mercury's challenging him to a duel in Act V, scene 1. This episode is very similar to the challenge directed at Sganarelle in Molière's *Le Mariage forcé* (1664), thereby demonstrating the vestiges of the hybridization approach to adaptations of Molière's plots. More significantly, Judge Gripus is another figure of corruption who both manipulates and is manipulated. In Dryden's *Amphitryon* the earthly female servant, Jupiter's servant, and the servant of the state are all predominantly self-serving. Whereas in Medbourne's *Tartuffe* the addition of Laurence works towards the denouement of the plot, in Dryden's *Amphitryon* the additional servant delays the resolution because the characters with whom she interacts become obsessed with their own concerns.

Yet the addition of Phædra does serve to intensify the satirical edge of the English *Amphitryon*, in which Jupiter's scheme is likened to the so-called Glorious Revolution of 1688 when the Catholic James II was overthrown by the Protestant William of Orange. Dryden, a Catholic convert, did not consider the revolution glorious. Michael Cordner, however, warns against reading *Amphitryon* as a clear allegory of this historical event:

> A simple matching of mythical and historical personages was never on Dryden's agenda. *Amphitryon* is, rather, fashioned as a teasingly suggestive meditation on the invasion of *'another's Realm'* by a force which cannot be withstood — constantly apposite, therefore, to the circumstances of post-1688 England, but scarcely ever commenting on them with naked directness.[32]

Rather than drawing parallels between the dramatic figures and historical figures, the relative social positions of the characters tell us more about the satirical focus of the work and their earthly interactions drive the plot. In Molière's play there is a rigid class structure amongst the characters that reflects the social structure of France at the time. The denouement of Molière's play is Jupiter's revelation of his true identity and Amphitryon's realization that he must accept his place in the hierarchy. Dryden, however, degrades the gods and questions the hierarchical structure more rigorously. The addition of the plot-thread involving Phædra, Mercury, Sosia, and Gripus works towards a deconstruction of the supposedly rigid structure.

The addition of Phædra does not serve as a catalyst for the resolution of the plot, but as a means of intensifying the theme of manipulation which is the basis of all the plot events. When Mercury first sees Phædra in Act II, scene 2, he declares, 'she's the Perquisite of my Place too; for my Ladies' waiting woman is the proper Fees of my Lords Chief Gentleman'.[33] In other words, Jupiter's chief servant deserves the 'perk' of pursuing Alcmena's waiting woman. Mercury's comment reinforces the analogous positions of the two characters; while Phædra is mortal and Mercury a god, they are equivalents in their grasping, mercenary nature, and the language of economic exchange indicates the personality match. In the mid seventeenth century the term 'perquisite' related specifically to a Lord of the Manor's profits beyond his yearly rents, but by the beginning of the eighteenth century it could refer to any casual gain from an office or 'place'.³⁴ To a large degree, the addition of Phædra in Dryden's text is born of the role of Mercury; Dryden had already articulated his belief that there must be a proliferation of characters in English drama of the time, so Mercury is given a love-interest in his version of the Amphitryon story. Mercury's 'perk of the job' is Dryden's means of complicating and thereby anglicizing Molière's plot.

Amphitryon in all its forms is a play which relies on both thematic and structural parallels. The pairing of Mercury and Phædra works as a subplot which parodies the pairing of Alcmena and Jupiter. Apart from Alcmena and Amphitryon, all of the other characters aim to manipulate each other to serve their own ends. It is the self-interest of the majority of characters that drives the plot. Mercury, commenting upon Phædra's extremely mercenary behaviour, claims that:

> Three thousand years hence, there will be a whole Nation of such Women, in a certain Country that will be call'd France; and there's a Neighbour Island too, where, the Men of that Country will be all Interest. Oh what a precious Generation will that be, which the men of the Island shall Propagate out of the Women of the Continent. (p. 19)

The reference to French women pairing up with British men reminds audiences of the controversial marriage of Charles I and France's Henrietta Maria. Given Dryden's support of the Stuart monarchy after the Restoration, this reading of the 'precious Generation' should not be considered exceptionally ironic, but the focus of Mercury's comment on the links between sexual politics and monetary concerns invites self-reflection from seventeenth-century audiences. Much of Dryden's *Amphitryon* is reminiscent of Jacobean citizen comedies in which the plot is saturated with characters motivated by money and lust. This resonance of a specific English plot-form is another means of anglicization. It is also compelling to read Mercury's comment as a comic metatheatrical reference to Dryden's construction of the play from a French source, as Molière's plot is interwoven with new plot threads that form an overall 'unity of interest' as it was to become known (see n. 20).

Variety and Intensification

The analysis of Medbourne's *Tartuffe* and Dryden's *Amphitryon* demonstrates that the addition of characters did not serve solely to increase the sense of variety for the English stage, although this was a major concern. The addition of characters could also intensify the satirical edge of plays that were reformulated for new temporal and geographical contexts. This could be achieved in starkly different ways, however. While the addition of the character Laurence serves to guide the other charcters and the audience through the plan to bring down the hypocrite in the denouement, the addition of Phædra in *Amphitryon* serves to complicate the parallel plot-structure in order to evoke a society full of self-interested schemers. What these characters share is their status as servants. Servants feature largely in Molière's plots because they promote comedy by highlighting the foibles of their masters, and many have a high level of agency. It is unsurprising, therefore, that the adaptors capitalize on this potential.

Though character additions that provide satirical intensification are the key aspects of these seventeenth-century adaptations of Molière, their overall prevalence in the period should not be overstated. Some adaptors simply add characters to increase the sense of variety, or to claim some originality. Thomas Shadwell's *The Miser* (1672) is another example of an adaptation in which additional characters affect the plot progression, though in this case no fewer than eight speaking character-roles and a handful of extra messenger-characters are added to the plot of *L'Avare* (1668). Shadwell claims in his preface that Molière's original had 'too few persons, and too little action for an *English Theater*', thereby emphasizing the link between character proliferation and intensification of plot. He follows this with the observation "Tis not barrenness of wit or invention, that makes us borrow from the *French*, but laziness; and this was the occasion of my making use of *L'Avare*'.[35] The fact that Shadwell took the trouble to add so many characters would seem to call into question his claim to be indolent, though he is intending to be comically provocative as well as self-defensive. It is not the adaptation as a whole which is meant to be viewed as a lazy literary exercise, but its initial conception. The fertility of wit and invention is meant to be found in the character additions and the resultant variety of action.

The significance of Shadwell's reference to the term 'to make use of' in his explanation of his reasons for adapting Molière is also double-edged. It can mean simply 'to utilize or employ', or it can mean 'to use as an expedient or to exploit for personal gain'. Some late seventeenth-century adaptors of Molière may well have been aware that both senses of the term applied to the work they carried out on the original French plots. But the view that such adaptations were a use and abuse of Molière's plots became dominant at the beginning of the 1700s and coincided with a drive to preserve Molière's characters in their original plots.

Molière's Plots Preserved for Posterity

In the early eighteenth century several dramatists started to highlight the fact that they had based their work on Molière's plots. In 1703 Susanna Centlivre used *Le Médecin malgré lui* (1666) as a basis for *Love's Contrivance; or, Le Médecin malgré lui*.[36] Her retention of the French title indicates the desire to emphasize the source. In the preface she makes the following reference to Molière: 'Some scenes I confess are partly taken from Molier [*sic*] [...] whoever borrows from them [the French], must take care to touch the Colours with an English Pencil, and form the Piece according to our Manners'.[37] Her mixture of metaphors is confusing; while the reference to 'touching the colours' seems to suggest that the French plot material is preserved but retouched in an English hue, the reference to forming the piece suggests more significant intervention. Her play is part-translation, part-adaptation of *Le Médecin malgré lui* and includes additional speaking roles. In Molière's play the young woman Lucinde is promised to one Horace, but he does not appear on stage. In Centlivre's version the intended husband is a fully-fledged old man in search of a young bride. As explored above, such character additions could constitute Centlivre's idea of 'forming the Piece according to our Manners'. It is not Centlivre's play itself which indicates a move towards preserving Molière's original plots, but the way she describes a *translation* process in the preface. Discussion of this kind, wherein principles of translation rather than adaptation or improvement are explored, became more common in the early 1700s.

A focus on translation and the carrying over of Molière's plots is also evident in *Monsieur de Pourceaugnac; or, Squire Trelooby* (1704). Like Centlivre, the self-defined translator of this work retains the French title and, significantly, places it ahead of the English title. The text includes a detailed preface outlining the method of translating Molière's *Monsieur de Pourceaugnac* (1669). It must be noted that the authorship history of this text is complex. A version was performed in London on 30 March 1704. Contemporary letters and accounts reveal that it was originally translated and adapted by William Congreve, John Vanbrugh, and William Walsh, but there is no surviving copy of their text.[38] In April 1704, however, an anonymous translation of *Monsieur de Pourceaugnac* was printed and the author explains that it was the success of the recent performance of the other writers' version that had triggered the publication of the text. It is likely that this translator was John Ozell because he had been working on a translation of some plays for his edition of Molière's works (published 1714) and the same *Squire Trelooby* was included in that edition.[39]

The preface of *Monsieur de Pourceaugnac; or, Squire Trelooby* opens with a clear statement on the nature of the text: 'The Author of the following Sheets has to acquaint the Reader that they contain an entire Translation, *mutatis mutandis*, of Mons. De *Pourceaugnac*, one of Molière's best Pieces'.[40] The use of the phrase *mutatis mutandis*, meaning 'with those things having been changed which need to be changed', points to adaptation but suggests a reluctance to make modifications to the plot unless it is essential. In this version the changes constitute character- and place-name alterations familiar to an English audience. The technical Latin term *mutatis mutandis* was used frequently in philosophy, law, and accountancy. This perhaps increases the likelihood that the translator is John Ozell, whose main occupation was that of an accountant. More significantly, it represents a deliberate and careful approach to preserving a Molière plot in such a way that an English reader could understand its comic significance. At the end of the preface the translator begs to be 'try'd by the Original' ($\pi 4^v$) and hopes that he has succeeded if the reader finds the English version as entertaining as the translator found the French. In this way, the preface reads as a justification for transmitting an entertaining dramatic plot, rather than a justification of elaborate adaptation.

Monsieur de Pourceaugnac; or, Squire Trelooby was reprinted ten years later in Ozell's six-volume *Works of Monsieur de Molière* (1714) which includes translations of thirty-three Molière plays, each retaining the original plots. It also includes an English translation of the lengthy preface that was attached to the 1682 first collected edition of the works of Molière in French. This preface expounds the idea that Molière had improved French comedy by giving it order, manners, taste, and characters.[41] This notion is extended further in the prefatory material to an eight-volume collection of Molière's works in English published in 1732. In *Select Comedies of Mr. de Molière* the translators admonish English dramatists by stating that they can learn from Molière:

> To understand what is meant by a *Whole* and *its Parts*; that to have *four or five independent Plots* in one Play is quite unnecessary, *one* being sufficient; and likewise not to put the *Players* to an unreasonable Expence, by obliging 'em to make new Clothes for double the *Number* of Characters that are wanted to carry on the *Design*, and provide new Scenes for a *Dozen* different Changes in *one* Performance, when a single *Dining-Room* would have done as well.[42]

This discourse points back to the theoretical debates in Dryden's *Essay of Dramatick Poesie*, and argues that numerous sub-plots, characters, and scene settings may be typical of English drama but are superfluous. It also points to the previous ways in which Molière's plays were adapted for English audiences. In the *Select Comedies*, however, Molière is specifically presented and cited for the first time as an exemplary model for plot formation.

The plays included in the *Select Comedies* are presented in the original French and English translation in a parallel text, thereby reinforcing the idea that they are to be considered exemplary. The translators advertise the Molière plots as pedagogical tools; they want the plays to be understood in English but for their overall form to match the original plots. This is in part because they are presenting their text as an innovative edition of Molière, but also because they recognize the powerful influence that Molière's plays had exerted on English plot formation in the preceding decades. That is not to state that adaptations of Molière plots ceased to be produced after the publication of the collected works. Rather, subsequent adaptations were made with reference to the original plots and to the close English translations of them.

Molière's plots were adapted more frequently than any other seventeenth-century French plots between 1663 and 1732. Towards the beginning of this period this was because Molière's one-act plays could be combined into hybrid, semi-original forms. Towards the middle of the period the prevalence of adaptations of Molière was partly a result of fashion and partly the result of the notoriety of his more satirically charged plays, such as *Le Tartuffe*. Adaptors realized that recontextualizations of Molière's plots could be an expedient way of creating satirical drama in English and often added characters to emphasize the new focus. Towards the end of the period there was a clear drive towards preserving Molière plots in their original form but translating them linguistically into English. This was in part owing to a growing interest in translating European literature, but also an interest in preserving the works of a dramatist who was now famous in both France and England and whose plots had formed the basis of many preceding plays.

This chapter began by considering the influence of French dramatic theory on English dramatic theory. On the surface, it seemed that English plot formation had adopted theoretical elements of French plot formation. An analysis of the practice of adapting Molière's plots for English audiences, however, reveals that the French plots themselves were subjected to a process of anglicization. Yet this practice required translators to recognize the French elements of the plots, be they structural or content-related, and so the French origins were not ignored. The array of ways in which the plots were adapted resulted to some degree from the compulsion of individual dramatists to offer original approaches, but also from continual experimentation in how to present and conserve plots that held the attention of audiences in both France and England.

Notes to Chapter 1

1. Aristotle, *Poetics*, trans. by Stephen Halliwell, in *Aristotle, 'Poetics', Longinus, 'On the Sublime', Demetrius, 'On Style'*, Loeb Classical Library, 199 (Cambridge, MA: Harvard University Press, 1995), 6. 1450^{a}38.
2. Antoine Furetière, 'Nœud', in *Dictionnaire universel*, 3 vols (The Hague & Rotterdam: Arnout and Reinier Leers, 1690), II, 731: 'se dit aussi de l'intrigue d'un Roman, d'un Poëme Dramatique, de l'endroit où les personnages sont les plus embarrassez [...] Dénouement: Ce qui sert à debrouiller, à demesler le nœud d'une Comedie, d'un Roman, d'une intrigue'. See also 'Nœud' in *Le Dictionnaire de l'Académie françoise dedié au Roy*, 2 vols (Paris: printed for Coignard, Veuve Jean-Baptiste, 1694), II, 123.
3. François Hédelin d'Aubignac, *La Pratique du théâtre*, ed. by Hélène Baby (Paris: Champion, 2001), p. 152.
4. Antoine Furetière, 'Épisode', in *Dictionnaire universel*, III: 'Histoire ou action detachée, qu'un Poëte ou un Historien insere et lie à son action principale, pour remplir son Ouvrage d'une grande diversité d'évenements. L'Histoire de Didon est un agreable *épisode* dans l'Eneïde. Les *épisodes* ne sont gueres bien receus dans le Dramatique'. The evolution of the definition can be seen in 'Épisode', in *Le Dictionnaire de l'Académie françoise*: 'Action que le Poëte adjouste et lie à son action principale pour l'embellir. *L'episode ne doit jamais estre si fort que l'action principale.*
5. Dramatic theorists came up with varying principles about the way these actions should be ordered. Jacques Scherer gathers a summary of these principles from ideas presented by dramatists and dramatic theorists including Corneille, d'Aubignac, Racine, André Dacier, and Morvan de Bellegarde. While Scherer provides a helpful overview, the points were not followed strictly by dramatists. See Jacques Scherer, *La Dramaturgie classique en France* (Paris: Librairie Nizet, 1986), p. 104.
6. Pierre Corneille, *Œuvres complètes*, ed. by Georges Couton, 3 vols (Paris: Gallimard, 1987), III, 174. Further references are given after quotations in the text.
7. John Dryden (1631–1700) worked for Cromwell's Secretary of State during the Interregnum. In 1660, however, he wrote a royal panegyric for Charles II and set about developing his reputation as the leading poet and literary critic of his times. He became poet laureate in 1668 but was deposed in 1688 when he refused to swear the oath of allegiance to William and Mary.
8. John Dryden, *Prose, 1668–1691, An Essay of Dramatick Poesie and Shorter Works*, ed. by Samuel Holt Monk and A. E. Wallace Maurer, The Works of John Dryden, 17 (Berkeley, Los Angeles, & London: University of California Press, 1971), p. 47. Further references are given after quotations in the text.
9. Jean Racine, *Théâtre. Poésie*, ed. by Georges Forestier (Paris: Gallimard, 1999), pp. 450–51. Racine also discusses the issue of 'une action simple' in the prefaces to *Britannicus* (1670) and *Mithridate* (1673).
10. William D'Avenant (1660–68) was a dramatist, poet, and theatre manager. He wrote several comedies and masques for the Caroline court, became poet laureate in 1638, and was knighted by Charles I in 1643. He followed the exiled court to Saint-Germain-en-Laye but was imprisoned in 1650 for his loyalty to the monarchy. After his release he started to develop London's theatre by promoting operatic works. In 1660 he applied to the Attorney-General to grant himself and Thomas Killigrew a monopoly for their respective acting companies. D'Avenant became manager of the Duke's Company and remained in this role until his death.
11. Act III of *A Playhouse to be Let* consists of D'Avenant's 1659 masque *The History of Sir Francis Drake*, and Act IV is his 1658 entertainment *The Cruelty of the Spaniards in Peru*. The play ends with the fifth 'audition', *Tragedy Travestie*, a burlesque of Katherine Philips's 1663 English verse translation of Pierre Corneille's *La Mort de Pompée* (1642).

12. William D'Avenant, *The Playhouse to be Let*, in *The Works of Sir William D'Avenant* (London: printed by T. N. for Henry Herringman, 1673), pp. 67–119 (p. 67). Corneille had likewise called his play *L'Illusion comique* (1636) 'un étrange monstre' (*Œuvres complètes*, I, 613).
13. Richard Flecknoe (c.1605–77) is believed to have attended the Catholic English College at St Omer and afterwards became a secular priest in London. As civil war loomed he left for the continent but returned ten years later to write poetry and plays. His relationship with theatre managers was strained; he argued that D'Avenant's production style was too elaborate. In the satire *Mac Flecknoe* (written around 1678) John Dryden attacks Thomas Shadwell by casting him as Flecknoe's literary heir.
14. In a diary entry for 15 September 1668 Samuel Pepys makes reference to an unpopular play he saw called *The Ladys à la Mode*, claiming it was a 'translation out of French by Dryden'. The title and date seem to suggest that it could have been a performance of Flecknoe's play and that Pepys had confused it with one of Dryden's Molière adaptations (Samuel Pepys, *The Diary of Samuel Pepys*, ed. by Robert Latham and William Matthews, 11 vols (London: Bell and Hyman, 1970–83), IX, 307).
15. Richard Flecknoe, *The Damoiselles à la mode* (London: printed for the author, 1667), A3^r. Further references are given after quotations in the text.
16. *Stratagème* is a key term in French farce. See Molière's *Les Fourberies de Scapin* (1671), *Œuvres complètes*, II, 1. 2. p. 374, 3. 1. p. 403, 3. 3. p. 410.
17. Plato, *Selected Dialogues of Plato: The Benjamin Jowett Translation*, rev. and intro. by Hayden Pelliccia (New York: Modern Library, 2001), p. 11.
18. John Dryden, *Plays: The Indian Emperour, Secret Love, Sir Martin Mar-all*, ed. by John Loftis and Vinton A. Dearing, The Works of John Dryden, 9 (Berkeley, Los Angeles, & London: University of California Press, 1966), p. 367.
19. Thomas Shadwell, *The Sullen Lovers; or, The Impertinents* (London: printed for Henry Herringman, 1668), (a)1^r (further references are given after quotations in the text). Shadwell (c.1640–92) was a dramatist who courted controversy. He argued with John Dryden on points of dramatic theory, resulting in Dryden's cutting satire on Shadwell, *Mac Flecknoe* (published in 1682). This embroiled Shadwell's fellow Whig writers in further quarrelling with Dryden's fellow Tory writers. Neverthless, Shadwell became poet laureate in 1688 and his interest in the role of music in drama helped to develop English opera.
20. By the eighteenth century Antoine Houdar de La Motte came up with a new unity he claimed was distinct from unity of action. La Motte's so-called *unité d'intérêt* does not require events to relate to each other so much as to particular characters. See Antoine Houdar de la Motte, *Suite des réflexions sur la tragédie où on répond à Mr. de Voltaire* (Paris: Dupuis, 1730; fac. repr. Millwood, NY: Kraus International, 1983), p. 12.
21. John Dryden, *Plays: The Tempest, Tyrannick Love, An Evening's Love*, ed. by Maximillian E. Novak and George R. Guffey, The Works of John Dryden, 10 (Berkeley, Los Angeles, & London: University of California Press, 1970), p. 212.
22. This is perhaps unsurprising given that Dryden used numerous sources for *An Evening's Love*, including Thomas Corneille's *Le Feint Astrologue* (1651), and Molière's *Le Dépit amoureux* (1656).
23. Matthew Medbourne (*bap.* 1637?, *d.* 1680) performed with the Duke's Company from 1661 until 1668, spent a season with the King's in 1670, and returned to the Duke's the following year. His Catholicism (and notoriety for brawling) made him a pawn in the Popish Plot, a frenzy caused by Titus Oates, who falsely claimed that several high-profile Catholics were plotting to assassinate Charles II. In 1678 Medbourne was imprisoned at Newgate, where he died two years later.
24. See Robert McBride, *Molière et son premier Tartuffe: genèse et évolution d'une pièce à scandale*, Durham Modern Languages Series (Durham: Durham University Press, 2005).
25. For an analysis of the satirically charged recontextualization of the play in the form of Medbourne's translation see Chapter 5.
26. For a full explanation of the different versions of *Tartuffe* see OC, II, 1361–89. See also McBride, *Molière et son premier Tartuffe*.
27. See Lori Sonderegger, 'Sources of Translation: A Discussion of Matthew Medbourne's 1670

Translation of Molière's *Tartuffe*', *Papers on Seventeenth-century French Literature*, 27.52 (2000), 553–72. Sonderegger argues that the two sections that are not highlighted by manicules (Act III, scenes 8 & 9) may not be additions at all, but scenes from Molière's original 1664 version that Medbourne had witnessed. In Act III, scene 8, Tartuffe describes his villainous plan to Laurence, who encourages him. Sonderegger puzzles over this apparent inconsistency in the character of Laurence, who supports the family in the other scenes in which he appears. In the following scene Madame Pernelle (Orgon's mother) and Flypote, her servant, rejoice at the thought that Damis will be disinherited in favour of Tartuffe. Sonderegger suggests that these are 'mirror scenes between master and servant which highlight the hypocrisy and criminality of Tartuffe, a theme central to Molière's play which met with opposition in France and acceptance in the radically different religious climate in England' (p. 568). Yet parallel-plots are a feature of the adaptation of French plays into English in the era. It is just as possible that they are additions by Medbourne but are not highlighted by manicules owing to accidental omission.

28. Matthew Medbourne, *Tartuffe; or, The French Puritan* (London: printed by H. L and R. B. for James Magnus, 1670), A3^r. Further references are given after quotations in the text.
29. According to Judith Milhous and Robert D. Hume the play was first performed in the autumn-winter season 1669–70: 'Dating Play Premieres', *Harvard Library Bulletin*, 22 (1974), 374–405 (p. 383). The editors of *The London Stage* record that it was performed in 1670 and 1671. See *The London Stage, 1660–1800: A Calendar of Plays, Entertainments and Afterpieces. Part I: 1660–1700*, ed. by William Van Lennep, Emmet L. Avery, and Arthur H. Scouten (Carbondale: Southern Illinois University Press, 1965), pp. 171, 179.
30. Anne Barbeau Gardiner, 'Medbourne's *Tartuffe* (1670): A Satire on Land-Acquisition during the Interregnum', *Restoration and Eighteenth-century Theatre Research*, 9.1 (1994) 1–16 (p. 1).
31. The addition of Phædra is not encapsulated in clearly defined sections. Dryden's adaptation of *Amphitryon* is not a straightforward translation of Molière's text with added scenes interspersed. He claims in his preface that around half of it is his own invention. There is a useful comparative chart for the acts and scenes of Plautus's, Molière's, and Dryden's versions of the play in John Dryden, *Plays: Albion and Albanius, Don Sebastian, Amphitryon*, ed. by Earl Miner, George R. Guffey and Franklin B. Zimmerman, The Works of John Dryden, 15 (Berkeley, Los Angeles, & London: University of California Press, 1976), pp. 554–56. In Dryden, Phædra features in ten of eighteen scenes that do not have any parallel scenes in Molière's text, thereby showing that her addition is the most significant source of plot-adaptation.
32. John Dryden, *Amphitryon; or, The Two Sosias*, in *Four Restoration Marriage Plays*, ed. by Michael Cordner and Ronald Clayton (Oxford: Oxford University Press, 1995), pp. xxxv–xxxvi.
33. John Dryden, *Amphitryon; or, The Two Socia's* (London: printed for J. Tonson, 1690), p. 17. Further references are given after quotations in the text.
34. Edward Phillips, 'Perquisites', in *The New World of English Words* (London: printed by E. Tyler for Nath. Brooke, 1658); John Kersey, 'Perquisite', in *A New English Dictionary* (London: printed for Henry Bonwicke and Robert Knaplock, 1702).
35. Thomas Shadwell, *The Miser, a Comedy* (London: printed for Thomas Collins and John Ford, 1672), A3^r. Further references are given after quotations in the text.
36. Susanna Centlivre (*bap.* 1669?, *d.* 1723) was an actress and playwright who wrote sixteen plays, three playlets, as well as several poems, satires, and prose pieces. Owing to her own acting career, she had a close relationship with those who performed her works. Her plays revealed her Whiggish political leanings but endured onstage long after her death.
37. Susanna Centlivre, *Love's Contrivance; or, Le Médecin malgré lui* (London: printed for Bernard Lintott, 1703), A2^v. Further references are given after quotations in the text.
38. See John C. Hodges, 'The Authorship of *Squire Trelooby*', *The Review of English Studies*, 4.16 (1928), 404–13.
39. John Ozell (*d.* 1743) was a London accountant. From 1711 onwards he published translations of writers including Cervantes, Racine, and Molière. In 1708 Ozell used his translation of Boileau's *Le Lutrin* to respond to Jonathan Swift's *The Battle of the Books* (1704), thereby revisiting the *querelle des anciens et des modernes*. Ozell reworked Boileau's writing to put forward Whig ideas, leading to satirical attacks from Tory writers.

40. Molière, *Monsieur de Pourceaugnac; or, Squire Trelooby*, trans. anon. [John Ozell?] (London: printed for Bernard Lintott, 1704), π2ʳ. Further references are given after quotations in the text.
41. Molière, *The Works of Monsieur de Molière*, trans. by John Ozell (and others), 6 vols (London: printed for Bernard Lintott, 1714), I, 1. Further references are given after quotations in the text.
42. Molière, *Select Comedies*, I, A10ᵛ.

CHAPTER 2

Translation Theory and Paratext

Seventeenth-century French writing had an influence not only on the practice of translation, but also on its theory. It was not the case, however, that there existed in early modern France or England a substantial body of written work on the theory of translation. Whereas the dramatic theory of Corneille and the abbé d'Aubignac had been discussed at length and indeed translated in late seventeenth-century England, writing on the practice of translating was treated less systematically and often formed the prefatory material to works that were the result of the process.[1] The majority of sources were of course classical Greek or Latin texts, not least because their translation had long since been at the core of education in both France and England, and a productive activity in literary and publishing circles.[2] Mid-seventeenth-century writers translating classical works for literary publication, however, turned away from the scholastic model of literal translation in order to grant the translator greater creative freedom.

This chapter will show that changing theoretical currents influenced the ways in which Molière's plays were first translated into English. Though the prefaces to Molière translations have hitherto been addressed in relation to cultural transfer and appropriation, they have not been read against translation theory in order to gauge the evolution of translation practice in the late seventeenth and early eighteenth centuries.[3] This chapter will fill this gap by examining the approaches of Molière's translators within the frames of both modern and early modern translation theory.

Translation Studies

In the prefatory material to late seventeenth- and early eighteenth-century translations and adaptations of Molière the roots of modern translation studies can be discerned, though early modern theoretical writings are shaped most frequently by translators' varying approaches to their work. The particular conditions of drama, produced for immediate effect in a collaborative process, meant that it was difficult to come up with a coherent theory of 'dramatic translation', particularly when translators of drama who sought recognition for creativity were reluctant to acknowledge themselves as translators in the first place. Furthermore, dramatic borrowings were rarely linear; a playwright might turn to Molière, but at the same time absorb other dramatic traditions, either from the source text itself (where Molière draws on Italian *commedia dell'arte* for example), or from a pertinent classical model such as Plautus. The idea that translation and adaptation could be complementary freed some writers from this concern at the beginning of the eighteenth century. The theory of translation continued to evolve and by the end of the eighteenth century a full essay on the principles of translation was published.[4] The complexities of translation have continued to invite numerous studies throughout the following centuries.

A systematic study of the theory of translation emerged in late twentieth-century 'Translation Studies'. This field is most concerned with modern attitudes to translation evolving in the present. Nevertheless, twentieth- and twenty-first-century translation theory offers some insightful terms and principles that can aid understanding of the methods by which Molière's plays were first translated.

Domestication

One significant difference between the translator in early modern England and the translator in modern England, is relative visibility. As the later sections of this chapter will show, the prefaces to the translations of Molière's works reveal that whether or not the translators were uneasy with their role, their presence was made clear. In modern translation, however, the translator is usually acknowledged, but does not claim a large amount of reader attention, particularly if the text is rendered by 'fluent translating', or translating that aims to disguise the foreignness of a source-text. Lawrence Venuti explains that fluent translation into English 'masquerades as true semantic equivalence when it in fact transcribes the foreign text with a partial interpretation, partial to English-language values, reducing if not simply excluding the very difference that translation is called on to convey'.[5] Venuti argues that the 'illusionism' of fluent translating and the invisible translator leads to an 'insidious domestication of foreign texts, rewriting them in the transparent discourse that prevails in English' (p. 17). The 'ethnocentric violence' of 'domestication', as Venuti terms it, is present in the late seventeenth-century translations of Molière, though this approach to translation is not concealed by translators; the 'Englishing' of the texts is often vaunted.

A 'domesticating' translation not only provides the means for a translator to demonstrate ingenuity in producing versions that read naturally in the target language, but it also has a broader social significance. Venuti argues that the prevailing aim of translation is:

> To bring back a cultural other as the same, the recognizable, even the familiar; and this aim always risks a wholesale domestication of a foreign text, often in highly self-conscious projects, where translation serves an appropriation of foreign cultures for domestic agendas, cultural, economic, political. Translation can be considered the communication of a foreign text, but it is always a communication limited by its address to a specific reading audience. (pp. 18–19)

This is all the more applicable to translation for the stage, which in the seventeenth and eighteenth centuries was expected to reflect the society with which theatre audiences were familiar. The prefaces to the first translations of Molière show that the domesticating influence was most dominant and often put to politically satirical effect. Matthew Medbourne's part-translation, part-adaptation of *Le Tartuffe, Tartuffe; or, The French Puritan* (1670), for example, deploys the French text to satirize religious affairs in England and to become part of a seventeenth-century English dramatic tradition of anti-Puritan satire. The first translations of Molière were frequently made to evoke a recognizable English world to English audiences.

The domesticating influence of translation in late seventeenth- and early eighteenth-century theatre was so dominant that audiences could expect to recognize aspects of their own culture in the English versions. A prime example of the domesticating tendency is offered in the first translation of Molière's *Monsieur de Pourceaugnac*. The writer of the preface to *Squire Trelooby; or, Monsieur de Pourceaugnac* (1704) addresses aspects of domesticating translation in detail as he compares his translation with another recent production on stage recorded in contemporary accounts as the work of the dramatists John Vanbrugh, William Walsh, and William Congreve:[6]

> Their Translation was not likely to be printed, tho' there have been Demands made for it, by the whole Town, who have taken up with wrong Conceptions of it as it was acted; some thinking it was a Party-Play made on purpose to ridicule the Whole Body of *West Country* Gentlemen. Now by this Translation it will be seen there was no such thing as any particular Character in this Kingdom aim'd at, 'tho I will not say the Cap may not fit some among us.
> Squire Trelooby of Penzance, in the county of *Cornwall*, is proper *English* enough for Monsieur *Pourceaugnac* of *Limoge* in the Province of *Gascony*, &c. (π4^r)

The performed version may have been interpreted as a 'Party-Play' because Vanbrugh, Walsh, and Congreve were Whigs. They may well have intended to satirize Tories and Jacobites, who had strong support in Cornwall at the beginning of the eighteenth century. The translator goes on to mention the inclusion of a well-known local London story in the Vanbrugh, Walsh, and Congreve version. So the passage demonstrates various nationalizing and localizing effects of domesticating translation, while at the same time recognizing the process undergone by the original French text.

Foreignization

Opposite to domestication is 'foreignization', in which the 'otherness' of the text being translated is detectable. Venuti explains that:

> Foreignizing translation signifies the difference of the foreign text, yet only by disrupting the foreign codes that prevail in the target language. In its effort to do right abroad, this translation method must do wrong at home, deviating enough from native norms to stage an alien reading experience. (p. 20)

This approach is alien to most seventeenth- and eighteenth-century translators of Molière. This is perhaps unsurprising given that Venuti proposes it as a new approach for an increasingly globalized world at the end of the twentieth century. Curiously, however, the first translation of a Molière play in English took a self-consciously 'foreignizing' approach. The contracted translation of *Le Cocu imaginaire* in William D'Avenant's *The Playhouse to be Let* (1663) is written in dubious yet comic French-accented English because it is supposedly being performed by French actors. There are no comparable examples of this foreignizing approach amongst the first translations of Molière for the stage; generally, theatrical experiences were designed to create familiarity rather than alienation.

Despite their apparent polarity, 'the domestic' and 'the foreign' were not wholly distinct concepts in the context of post-Restoration Anglo-French relations. After the restoration of Charles II, who had been in exile in France, French fashions and literature were rapidly absorbed into the urban culture of London. This had a profound effect on language. In the seventeenth century many French words passed into English (*galanterie*; *mode* as in 'prevailing fashion'; *libertin* as in 'free-thinker in religion'; *hypochondriaque* as in 'melancholic'; *bourgeois* as an identifier for a citizen of a French town or borough); their meanings were fluid.[7] Translators of Molière could retain some of the French words of the original texts provided that they were starting to be used in English. These words could be regarded as both foreign and domestic depending on the knowledge or experience of audiences which, at the time, were confronted with French imports of many kinds.[8]

Given that translation theory tends to conceive of the source-language and the target language in distinct terms, it can be helpful to consider blurred boundaries between the domestic and the foreign in relation to the theory of adaptation. The fundamental meaning of *adaptation* is the process of altering something to suit a particular purpose or new environment. In this sense, the process of translation is itself a process of adaptation. The modern field of 'Adaptation Studies' has now emerged. It began with studies of the adaptation of novels for film in the mid-twentieth century, but has since broadened to include a wide range of adaptations for various media. Though it is a separate field from translation studies in that a bilingual element is not a crucial component, much of the critical discourse in both areas is interlinked. The editors of *Adaptation Studies: New Challenges, New Directions* note that:

> A central — perhaps even *the* central — question of adaptation studies has been that of fidelity, or the relationship between what has been considered an original and the more-or-less faithful rendering of that form or content into a new product. From the very outset of adaptation criticism [...] scholars have criticized the idea that faithfulness is the most interesting and productive instrument with which to confront adaptations [...]. Although fidelity discourse has been abandoned, the issue of similarities and differences is still very much present in contemporary research. Adaptation must necessarily incorporate some kind of comparative element — seeing one text in relation to another — and the strategic and almost universal move in the field has been to 'translate' fidelity into the more neutral, and thus useful, measure of similarity and difference on various levels of the compared texts.[9]

This echoes discussion of translation in relation to the Renaissance practice and principle of imitation. It also reflects the ideas of fidelity and infidelity that emerged strongly in the seventeenth-century French and English theoretical writings on translation. The first translations of Molière's plays into English were shaped by the tension between similarity and difference and resulted in the writing of some justificatory prefaces that attempted to explain the competing forces of 'fidelity' and 'originality', and some that ignored them.

Translation Terms

The complexity of translation is reflected in the etymology of its descriptors. The term 'translation' derives from the classical Latin *trānslātiō*, meaning the act of transferring something from one place to another, the shifting of ideas or concepts from one context to another, and by extension the transformation of words in one language into words in another. The stem *trānslāt-* comes from the past participle of *transferre*, 'to transfer, carry across', and the word 'translation' may have entered English via the Latin-derived Old French verb *translater*, which from the twelfth century to the fifteenth century was used to describe conveyance and the process of translating from one language to another.[10]

By the sixteenth century the French verb *traduire*, formed from the Latin *trādūcĕre* 'to transport, lead across', had replaced *translater*.[11] Seventeenth-century dictionary definitions of the French word *traduire* and its related noun *traduction* refer to the process of turning writing in one language into writing in another language, 'tourner d'une langue en une autre'.[12] The French verb *tourner* could also be used as a substitute for *traduire*. These French words came to replace the older term *vertir*, the Latin root of which is the equivalent of the Greek *tornos* meaning 'lathe or circular movement'. In both Furetière's 1690 dictionary and Thomas Corneille's 1694 dictionary it is noted that *vertir* was an old word meaning 'traduire d'une langue en une autre'.[13]

Seventeenth-century English definitions of translation arrived via French and are therefore comparable. By the end of the sixteenth century the process of linguistic translation was being articulated in increasing detail. John Rider's *Bibliotheca scholastica* includes the entry 'To Translate from one language to another: to interprete', which draws attention to the explanatory role of translation in the listing of the synonym.[14] Edward Phillips's entry for 'translation' in *The New World of English Words* (1658) reads: '(lat.) a changing from one place or thing to another, a turning out of one language into another'.[15] The English verb 'to turn', like the French *tourner*, could likewise be used as a substitute for 'to translate' throughout the seventeenth century. There was no equivalent verb to the term *vertir*, but the derivative word *version*, in French and English respectively, could be used by seventeenth-century writers to refer quite specifically to a translation from one language into another.[16] In modern English usage, 'version' can be applied more loosely to texts which are derivative of previous works, whereas the word 'translation' is reserved for works which bear a close resemblance to the source in terms of signification. If the means of referring to the general process of translation are complex, the distinctions between different methods of translation are more complicated still. Nevertheless, early modern writers attempted to identify, and in some cases to categorize, different types of translation.

Early Modern Theoretical Writings on Translation

As the comparisons between Venuti's principles and the examples of early Molière translations suggest, Translation Studies is not a wholly original field of criticism. There are further parallels to be drawn between modern theory and early modern critical writings. Significant sustained interest in the process of translation grew rapidly in Renaissance Europe. Much theoretical discussion of translation grew out of the humanist educational concept of *imitatio*. This was the principle that held that scholars should copy the style or rhetorical devices of classical Latin or Greek writers in order to train themselves to write well and to produce literary works of a high quality. Such imitation does not produce carbon copies of the original; humanist imitation is based on the seemingly paradoxical notion that the copies should be different and yet somehow the same as original source-texts.

Valerie Worth-Stylianou points out that the tension between similarity and difference meant that the terminology surrounding Renaissance imitation was varied, stating that the 'language of criticism contains a range of terms, such as emulation, *remaniement* [reworking], paraphrase, and finally translation, to define degrees of similarity or difference between the two texts'.[17] She goes on to point out that though translation contributed to the practice of 'imitation' it was also considered a separate field in its own right, distinct from other forms of imitation because it is an exercise that involves two languages and a sustained close engagement with the source, usually from beginning to end. This engagement involves choice:

> The translator must, albeit unconsciously, impose his own reading on the source text and produce a rewriting of it. In this way, translation [...] depends upon the implied presence of a series of choices which guarantee the individual character of every work. Similarity to the source text may be an element integral to the process of translation but difference from the model is the prerogative of the individual translator. And because there are no hard-and-fast normative rules, he is continually practising and thereby defining his art. (p. 4)

The roots of translation theory lie in the justifications and explanations of individual choices made by practising translators.

Concentration on the classics as models for philosophical and poetic writing endured into the mid-seventeenth century and led to a proliferation of translations and discussions of the method of translation best suited to literary output. In France, Nicolas Perrot d'Ablancourt demonstrated innovative principles in the theory of translation, though his ideas were shaped to some degree by the ambitions of the Académie française. His remarks on translation varied depending on the type of work he was translating. In rendering Tacitus, for example, he considers that the historical nature of the work demands respect for facts. He writes at length in a 1658 preface about the retention of details relating to Roman life, dates, and personal names. On the other hand, he notes that over-scrupulousness could diminish the pleasure to be had from reading the text: 'Il faut [...] prendre garde qu'on ne fasse perdre la grace à son Auteur par trop de scrupule, & que de peur de luy manquer de foi, on luy soit infidèle en tout'.[18] The ideas of 'fidelity' and 'infidelity' occur frequently in d'Ablancourt's writing on translation and he advocates both of them depending on the effect he wishes to create.[19]

In the preface to his translation of Lucian, d'Ablancourt allows more intervention from the translator in rendering the fables. Given the simultaneous didactic and entertaining purpose of the fables, d'Ablancourt is, unsurprisingly, concerned that they be understood within his contemporary context and in accordance with contemporary manners:

> J'ai retranché ce qu'il y avait de plus sale, et adouci en quelques endroits, ce qui était trop libre [...] voilà mon dessein assez bien justifié par tant d'avantages qui peuvent revenir au public, de la lecture de cet Auteur. Je dirais seulement que je lui ai laissé ses opinions toutes entières, parce qu'autrement ce ne serait pas une Traduction, mais je réponds dans l'Argument ou dans les Remarques, à ce qu'il y a de plus fort, afin que cela ne puisse nuire.[20]

According to d'Ablancourt, the translator is not a passive figure who merely re-encodes a language, but an arbiter of taste who ought to sanitize the original text where it does not complement contemporary manners. The initial step of translation is to select a work to be translated; the translator is held responsible for the choice, but can mitigate criticism by translating the source text with sensitivity to the target audience. D'Ablancourt also points out, however, that he cannot tamper with Lucian's own views, or the text would no longer be a translation. The only way to demonstrate his concern for upholding his contemporary social mores is to discuss any controversial views in paratextual material. The informal nature of the language in the fables also calls for some ingenuity on the part of the translator, because it includes Homeric verses, hackneyed allusions, old-fashioned proverbs, and examples that must be modernized in order to entertain the readers of the translation. What d'Ablancourt demonstrates above all is the manner in which translation technique may change according to the type of work selected as a source-text.

D'Ablancourt's ideas about translation passed into England. Echoes of passages of his prefaces are found in Sir John Denham's preface to the 1656 edition of *The Destruction of Troy*. Denham had been a royalist exile in France, so had most probably come into contact with the discussion concerning the loose translations that were being produced by d'Ablancourt. Denham defines the 'new way' of translating in relation to the supposed errors of the 'old way':

> I conceive it a vulgar error in translating Poets, to affect being *Fidus Interpres;* let that care be taken with them who deal in matters of Fact, or matters of Faith: but whosoever aims it in Poetry, as he attempts what is not required, so he shall never perform what he attempts; for it is not his business alone to translate Language into Language, but Poesie into Poesie.[21]

The notion that translation was becoming a literary pursuit and art in its own right became increasingly prevalent in the 1650s. Abraham Cowley, who also returned to England from exile in France, writes in his preface to *Pindarique Odes* (1656) that:

> It does not at all trouble me that the *Grammarians* perhaps will not suffer this libertine way of rendering foreign Authors, to be called *Translation*; for I am not so much enamoured of the *Name Translator*, as not to wish rather to be *Something Better*, though it want yet a *Name*.[22]

Elsewhere in the preface Cowley suggests the word 'Imitation' as a means of describing the new 'libertine' approach to translation. He does not address, however, exactly how far 'imitation' strays from an original source text. It was left to John Dryden to attempt to draw up categories from the approaches to translation that had been outlined in loose metaphorical terms by Cowley and his contemporaries.

Dryden outlined three essential types of translation. Like the translators before him, he made his observations in a preface to a translation of a classical work, *Ovid's Epistles* (1680):

> All translation, I suppose, may be reduced to these three heads.
> First, that of metaphrase, or turning an author word by word, and line by line, from one language into another. [...] The second way is that of paraphrase, or translation with latitude, where the author is kept in view by the translator, so as never to be lost, but his words are not so strictly followed as his sense [...] The third way is that of imitation, where the translator (if now he has not lost that name) assumes the liberty, not only to vary from the words and sense, but to forsake them both as he sees occasion.[23]

Dryden goes on to express his favour for paraphrase over metaphrase and imitation:

> Since every language is so full of its own proprieties, that what is beautiful in one, is often barbarous, nay sometimes nonsense, in another, it would be unreasonable to limit a translator to the narrow compass of his author's words: 'tis enough if he choose out some expression which does not vitiate the sense. (p. 118)

Yet Dryden himself concludes the preface by noting that he has 'transgressed' the 'rules' he has offered, thereby suggesting that they can only be guidelines. He claims he has 'taken more liberty than a just translation will allow' (p. 119). A 'just translation', then, is a practice that grants the translator *some* liberty, but not too much liberty. In Dryden's critical writing the term 'just translation' signifies limited paraphrase, but a clear explanation of the requisite restrictions on paraphrase eludes him. Rather, the ideal of a 'just translation' acts as a benchmark against which Dryden can measure his various translations.

Dramatic Translation and Theory

The most detailed remarks on the theory of translation in the seventeenth century are found in prefaces to translations of classical poetry or philosophy. Classical drama likewise had a strong influence on both French and English drama of the seventeenth century, but the manner in which it was treated as a source for translation is complex. While some plays were translated closely and presented in parallel texts for scholarly and leisurely reading, others were adapted for new stage productions. Liberties could be taken to shorten the latter, or to add to them music, song, or dance. In seventeenth-century Europe there was a long tradition of borrowing plots, or plot mechanisms, stories, or characters from either classical or near-contemporary sources and across borders. Seventeenth-century French comedy, for example, was shaped by a range of contemporary as well as classical influences, including Spanish comedy, Italian *commedia dell'arte*, novels, and traditions of farce. Molière's plots were chopped, changed, and combined in the first appearances of his work on the English stage (see Chapter 1). Making a distinction between translation and adaptation was both difficult and counterproductive for dramatists who wanted to claim some originality for a work and to avoid the charge of plagiarism.

Those who translated drama for stage productions sought the acclaim of audiences first and foremost. According to those who adapted Molière's plots in English, this acclaim was dependent on the level of variety in the intrigue. But some of those adaptors still translated sections of Molière's dialogue. Many avoided explaining the interplay between plot adaptation and linguistic translation as they wanted to lay claim to originality. Likewise, those who translated Molière line-by-line, without adding or rearranging sections, often evaded describing their translation process, partly because they wanted to protect their status as creative dramatists and partly because there was little existing theoretical discourse on the translation of drama. Drama, particularly comedy, was meant to reflect the contemporary society in which it was performed; unlike translations of the classical authors, which were intended for posterity, much translation of contemporary drama in the seventeenth century was intended to make an impact in performance, and this had consequences for the way it was translated.

Seventeenth-Century Evasion of Theory

Many of the first translators of Molière were creative in the way they avoided the term 'translation', even if a reading of their texts shows that they did translate either all or parts line-by-line from the French. An analysis of the terms used to describe those texts that do include direct translation from Molière is a helpful tool for gauging changing attitudes towards the translation of drama. If seventeenth-century dramatists were reluctant to declare that they had simply translated Molière, by the beginning of the eighteenth century a more direct acknowledgment of the translation process was typical, perhaps because literary translation was being discussed in more detail, particularly after Dryden had recorded his three basic guiding principles.

In the preface to Richard Flecknoe's *The Damoiselles à la mode* (1667), a hybrid of *Les Précieuses ridicules* and *L'École des maris*, translation is described as 'Englishing':

> For the Language of the *Pretieuse*, it may be wondered that I durst attempt the *Englishing* of it (so often attempted by our best *English* wits, and as often despaired of) it being a Language even new unto the *French* themselves, and so little understood by most of them, as they are forc'd to make a Dictionary for it apart; which notwithstanding I have done, and I hope with success, as I have not only made the Language of the Author, *English*, but even the spirit, life, and quickness of it too. (A3^v)

This is the only part of the preface that addresses the linguistic changes Flecknoe had made to the original French text. Elsewhere Flecknoe uses an elaborate metaphor of jewel-setting to describe the way he combines different plots. The term 'Englishing' can apply to both the plot adaptation and the translation, though in the section above it is used in relation to one particular difficulty of translation. Flecknoe uses the term to emphasize his ingenuity; he has not merely translated a difficult type of language so that it is understandable to his audiences, he has also made it fit into the English language.

Ironically, a reading of the text shows that Flecknoe 'Englishes' the play by 'Frenchifying' much of the language. This, however, is representative of the way that French words were absorbed into English within particular fashionable and urban contexts in the late seventeenth century. The idea that characters should be speaking in a recognizably English way was particularly important in comedy of the time, which was supposed to reflect contemporary society and mores. It is difficult, if not impossible, to define what the 'spirit, life and quickness' of the 'Author's [Molière's] Language' are, though the comment acknowledges the reputation of the author of the source-text and thereby demonstrates the translator's discernment in having picked out the text. Other dramatists openly declare that their translation has been a theft or exploitation of the source text, though such admissions are often presented comically. Thomas Shadwell adapted several of Molière's plays and translated some sections directly. In *The Sullen Lovers* (1668) the only reference made to any translation of *Les Fâcheux* (1661) is the remark 'I made use of but two Short Scenes' (A3^v). The evasive term 'to make use of' appears in his address to the reader of *The Miser* (1672), in a provocative observation quite typical of Shadwell:

> I think I may say without vanity that *Moliere's* part of it has not suffer'd in my hands, nor did I ever know a *French* Comedy made use of by the Worst of our Poets, that was not better'd by them. (A3^r)

Setting aside the deliberately incendiary nature of the comment, Shadwell demonstrates a trend for Molière's translators to define their works in negative terms; rather than defining what the translation has done to the source-text, many translators or adaptors merely state that no harm has been done to it in the process. Even several decades later in 1703, the preface to Susanna Centlivre's *Love's Contrivance; or, Le Médecin malgré lui* reads similarly in the comment 'I dare be bold to say it has not suffered in the Translation' (A2^v). Significantly, this is one of the few references to translation found in the late seventeenth- and early eighteenth-century translations of Molière's plays. In Centlivre's comment, however, 'in the Translation' could be read as 'in the carrying over'; she means she considers that the text has been unharmed in transit. Although she goes on to write that she has 'touched the Colours with an English Pencil' and 'formed the Piece according to our Manners', she offers no description of the translation technique she has adopted, whether paraphrase, metaphrase, imitation, or a mixture of all three.

In contrast, John Dryden, having defined three types of translation technique in 1680, subsequently used his own terms to refer to his translations or adaptations, measuring them by the principles he had set out. Thus, in the preface to *Amphitryon* (1690) he writes: 'the World will too easily discover that more than half of it is mine, and that the rest is rather a lame Imitation of their Excellencies than a just Translation' (A3^r). Dryden, having supposedly dismissed imitation in the preface to *Ovid's Epistles*, here claims that he had used the technique. Perhaps this is because he allows a greater freedom when translating or adapting plays than when translating Latin lyrics.[24] His choice of adjectives, however, demonstrates that he still considers the 'just translation' the ideal. His recourse to 'lame imitation' is perhaps due to the heavy adaptation process he undertakes when combining plot elements from Plautus and Molière. Above all, Dryden demonstrates that the theory of translation was more complex than he had acknowledged by his categorizing principles; they do, however, remain helpful in identifying the dominant translation techniques used by other writers.

Eighteenth-Century Engagement with Theory

At the beginning of the eighteenth century there was a strong interest in translating Molière closely, though whether this was to be achieved by paraphrase or metaphrase was still open to debate. *Monsieur de Pourceaugnac; or, Squire Trelooby*, believed to be by John Ozell, has a preface setting out in detail the differences between the published translation and the unpublished version that had been produced for the stage the same year:

> I call this an entire Translation, because the other that was play'd was not so; there being omitted the long Debate of the two Doctors [...] entirely and also the Eleventh Scene of the second Act [...] unless it can be shewn me that the other was anything other than a Translation, which nobody can ever say that ever read *Pourceaugnac* before they saw *Trelooby* [...] I believe I shall not incur the Pique of the other Gentlemen. (π3–3ᵛ)

This comment demonstrates the way that texts translated for theatre were often altered, in this case to cut down the play. It also demonstrates that translation was popular and that a writer could only claim originality 'rights' through significant imitation or adaptation. It should be noted that this play was intended for publication alone. The translator capitalizes on the success of the recent theatre version by linking his translation with it and thereby emphasizing its immediate topicality. Translation of a Molière play for print, however, demonstrates the growing trend towards 'just translation' that Ozell was to strengthen in his *Works of Monsieur de Molière* (1714).

Those early eighteenth-century writers who did not translate closely from Molière defined their publications in relation to translation. In the preface to *The Quacks; or, Love's the Physician* (1704/5), Owen McSwiny notes that he cannot 'style it a Translation' because he has added a part, altered characters, and changed the 'contrivance'.[25] His preface also indicates the way that different approaches to translation or adaptation could be typified by theatrical groups:

> As for the Gentlemen of the other House, who are to reform the Stage, purify our Diversions and Naturalize all the Wit of Moliere (for beginners shou'd have a Fond) I shall only say [...] they are the properest Persons in the World to reform the Stage, having known so well what it is to corrupt it.[26]

McSwiny refers to the Lincoln's Inn Fields Theatre where the translation of *Monsieur de Pourceaugnac* called *Squire Trelooby* had been performed the previous year.

McSwiny's comment points to another emerging facet of translations of Molière: the idea that the French plays can be used as models for English playwrights. Clearly McSwiny disregards this view, arguing that only fledgling dramatists would need to ape the style of foreign drama, despite the fact that he translates from Molière. But the reference to the naturalizing of Molière's wit indicates a change in attitudes towards the source-text; rather than the English dramatists having an important influence on the source-text, the original source has a significant influence on the work of English dramatists. This attitude was not shared by all the writers who translated Molière, but it did become increasingly prevalent as later translators sought to find an alternative route to the freewheeling translators that first reworked Molière's plays.

The assertion that translation could offer English dramatists exemplary models was strengthened by publications of collected works. John Ozell published his *Works of Monsieur de Molière* in 1714 and Henry Baker, James Miller, and Martin Clare produced a parallel text in several volumes entitled *Select Comedies of Mr. de Molière* in 1732. Both works are described as translations of the originals. In the preface to the *Select Comedies* the translators describe their work in terms that echo Dryden's ideal of a 'just translation':

> The *School-Boy* will be assisted to *construe* and understand *Moliere*, seeing we have almost constantly observ'd his *Words* as well as his *Sense* [...]. The *Scholar* will be entertain'd to find him speak so good *English* tho' so closely translated, and marvel how the *Spirit* and the *Letter* of the *Original* could be at once so well preserv'd. (I, A11^v–A12^r)

Seventeenth-century translation theory had developed as a rejection of the pedagogical function of close translation in order to allow literary translators to employ creativity in their vernacular versions of the classics. Baker, Miller, and Clare, however, turn back to the educational model in translating Molière's plays.[27] They do acknowledge the importance of entertainment, however, and point to the practice of paraphrase; the plays cannot be translated word for word exactly, or the English would not read naturally.

Though the translators of the *Select Comedies* aim to establish the text as an original and important printed work, they present it as complementary to the work of the theatre, arguing that although their translations 'may be thought too literal and close' to be put on the stage, dramatists could 'model and adapt them to our Theatre and Age' (I, A4^r). The idea that close translations needed to be reshaped to entertain audiences was still maintained at the beginning of the eighteenth century. Rather, two literary branches, translation and adaptation, were presented as working in a symbiotic manner. In the preface to *The Mock Doctor*, 'done from Moliere', Henry Fielding refers to the *Select Comedies*, though he does not suggest that he has worked from the translation in the collection:[28]

> I wish I had been as able to preserve the Spirit of *Moliere*, as I have, in translating it, fallen short even of that very little Time he allowed himself in writing it [...]. One Pleasure I enjoy from the Success of this Piece, is a Prospect of transplanting successfully some others of *Moliere* of great Value. How I have

done this, any *English* Reader may be satisfy'd by examining an exact literal Translation of the *Medecin malgrè* [sic] *Lui*, which is the Second in the Second Volume of *Select Comedies of Moliere,* just published by *John Watts*.²⁹

It is significant that Fielding changes the verb he uses to describe his work from 'translating' to 'transplanting'. Clearly the boundaries between translation and adaptation are still indistinct. He has the tool of the *Select Comedies*, however, to measure how far he has strayed from an 'exact literal' translation. Of course, it is possible that this reference is little more than a marketing technique, but it demonstrates a profound change of attitude towards translation when compared to views expressed in the first English versions of Molière in the 1660s.

(Not) Translating Dramatic Verse

In addition to assessing what Molière's translators said about their work, it is also telling to consider what they omitted to say. Seventeenth-century theoretical writing on literary translation related most often to classical verse. When addressing this genre, translators referred to the metrical form of the works being translated, though not often in great detail. In his preface to *The Pindarique Odes* Abraham Cowley notes that:

> Our Ears are strangers to the Musick of his [Pindar's] *Numbers*, which sometimes (especially in *Songs* and *Odes*) almost without anything else, makes an excellent *Poet*; for though the *Grammarians* and *Criticks* have laboured to reduce his Verses into regular feet and measures (as they have also those of the *Greek* and *Latin Comedies*) yet in effect they are little better than *Prose* to our Ears. (Aaa2ʳ)

Cowley's comment blurs the distinction between verse and prose. Molière's *bourgeois gentilhomme*, Monsieur Jourdain, is sincerely impressed by the information provided by his philosophy tutor: 'tout ce qui n'est point Prose, est Vers, et tout ce qui n'est point Vers, est Prose' (II.4; *OC*, II, 283). According to Cowley, however, a verse-form in a foreign language will have little metrical resonance in another language. His comments relate to the complicated metrical structure of Pindar's odes. He notes that strict grammarians have attempted to make the verse more regular, but that the musical effect of the original odes has been lost in this process and that it therefore resembles prose when heard or read.

Cowley also notes that grammarians have 'reduced' the verses of Greek and Latin comedies to 'regular feet and measures'. Plautus's comedies, for example, were composed with at least three metrical forms (the parts recited without *musical* accompaniment were in iambic senarii, the recitatives with music were in trochaic septenarii and the singing parts were composed in various metres).³⁰ Cowley refers to such complex verse-forms being 'reduced' both in the sense of being simplified and in the sense of their aesthetic impact being diminished. Nevertheless, he advocates using English verse to translate classical verse, be it poetry or drama. The Earl of Roscommon likewise notes in his *Essay on Translated Verse* (1684) that he and his contemporary English translators go further than the French translators of classical literature to:

> [...] shew the world a nobler way,
> And in *Translated Verse* do more than *They*.
> Serene and clear harmonious *Horace* flows,
> With sweetness not to be expressed in *Prose*;
> Degrading *Prose* explains his meaning ill,
> And shews the *Stuff*, but not the Workman's skill.[31]

This enthusiasm for translation in verse, however, did not extend to the practice of translating French dramatic poetry.

Seventeenth-century French drama was often written in rhyming couplets of alexandrines (twelve-syllable lines). Molière used this verse-form for all or parts of fourteen of his plays. His first English translators, however, shied away from translating the French verse into English verse. Many turned to Molière's prose plays. Those who did translate the verse plays either rendered them into English prose, or blank verse. The seventeenth-century translators omit to explain why they have translated French verse into prose, perhaps because they are reluctant to admit defeat, or rather are trying to avoid it. Matthew Medbourne, for example, invites readers to compare his translation of *Le Tartuffe* with the original, but does not point out that he has converted French alexandrine couplets into loose blank verse (A3ʳ). Later critics have not failed to notice the change, however. Dudley H. Miles observes that Medbourne's text 'is a translation into the blankest of miserable blank verse, in an ignorantly literal manner, scene by scene, the only changes being the addition and advantage modestly confided to the reader by the title-page'.[32] Given the frequency with which French drama was being translated at the time, careful consideration of verse-form was not a priority.

Even the early eighteenth-century translators who composed collected works of Molière in English did not take up the challenge of translating into verse. The translators of the *Select Comedies* of 1732 were obliged to make some comment on their verse-avoidance because their work is a parallel text and the discrepancy is immediately evident:

> In one respect, indeed, he [Molière] was very unfortunate, which was, being under a Necessity of writing in *Rhyme*. He knew better than approve of such a villainous Practice, but 'twas the Taste of *Moliere's* Judges *then*, as 'twas of *Dryden's* in *his Time*, and not a *Line* would go down but what was tag'd at the End. *Rhyme* in *Tragedy* is ridiculous enough, but to put *Comick Humour* and *Common Conversation* into Epick Verse and Gingling [*sic*] Couplets, is such a monstrous Absurdity, that 'tis inconceivable how so polite and judicious a Nation could endure it, much more demand it. It must not be wonder'd at if we are a little warm on this point, when it has prov'd such a Clog to us in our Translation; forasmuch as it often oblig'd us to quit our Author's Expression more than we chose to do, or else to give our Stile a stiff and poetical Turn. (A9ʳ)

In fact, the tension between a regular verse-form and the comic irregularity of human characters in 'common conversation' frequently enhances Molière's comedy.[33] The translators of the *Select Comedies* exaggerate Molière's supposed discomfort with rhyme to justify their avoidance of it. They do explain, however, the difficulty of translating rhymed verse in relation to their aim to keep the sense of the words as close as possible to the original French. Instead of acknowledging that the loss of rhyme diminishes the aesthetic and comic effect, they claim that they have dispensed with something troublesome in the original.

The translators of the *Select Comedies* also suggest that the decision as to whether to translate into rhyming verse or into prose is subject to the prevailing literary fashions. The preface echoes the various views on rhyme put forward in Dryden's *Essay of Dramatick Poesie*. In this work, Neander, the critic most closely associated with Dryden, argues against Lisideus's criticism of rhyme:

> You say the Stage is the representation of Nature, and no man in ordinary conversation speaks in rhime. But you foresaw when you said this, that it might be answer'd; neither does any man speak in blank verse, or in measure without rhime. Therefore you concluded, that which is nearest Nature is still to be preferr'd. But you took no notice that rhime might be made as natural as blank verse, by the well placing of the words. (p. 70)

Despite the claims in the *Select Comedies*, there was no clear consensus on the most appropriate literary form for drama in the late seventeenth century. Dryden experimented with rhyme and prose in his adaptation of *Amphitryon* and was perhaps inspired by Molière's mixing of verse-forms in his French version of the play. *Amphitryon*, however, is an adaptation of Plautus and Molière, not a straightforward translation. As the translators of the *Select Comedies* attest, translating into rhyming verse can threaten the fidelity to the words of the original. On the other hand, the aesthetic and dramatic effects of rhymed verse are fundamental to a play, and are inevitably lost in translation into blank verse or prose. Many of Molière's first English translators omit to discuss this problem in their prefaces because there is no wholly satisfactory way of solving it.

Amongst the first English translations of Molière's plays the boundary between translation and adaptation is blurred. It is still helpful, however, to conceive of these concepts as a sliding scale that enables an understanding of the various ways in which Molière's texts were 'Englished' in the late seventeenth and early eighteenth centuries. On the one hand, the concept of adaptation is particularly applicable to the translation of drama, because it involves a change in media; work produced for one kind of stage is reworked for another kind of stage. On the other hand, the linguistic translation that is required in this process is a specific kind of adaptation in which terms in one language are changed into the terms of another so that they will resonate with the target audience.

Translation theory itself adapts to the era and environment in which it is being addressed. In the prefaces to seventeenth-century translations of Molière, the process of adaptation and alteration was emphasized. In the early eighteenth century there was a shift by which the concept of close translation of the source-text was prioritized as individuals became increasingly interested in the commercial power of print and the historical interest of well-known French plays. Despite the change in focus, both seventeenth- and early-eighteenth-century approaches to translating Molière were shaped by the strong French influence in post-Restoration English society.

This circumstance contributed to the blurring of another theoretical boundary; domesticating translations and foreignizing translations were not straightforwardly distinguishable. All translations of Molière in the period demonstrated anglicization of the French texts, but they also simultaneously explored the gallicized elements of English language and culture.

Notes to Chapter 2

1. The ideas in Corneille's *Trois discours*, especially from the third discourse on the unities are discussed in John Dryden's *Essay of Dramatick Poesie*, in Dryden, *Prose 1668–1691*. François Hédelin, abbé d'Aubignac, *The Whole Art of the Stage, Made English*, trans. anon. (London: printed for the author, 1684).
2. See France, *The Oxford Guide to Literature in English Translation*; Valerie Worth-Stylianou, 'Translatio and Translation in the Renaissance: From Italy to France', in *The Cambridge History of Literary Criticism, III: The Renaissance*, ed. by George Alexander Kennedy and Glyn P. Norton (Cambridge: Cambridge University Press, 1999), pp. 127–35.
3. See Paulina Kewes, *Authorship and Appropriation: Writing for the Stage in England, 1660–1710* (Oxford: Clarendon Press, 1998).
4. Alexander Tytler, *Essay on the Principles of Translation* (London: printed for T. Cadell; and W. Creech, Edinburgh, 1791).
5. Lawrence Venuti, *The Translator's Invisibility* (London & New York: Routledge, 1995), p. 21.
6. See Hodges, 'The Authorship of *Squire Trelooby*'.
7. See Terttu Nevalainen, 'Early Modern English Lexis and Semantics', in *The Cambridge History of the English Language*, ed. by Roger Lass, 6 vols (Cambridge: Cambridge University Press, 2000), III, 332–498 (pp. 368–70).
8. See, for example, the ambiguous uses of the term *galanterie* / 'gallantry' in late seventeenth- and early eighteenth-century English in Chapter 4. 'Gallantry' could refer to courteous and refined behaviour, but it also came to refer to the illicit amorous intrigues to which such behaviour could lead. The term and the conduct it represents were thus associated with French fashions.
9. *Adaptation Studies: New Challenges, New Directions*, ed. by Jørgen Bruhn, Anne Gjelsvik, and Eirik Frisvold Hanssen (London: Bloomsbury, 2013), p. 5.
10. Frédéric Godefroy, 'Translater, verbe', in *Dictionnaire de l'ancienne langue française*, 8 vols (Paris: F. Vieweg, Émile Bouillon, 1881–1902), VIII, 17–18.
11. Robert Estienne, 'Traduire', in *Dictionnaire françois-latin, augmenté* (Paris, 1539), p. 494.
12. 'Traduire', in *Dictionnaire de l'Académie françoise*, II, 724.
13. Furetière, 'Vertir', in *Dictionnaire universel*, III, 804; Thomas Corneille, 'Vertir', in *Le Dictionnaire des arts et des sciences*, 2 vols (Paris: Jean Baptiste Coignard, 1694), III, 563.
14. John Rider offers a range of synonyms, related terms, and Latin roots in this entry: 'A translation. 1 Interpretatio, f. interpretamentum, n. 2 Translatio, versio, f. A translation of words from their owne proper signification into another, as Video pro intelligo. 1 Metaphora, f.'. John Rider, 'To Translate from one language to another: to interpret', in *Bibliotheca scholastica* (Oxford: printed by Joseph Barnes, 1589).
15. Phillips, 'Translation', in *The New World of English Words*.
16. John Florio, 'Versióne: "a turning or version. Also a translation"', in *Queen Anna's New World of Words; or, Dictionarie of Italian and English Tongues* (London: printed by Melchisedec Bradwood, 1611), p. 596.
17. Valerie Worth-Stylianou, *Practising Translation in Renaissance France: The Example of Étienne Dolet* (Oxford: Clarendon Press, 1988), p. 2.
18. Nicolas Perrot d'Ablancourt, *Les Œuvres de Tacite de la traduction de N. Perrot sieur d'Ablancourt*, 2 vols (Paris: Augustin Courbé, 1658), I, A3^{r-v}.
19. In 1740 the critic Gilles Ménage described one of d'Ablancourt's translations as a 'belle infidèle'. The term came to refer to translations that adapt to the prevailing aesthetics of the translator's era. Roger Zuber explores this translation technique with reference to d'Ablancourt and his

contemporaries in *Les Belles Infidèles et la formation du goût classique* (Paris: Colin, 1968; rev. edn Paris: Michel, 1995).

20. Nicolas Perrot d'Ablancourt, *Lucien, de la traduction de N. Perrot, sr. d'Ablancourt*, 2 vols (Paris: Augustin Courbé, 1654), I, ě2^v.
21. John Denham, *The Destruction of Troy: An Essay upon the Second Book of Virgils Æneis, Written in the Year, 1636* (London: printed for Humphrey Moseley, 1656), A2^v.
22. Abraham Cowley, *Pindarique Odes*, in *Poems: i. Miscellanies. ii. The Mistress. iii. Pindarique Odes. iv. Davideis* (London, 1656), Aaa2.
23. Dryden, *Poems, 1649–1680*, p. 114.
24. Marie-Claude Canova-Green reads Dryden's comment as a means of minimizing the debt to Molière by drawing attention to the fact that Molière himself adapted from ancient sources. As the title of her paper suggests, Canova-Green takes a sceptical view of the English translators' prefaces, arguing that the English dramatists were motivated to denigrate Molière's plays in order to counter accusations of plagiarism and to reflect anti-French feeling following episodes of political animosity such as France's support of Holland in the second Anglo-Dutch War (1665–67). Marie-Claude Canova-Green, 'Molière, ou comment ne pas reconnaître sa dette: le théâtre de la Restauration en Angleterre', in *La France et l'Europe du Nord au XVIIe siècle: de l'Irlande à la Russie*, ed. by Richard Maber, Biblio 17 (Tübingen: Narr Francke Attempto, 2017), pp. 109–20.
25. Owen McSwiny [Swiny] (1676–1754) was an Irish theatre impresario who worked with Christopher Rich at Drury Lane. In 1706 he rented the Queen's Theatre, but licensing rights changed so that only opera could be performed there. McSwiny was transferred back to Drury Lane and then back to the Queen's Theatre, where he failed to revive the opera. He became bankrupt and moved abroad. He returned in 1735 and remained involved in theatre, helping to organize a French troupe's stay in London in 1749.
26. Owen McSwiny, *The Quacks; or, Love's the Physician* (London: printed for Benjamin Bragg, 1705), π2^v. Further references are given after quotations in the text.
27. Henry Baker (1698–1774) finished an apprenticeship with a bookseller in London in 1720 and was engaged as a tutor. This experience led to his principal occupation as a teacher of deaf people. He sustained his literary interests by writing works on natural philosophy and translating. In 1741 he became a fellow of the Royal Society to which he left money for the annual Bakerian Lecture. James Miller (1704–44) was a preacher in London. While at university he wrote the comedy *The Humours of Oxford* which was performed at Drury Lane in 1730. Following his involvement in the *Select Comedies of Mr. de Molière* he adapted other plays for the stage (his 1734 play *The Mother-in-law; or, The Doctor the Disease* was based on *Le Malade imaginaire* and *Monsieur de Pourceaugnac*). Miller's involvement in the theatre led to criticism from fellow churchmen. Martin Clare (d. 1751) was founder of the Soho Academy, a boarding school which specialized in commerce but also had a good reputation in the arts. Clare was a freemason and became a fellow of the Royal Society in 1736.
28. Henry Fielding (1707–54) was a writer and magistrate credited with developing the modern novel. He began his career as a playwright. Following *The Mock Doctor* (1732), he wrote a popular version of Molière's *L'Avare* (*The Miser*, 1733). In 1736 Fielding managed his own acting company, but the 1737 Theatrical Licensing Act prompted him to turn to law and to devote time to writing political works and novels.
29. Henry Fielding, *The Mock Doctor; or, The Dumb Lady Cur'd. A Comedy. As it is Acted at the Theatre-Royal in Drury Lane, by His Majesty's Servants. With the Musick prefix'd to each Song* (London: printed for J. Watts, 1732), A3^v (further references are given after quotations in the text). I give the title of this first edition in full because there was a 1732 pirated edition that did not include the music to the songs, the dedication, or the preface.
30. See Gian Biagio, *Latin Literature: A History*, trans. by Joseph Solodow (Baltimore, MD, & London: John Hopkins University Press, 1994), p. 35.
31. Wentworth Dillon, Earl of Roscommon, *Essay on Translated Verse* (London: printed for J. Tonson, 1685), pp. 3–4.
32. Dudley H. Miles, 'The Original of the Non-Juror', *Publications of the Modern Languages Association*, 30.2 (1915), 195–214 (p. 197).

33. See W. D. Howarth, *Molière: A Playwright and his Audience* (Cambridge: Cambridge University Press, 1982), pp. 235–56.

CHAPTER 3

Rhythm, Rhyme, and Song

Molière wrote thirteen plays entirely in verse and one in both prose and verse. The first translations into English took many different forms. Some translators transformed Molière's alexandrines into blank verse, others converted them into prose, or a mixture of verse and prose. It is important to consider the way that the sound of language, its rhythms and patterns, affects an audience's interpretation of dramatic dialogue. Save brief reviews from theatregoers such as Samuel Pepys, there is little evidence of the ways that the first translations of Molière were performed or received by spectators.[1] But an analysis of the methods by which rhythmic, rhyming, and musical elements of Molière's plays were reconfigured in translation can offer insights into the ways that translations affect verbal performance, or imagined verbal performance in the case of those translations that were intended for print.

This chapter is entitled 'Rhythm, Rhyme, and Song' to signal the breadth of techniques that translators adopted to preserve or complement Molière's attention to prosody. Although these three terms provide the subheadings for this chapter, it should be noted that they often work together to influence the rhetorical power or comic effect of characters' dialogue. So the extended chapter-section on rhyme, for example, also includes analysis of rhythm and sound patterning, particularly when addressing the ways in which Molière's rhymes are replaced with prose.

The first section on rhythm addresses the first English translations of Molière's early comedy *Le Cocu imaginaire* (1660) and considers the ways in which the translators either bypassed or dealt with the problematic task of transforming French alexandrines into patterned language in English. The second section on rhyme assesses both the gains and the losses of the English translators' sparing use of rhyme, using Medbourne's *Tartuffe; or, The French Puritan* (1670) and Dryden's *Amphitryon* (1690) as case studies. The third section considers the translators' attention to song. While rhyme and rhythmic elements such as metre or repetition were disregarded in some prose translations, songs were not. The chapter ends with an overview of the ways that songs not only suited the English theatre's taste for variety, but also offered a reminder to both audiences and readers that Molière's plays had been translated with an eye, or rather an ear, to the performance and reception of plays that gave voice to the preoccupations of the societies in which they were presented.

Rhythm

The most evident challenge faced by translators of Molière was how to render alexandrines in such a way that they carried prosodic emphasis in English. It is no coincidence that many of his first translators chose to translate his prose rather than verse comedies. The first English dramatist to translate Molière, however, cheated his way out of the bind. William D'Avenant, who included a translation of the one-act *Le Cocu imaginaire* in *The Playhouse to be Let* (1663), came up with the ploy of translating Molière's play for a group of mock French actors visiting England. He therefore dispensed with the concerns of traditional English dramatic rhythm by writing in mock French-accented English. Thus neither standard French nor English metrical patterning needed to apply. In the printed text, however, the lines are set out as verse. Sganarelle's first confrontation with his wife in *Le Cocu imaginaire*, for example, is translated thus in *The Playhouse to be Let*:

> Tu ne m'entends que trop Madame la carogne,
> Sganarelle est un nom qu'on ne me dira plus,
> Et l'on va m'appeler Monsieur Corneillius.
> J'en suis pour mon honneur [...]. (6.190–93; OC, 1, 50)
>
> Goody slutt you understand me too vell.
> My name sall be no more *Monsieur Sganarelle*,
> But mi lore Cuckol; mi sall make your body lesse
> By vone arme, ande two ribe. (p. 79)

While decasyllabic lines are the most common throughout D'Avenant's translation of *Le Cocu imaginaire*, there are several longer and shorter lines and no consistent patterns of stress. The quotation above demonstrates the irregularity. Why, then, is the text presented as verse at all? D'Avenant was perhaps making a gesture to the verse-form of the original play in French. Another way of accounting for the form is to consider the hybrid nature of *The Playhouse to be Let* alongside the pre-existing verse-plays *The History of Sir Francis Drake* (1659) and *The Cruelty of the Spaniards in Peru* (1658), as well as the new *Tragedy Travestie* in verse. So D'Avenant may have sought to give some rhythmical patterning to the translation of *Le Cocu imaginaire* in order to provide a veneer of overall consistency in the play. Another explanation is that the compositor of the text set out D'Avenant's play as verse when the manuscript may have been in prose. This was not an uncommon occurrence in the early modern period, when compositors would set up lines for printing by recalling blocks of text by rote.[2] It should be noted that *The Playhouse to be Let* was not published until 1673, after D'Avenant's death, so the author/translator was not available to oversee the printing process. Even if we read the lines in the printed text as extremely irregular verse, the unusual rhythmical elements serve his comic device of Frenchifying spoken English, rather than finding equivalent uses of prosody to those found in Molière's plays. Subsequent translators used more sophisticated rhythmical patterning in order to emphasize the comic contradictions presented in Molière's dialogue.

Thomas Rawlins translated large sections of *Le Cocu imaginaire* in *Tom Essence; or, The Modish Wife* (licensed for performance in 1676 and published in 1677).[3]

Rawlins used a mixture of prose and verse to demonstrate the mismatch in characters' emotions. The central misunderstanding in Molière's play leads to a chain of misinterpretations. The young woman Célie, for example, is appalled when Sganarelle tells her that Lélie, her beloved, is the cuckold-maker. Sganarelle wrongly believes that her sorrow and anger are born out of sympathy for his own plight, whereas Célie is in fact bemoaning the apparent infidelity of Lélie. Célie essentially performs a monologue within a dialogue, to which Sganarelle responds by jumping in with his assertions of the false nature of the accusation.

In Molière's play Sganarelle and Célie share lines of verse, most of which serve to show that Sganarelle is hastily filling in the gaps of knowledge (albeit with false information, as the audience knows). Chiastic constructions such as 'Il adore ma femme, et ma femme l'adore' (l. 378) highlight Sganarelle's misguided assurance in his observations; this particular example also completes a rhyme with 'il me déshonore' (l. 377). The repetition of 'adore' gives the impression of confident insistence. Repetition serves a different purpose in Célie's lines; her reference to 'quelque lâche tour' at first signals an uncertain sense of weak conduct on the part of Lélie, whereas the repetition of 'lâche' in 'ta lâche action' shows that Célie's anger is taking over as she addresses the absent Lélie in an apostrophe. Her exclamation 'Ô Ciel est-il possible?' shares a line with Sganarelle's typical self-centred response, 'il est trop vrai pour moi' (l. 391) and is followed by Célie's continued address to Lélie: 'âme double et sans foi' (l. 392). So although the lines fit metrically and rhyme, the characters are both preoccupied with their own trains of thought. The mismatch between the symmetrical form of the language and the 'crossed wires' of the interaction enhances the dramatic irony. Rawlins's translation, presented in parallel with the French in the following pages, includes different techniques to represent the discrepancy in the characters' concerns (I have highlighted chiasmus, repetition and sound patterning in bold):[4]

The most evident difference between the French and English is that the French is all in rhymed verse whereas the English is a mixture of prose and blank verse. Rawlins's Sganarelle-character, Tom Essence, always speaks in prose, whereas his Célie equivalent, Theodocia, sometimes speaks in prose and sometimes in blank verse, depending on the characters to whom she is speaking or the topic of conversation. When she talks of her love for the appropriately-named Courtly, for example, she speaks in verse, in part to emphasize the quality of her love and in part to show a comic contrast to the ramblings of Tom Essence.

Although the rhymes are not carried over into the English, there is word- and sound-repetition that is designed to underscore the anguish of the young female character in both the French and the English, even if this is not as carefully crafted in the English as in the original rhyming alexandrines. In the French, the repetition of 'lâche' in relation to Lélie is contrasted with the repeated reference to 'cœur' and its echo in 'j'y cours', towards the end of Célie's speech. All the references to 'cœur' are applied to Célie; the first relates to her steadfastness, the second to the seat of her love and therefore pain, and the third to her resolve and courage to seek revenge, thereby aligning the concept of *cœur* with *courage*. Whereas in the French

SGANARELLE	Ce Damoiseau, parlant par révérence,
	Me fait cocu Madame, avec toute licence,
	Et j'ai su par mes yeux avérer aujourd'hui
	Le commerce secret de ma femme et de lui.
CÉLIE	Celui qui maintenant...
SGANARELLE	Oui, oui me déshon**ore**,
	Il **adore ma femme**, et **ma femme** l'**adore**.
CÉLIE	Ah j'avais bien jugé que ce secret retour
	Ne pouvait me couvrir que quelque **lâche** tour,
	Et j'ai tremblé d'abord en le voyant **par**aître,
	Par un **p**ressentiment de ce qui devait être.
SGANARELLE	Vous **p**renez ma défense avec trop de bonté,
	Tout le monde n'a pas la même charité,
	Et **p**lusieurs qui ont bientôt a**p**pris mon martyre
	Bien loin de **p**rendre **p**art, n'en ont rien fait que rire.
CÉLIE	Est-il rien de **p**lus noir que ta **lâche** action,
	Et **p**eut-on lui trouver une **p**unition:
	Dois-tu ne te **p**as croire indigne de la vie?
	Après t'être souillé de cette **p**erfidie?
	Ô Ciel est-il possible?
SGANARELLE	Il est trop vrai pour moi.
CÉLIE	Ah ! traitre, scélérat, âme double sans foi.
SGANARELLE	La bonne âme.
CÉLIE	Non, non, l'Enfer n'a point de gêne
	Qui ne soit pour ton crime une trop douce peine.
SGANARELLE	Que voilà bien parler !
CÉLIE	Avoir ainsi traité
	Et **la même** innocence et **la même** bonté !
SGANARELLE	*Il soupire haut*
	Hay
CÉLIE	Un **cœur** qui jamais n'a fait la moindre chose
	À mériter l'affront où ton mépris l'expose.
SGANARELLE	Il est vrai.
CÉLIE	Qui bien loin ... Mais c'est trop et ce **cœur** ...
	Ne saurait y songer sans mourir de douleur.
SGANARELLE	Ne vous fâchez pas tant ma très chère Madame,
	Mon mal vous touche trop et vous me percez l'âme.
CÉLIE	Mais ne t'abuse pas jusqu'à te figurer
	Qu'à tes plaintes sans fruit je veuille demeurer,
	Mon **cœur** pour se venger sait ce qu'il te faut faire,
	Et j'y **cours** de ce pas, rien ne m'en peut distraire.

(16.373–406; OC, I, 64–66)

TOM ESSENCE	That Rogue; he has Feloniously stolen the precious Jewel of my life; my Rep, in fine, he has Cuckold me; now 'tis out, my heart is somewhat eas'd.
THEODOCIA	It is impossible, can *Courtly* be so base?
TOM ESSENCE	Oh 'tis too true, these eyes, but now, Were witnesses of his and my Wife's familiarity: to conclude, he lyes with my Wife; now you have the sorrowful truth of my Woe.
THEODOCIA	All my prophetick fears were but too true, And *Courtly's* treacheries too evident: Me-thoughts his looks, as he past by, betray'd An inward guilt. If thou art False, where shall I find one Just? For, with such seeming Honesty, he swore, And with such Imprecations on himself, If in the least he Violated Love, Or broke his **Vows**, those **Vows** he made to me, I durst to have sworn, he really design'd That Constancy he **Vow'd**: But blinded by my Love, I finde too late, He's like the rest of the perfidious Race
TOM ESSENCE	Sweet Mrs *Theo.* Queen of Diamonds, moderate thy passion. Your Charity to me is too great, and since so cordially you espouse my afflictions, I'me grieved that you are not a man; if you were, *I* should have entreated the favour of you, that you would cudgel him for my sake; but seeing that cannot be, I'le drown my self in Tears, and lay my death to his charge: oh, oh, oh *(crys)*.
THEODOCIA	Oh that *I* were a man, *I*'de soon redress My wrongs: His Life shou'd pay the forfeit of his Vows, And he shou'd fall a Victim to my rage.
TOM ESSENCE	Good Saint!
THEODOCIA	But oh *I* rave; For *Courtly's* generous soul cou'd ne're admit A thought so **base** to harbour in his **brest**, Much **less** wou'd execute so **vile** an act; Heaven's! 'tis impossible! *Courtly* false? it cannot be.
TOM ESSENCE	Oh yes, Madam; yes, too true he's false; but how shall we curb his Leachery?
THEODOCIA	Sure hell itself has not a torment equal to thy Crime.
TOM ESSENCE	Sweet Soul!
THEODOCIA	To wrong a person never injur'd thee — [...] But my complaints are vain, I'le tear this Viper from my brest, and then Study a just Revenge to scourge his soul, For Violations done to Sacred Love. (pp. 28–29)

there are plosives in 'punition', 'perfidie', and 'possible' that emphasize Célie's anger, intensified in her last lines with the use of fricative consonants in 'figurer', 'fruit' and 'faut faire', the English instead repeats the phonemes /v/ and /l/ of 'Violated Love' ('Vows', 'Vowed', 'Victim', 'late', 'Life') to highlight Theodocia's focus on the hurtful idea that Courtly has betrayed her. As the repetition of 'cœur' represents a transition from pain to anger in the original French, the alliteration at the end of Theodocia's speech shows that she has moved from disbelief to rage; the sibilance in 'brest' is transferred into 'Study' and then adapted into the phoneme /sk/ in 'scourge', which is in turn reflected in love's new religiously connoted epithet 'Sacred'. The use of verse and repetition is intended to represent anguish on the part of Célie/Theodocia, but this scene is also comic because Sganarelle/ Tom Essence believes that the young woman is responding to his concern and sympathizing with him. This comic element is conveyed with the assistance of the prosody. While Sganarelle and Célie share certain alexandrine lines, it is only Sganarelle who sees their conversation as a meeting of minds; Célie is in her own world. The comedy of the misconstrued sympathy is reinforced by the shared line in which Sganarelle offers praise ('Que voilà bien parler') and Célie focuses on Lélie's alleged behaviour ('avoir ainsi traité'). The phoneme /e/ is also shared and necessarily repeated in the following line to observe the rules of the alternations of masculine and feminine rhymes in alexandrine lines ('la même bonté'). But there is extra comic energy when Sganarelle responds with a dramatic sigh and utters the interjection 'Hay' at the beginning of the following line thereby repeating the /e/ phoneme of the masculine rhyme, apparently in sympathy with Célie. While 'hay' could just be interpreted as an exclamation with flexible meaning, it was also used as a way to drive on beasts of burden, so there is a sense that Sganarelle is whipping up Célie's tirade. The reinforcement of the masculine rhyme also contrasts with the following feminine rhyme in which Célie laments that her heart has remained constant ('Un cœur qui jamais n'a fait la moindre chose | À mériter l'affront où ton mépris l'expose').

Given that Rawlins's Tom Essence speaks in prose and his Theodocia speaks in blank verse, the mistaken cuckold's pleasure in sympathy is conveyed more bluntly in the English text. Tom Essence expresses the wish that Theodocia were a man so that she could take his place in physical rather than verbal combat. Essence also adopts a stereotypical feminine response by crying, stating that he will drown himself in tears, and that he will perish. This contrasts with Célie's defiant response in measured verse, in which she repeats the phonemes of 'Violated Love' with a sense of fury rather than sorrow ('His Life shou'd pay the forfeit of his Vows, | And he shou'd fall a Victim to my rage'). This attitude re-emerges in her final lines of this section.

So, although on the surface the form of the language would appear to be starkly different in the French and the English, the variations are nonetheless produced with a mind to the dramatic effects of the rhythms in the original. The woe and anger of the young woman apparently scorned is acute in both the French rhymed verse and the English blank verse, and the confusion of the mistaken cuckold is as comically stark in the English prose as it is in the French alexandrines. Be that as it may, the first translators of Molière were not concerned with finding close prosodic equivalents to the French verse form. Neither D'Avenant nor Rawlins translated Molière's verse play in consistent iambic pentameter to match closely the regular crafted alexandrines. The rhythms of the English translations are marked by a spontaneity that was partly the result of the expediency of the hurried translations and partly a reflection of English theatre's tolerance of blurring boundaries between prose and verse and its promotion of 'naturalness' of language onstage.

Rhyme

While a seventeenth-century French comedy could consist entirely of rhyming alexandrines, English comedy of the same period tended to be in prose or blank verse, even if a few experimented with rhyme. The various views on the use of rhyme in English dramatic verse have been explored in Chapter 2, but it is worth recalling that the supposed 'unnaturalness' of rhyme was more often cited in early modern English critical writing about drama than in French. That is not to state, however, that rhyme was completely absent from comedy in English, but it was most often used sparingly for isolated effects. Its occasional use in late seventeenth- and early eighteenth-century translations of Molière was therefore for specific dramatic or comic purposes.

Sir Robert Howard noted in his preface to *Four New Plays* (1665) that rhyme may well be suitable for poetry, but not for drama:

> Another way of the Ancients which the *French* follow, and our Stage has now lately practis'd, is to write in Rhime; and this is the dispute betwixt many ingenious Persons, whether Verse in Rhime, or Verse without the sound, which may be call'd Blank Verse, (though a hard Expression) is to be preferr'd? [...] A Poem being a premeditated form of Thoughts upon design'd occasions ought not be unfurnished of any harmony in Words or Sound: The other is presented as the present Effect of Accidents not thought of [...] unless it were possible that all persons were born so much more than poets, that verses were not to be composed by them, but already made in them.[5]

Howard is particularly averse to couplets shared by two speakers, 'the smartness of a Reply, which has its beauty by coming from sudden Thoughts, [...] seems lost by that which rather looks like a Design of two, than the Answer of one' (a4ʳ). The example from *Sganarelle* shows that the 'design' of shared rhymed lines can contribute to the presentation of comic character interaction by establishing a contrast between the dialogue's constructed form and the miscommunication that it presents. Many of the first translators of Molière, however, shared Howard's view, not least because translating Molière's French verse into English verse posed a considerable challenge.

Matthew Medbourne made use of blank verse in his translation-adaptation of *Le Tartuffe*. The quality of the blank verse has been criticized by scholars such as Dudley H. Miles, but the English work does incorporate some comic use of occasional rhyme.[6] When Valère and Mariane prepare to overcome the obstacles to their marriage, for example, Medbourne makes use of a rare section of rhyme. The conversation in Molière's model is followed by Medbourne's translation:

VALÈRE	*à Mariane*	
	Quelques efforts que nous préparions tous,	
	Ma plus grande espérance, à vrai dire, est en vous.	
MARIANE	*à Valère*	
	Je ne vous réponds pas des volontés d'un père;	
	Mais je ne serai point à d'autre qu'à Valère.	
VALÈRE	Que vous me comblez d'aise! Et quoi que puisse oser...	
DORINE	Ah! jamais les amants ne sont las de jaser.	
	Sortez, vous dis-je.	
VALÈRE	*il fait un pas et revient*	
	Enfin ...	
DORINE	Quel caquet est le vôtre !	
	Tirez de cette part; et vous, tirez de l'autre.	
	(II.4.815–22; *OC*, II, 140)	
VALERE	What Force soever we can now prepare;	
	In you is all my Hope, for you my Care.	[*to* Mariana.
MARIANA	I cannot answer for a Father's Will;	
	But be assur'd, I am my Valère's still.	[*to* Valere.
VALERE	How I'm o'erwhelmed with Joy? and now I dare —	
DORINA	Lovers are never weary of Discourse:	
	Go, get you gone, I say. [Valere *goes a Step and returns*	
VALERE	Well, to conclude —	
DORINA	No more of this Discourse.	
	Here part, dear Friends, and banish all your Fears;	
	Go, go, divide. Courage till our next meeting. (p. 25)	

Dorine clearly becomes exasperated with the fawning of the young lovers, as indicated by her interruption of Valère's attempt to continue his honeyed words. The idea that rhyming is a form of amorous, effusive, and possibly affected discourse comes through in Medbourne's translation of this section, in which Valère and Mariane's alexandrines are transformed into two rhyming couplets. In the English, Valere responds to Mariana's couplet rhymes with his own couplet and therefore suggests that were it not for Dorina's interruption he might keep speaking in continuous rhyme. In both the French and the English the maid is presented as wearied by the affected conversation of the lovers and keen to put an end to it. Medbourne's translation of the verb 'jaser' and the noun 'caquet' with reference to 'discourse' rather than 'prattle' also suggests that the language the lovers employ is self-conscious and carefully constructed (as it is by Medbourne who makes it rhyme). Medbourne's rare use of rhyme in his translation of *Le Tartuffe* here allows him to emphasize the comically amorous behaviour of Valere and Mariana. He includes the physical comedy of the characters' interaction by showing the suitor's resistance to leaving, but emphasizes their affected behaviour by including blatant rhymes.

While Sir Robert Howard questions the validity of rhyme in drama because of its unnaturalness, the very artificiality of rhyme can complement characterization when characters are shown to behave in line with certain social conventions. Clive Scott argues not only that Howard's assertion is inapplicable to French tragedy because 'it is precisely the function of rhyme [...] to imply that all has already been thought of, that the accidents and spontaneities of speech are an illusion, [and] have already been foreseen as part of a preordained design', but he also argues that rhyme's unnaturalness can enhance comedy too.[7] Scott notes that rhyme serves the comic 'trends' of both 'the improvised, the unpredictable, the punctual' and 'the long-term, the designed, and the mechanical' (p. 181). While the latter is borne out in the restoration of order through marriage, the former is borne out in 'the punctual associative mechanism we call "wit", where a first line is the shoulder upon which the second line climbs, where the first line is a bid which the second line outbids'. This comment may be true of Dorine's witty interruption of Valère where she responds to his tentative 'quoi que puisse oser' with the more direct and plain 'jamais les amants ne sont las de jaser', but in the English translation Dorina abandons rhyme when interrupting the pair, exasperated by its ostentation. Valère's step away from Mariane, only to return, is a visual representation of the rhyming discourse he has just performed with her; it is predictable and therefore comic. It also relates to the overall design of comedy, in which order will be restored mechanically through marriage; as Medbourne's Dorina asserts, the pair will need to part and divide themselves (and cut off their 'discourse') in order to be reunited.

In his translation of *Le Tartuffe* Medbourne includes other hints that the disorder will become order; he uses rhyme to do so. He includes, for example, Shakespearean-style 'leaving couplets' in which the final lines of a character about to exit the stage are rhymed. Thus the final alexandrine of Act I, scene 5, of *Le Tartuffe* is translated with a couplet:

ORGON	Adieu
CLÉANTE	Pour son amour, je crains une disgrâce,
	Et je dois l'avertir de tout ce qui passe. (1.5.425–26; *OC*, II, 116)

ORGON	Farewell.
CLEANTHES	The Love I bear him makes me fear his Fate,
	And binds me too to tell him what I hate. (p. 11)

The rarity of rhyme in the English version invites a reading of this couplet as a self-defensive apology on the part of Cleanthes, who can be viewed as a comically sermonizing character.[8] In line with the English distaste for long discourses Medbourne breaks up Cleanthes's lines with interruptions from Orgon, but the conspicuousness of this couplet warns the audience not only that Cleanthes will have much more to say, but that he will be proven right and contribute to the resolution of the play.

In Medbourne's *Tartuffe*, then, the use of rhyme centres more on the 'designed and mechanical' than on the 'improvised and unpredictable', perhaps in part as a comic signal that the translated play is a retelling of an existing comedy. The expediency of the ending of Molière's *Le Tartuffe* in which Louis XIV, via an officer of court, intervenes at the last moment to save the day, was criticized as soon as the play was authorized, but the reiteration of this in a slightly different guise is self-consciously flagged up in its first English translation. When the family learns of Tartuffe's arrest in Molière's play the women respond thus:

DORINE	Que le Ciel soit loué!	
MADAME PERNELLE		Maintenant je respire.
ELMIRE	Favorable succès!	
MARIANE		Qui l'aurait osé dire?
		(v.7.1945–46; *OC*, II, 189–90)

This unusual use of two consecutive shared alexandrines emphasizes the shock of the characters and their final united front against Tartuffe. Any irony detected in Mariane's comment in the French play would be tempered by the understanding that the ending of the play is intended to flatter Louis XIV who had finally allowed it to be performed. In Medbourne's version each female character is given a line of verse, though a dubious use of contraction is made to fit the words into the decasyllabic scheme of English verse:

DOR.	Oh *Laurence*! I am ravish'd with my Joy.
PERN.	Truly, la! I am Comforted agen.
ELM.	O most propitious Stars! most blest Success!
MAR.	Who could have dar'd to've hop't this Happiness? (p. '62', *recte* 64)

In translation, Mariana's comment is more difficult to read in a non-ironic way because the use of rhyme is rare and self-conscious. Alongside Elmira's comment about the propitious stars, the rhyming of 'success' and 'happiness' points to the inevitable restoration of order through marriage in comedy. Indeed, the women's lines in the translation follow an addition by Medbourne in which Orgon gives Valere to his daughter.

Mariana's rhetorical question at the end of Medbourne's *Tartuffe* actually invites the response from the audience: '*we* dared hope, and indeed expected, this happiness, even if the exact means of the happy ending was unforeseeable'. As Scott argues:

> Comedy cares little how justice is done as long as, ultimately, it is done; and more often than not, comedy seems to accept that the world must be, and continue to be, what it already is, and to concern itself with showing us what it is and with satisfying our need for reassurance by allowing us to turn away with the vague promise of a 'happy ever after' [...] it is only by making the conventionality of that marriage obtrusive, by reminding us that artifice is necessary to human happiness, that the comic author can pull us up with a 'Not so fast', can install his cautionary 'There, but for the grace of God...'. (pp. 178–79)

The moments of artifice presented in the couplets in the final scene of Medbourne's translation draw attention to the idea that the family has had a 'near miss' once again. Medbourne did not shy away from the fact that he had reworked Molière, and sought to capitalize upon it. His infrequent retention of rhyme plays on dramatic conventions in French and English tradition and therefore adds a comic dimension.

Replacing Rhymes

Molière did not write all of his plays in continuous rhymed alexandrines. He experimented most liberally with verse-form in *Amphitryon* (1668). This was part-translated, part-adapted into verse and prose in Dryden's *Amphitryon, or The Two Socia's* in 1690. Molière's opening demonstrates his prosodic inventiveness. A reading of it in parallel with Dryden shows the English adapter making use of prosodic elements in prose to convey the negotiations of Mercury and Night, who are both called upon to assist Jupiter in his plan to bed Alcmena, wife of the eponymous Amphitryon. The following parallel quotations are contracted:

MERCURE	Tout beau, charmante Nuit; daignez vous arrêter.
	Il est certain secours, que de vous on désire:
	Et j'ai deux mots à vous dire,
	De la part de Jupiter.
LA NUIT	Ah, ah, c'est vous, Seigneur Mercure!
	Qui vous eût deviné là, dans cette posture?
MERCURE	Ma foi, me trouvant las, pour ne pouvoir fournir
	Aux différents emplois où Jupiter m'engage,
	Je me suis doucement assis sur ce Nuage,
	Pour vous attendre venir.
	[...]
	Que vos Chevaux par vous au petit pas réduits,
	Pour satisfaire aux vœux de son Âme amoureuse,
	D'une Nuit si délicieuse
	Fassent la plus longue des Nuits.
	[...]
LA NUIT	Voilà sans doute un bel emploi,
	Que le grand Jupiter m'apprête:
	Et l'on donne un nom fort honnête
	Au service qu'il veut de moi.
MERCURE	Pour une jeune Déesse,
	Vous êtes bien du bon temps!
	Un tel Emploi n'est bassesse,
	Que chez les petites Gens.
	Lorsque dans un haut Rang on a l'heur de paraître,
	Tout ce qu'on fait est toujours bel, et bon;
	Et suivant ce qu'on peut être,
	Les choses changent de nom.
LA NUIT	Sur de pareilles matières,
	Vous en savez plus que moi:
	Et pour accepter l'Emploi,
	J'en veux croire vos lumières.
MERCURE	Hé, là, là, Madame la Nuit,
	Un peu doucement je vous prie.
	Vous avez dans le Monde un bruit,
	De n'être pas si renchérie.
	On vous fait Confidente en cent Climats divers,
	De beaucoup de bonnes Affaires;
	Et je crois, à parler à sentiments ouverts,
	Que nous ne nous en devons guères.

LA NUIT	Laissons ces contrariétés, Et demeurons ce que nous sommes. N'apprêtons point à rire aux Hommes, En nous disant nos vérités.

MERCURE	Adieu, je vais là-bas, dans ma Commission,
	Dépouiller promptement la forme de Mercure,
	    Pour y vêtir la Figure
	    Du Valet d'Amphitryon.

LA NUIT	Moi, dans cet Hémisphère, avec ma Suite obscure, Je vais faire une Station.
MERCURE	Bon jour, la Nuit. (*Prologue*, 1–154; *OC*, I, 851–56)

MERCURY	Madam *Night*, a good Even to you: fair and softly, I beseech you Madam: I have a word or two to you, from no less a God than *Jupiter*.
NIGHT	O, my nimble finger'd God of Theft, what make you here on Earth, at this unseasonable hour? What Bankers Shop is to be broken open to Night? Or what Clippers, and Coiners, and Conspirators, have been invoking your Deity for their assistance?
MERCURY	Faith none of those Enormities; and yet I am still in my Vocation: for you know I am a kind of Jack of all Trades: at a word, Jupiter is indulging his Genius tonight, with a certain noble sort of Recreation, call'd Wenching [...] He has sent me to will and to require you to make a swinging long Night for him, for he hates to be stinted in his pleasures
NIGHT	Tell him plainly I'll rather lay down my Commission: What wou'd he make a Bawd of me?
MERCURY	Poor Ignorant! why he meant thee for a Bawd when he first made thee. What art thou good for, but to be a Bawd? Is not Day-light better for Mankind, I mean as to any other use, but only for Love and Fornication? Thou hast been a Bawd too, a Reverend Primitive Original Bawd, from the first hour of thy Creation! [...]
NIGHT	Well, I am edified by your discourse; and my comfort is, that whatever work is made, I see nothing.
MERCURY	About your business then: put a Spoke into your Chariot Wheels, and order the Seven Stars to halt, while I put myself into the habit of a Serving-man; and dress up a false *Sosia*, to wait upon a false *Amphitryon*. Good night, *Night*. (pp. 5–6)

The experimentation in verse form is evident from the prologue of Molière's *Amphitryon*, in which he includes various sequences of alexandrines, heptasyllabic lines, and octosyllabic lines. Dryden adapts these variations in this section into prose, but uses blank verse and rhymed verse elsewhere in the play. In this exchange between Mercury and Night Dryden replaces the *rimes embrassées* (ABBA) and *rimes croisées* (ABAB) of Molière's characters with lyrical prose.

In Molière's play, the initial surprise of La Nuit's encounter with Mercure is indicated by the interjection 'Ah, ah, c'est vous Seigneur Mercure!', and the use of rhyme to pair this octosyllabic line with the following alexandrine ending 'dans cette posture'. It is as though by finding the rhyme, La Nuit is recovering her composure and preparing to listen to Mercure's request. This is translated into the English with a densely alliterative and rhythmical sentence that demonstrates Night's attempts to guess Mercury's intentions in advance: 'Or what Clippers, and Coiners, and Conspirators, have been invoking your Deity for their assistance?'. The progression from the two-syllable words 'Clippers' and 'Coiners' (people dealing in unlawful monetary practices) to the four-syllable 'Conspirators' serves to suggest Night's mounting apprehension at the business that Mercury might be seeking to pursue, thereby complementing the initial surprise expressed by 'La Nuit' in her pairing of an octosyllabic line and an alexandrine.

As the passage continues, Molière suggests La Nuit's sense of decorum by making her speak in several regular self-contained quatrains of octosyllabic lines in *rimes embrassées* that include repeated rhyme words ('emploi', 'm'apprête', 'honnête', 'de moi' / 'matières', 'que moi', 'l'emploi', 'lumières'). Mercury's verse, on the other hand, is more flexible, as he tries different lines of reasoning to persuade Night to help his master in his endeavours. His relentless consecutive rhyming in his final argument ('Nuit', 'prie', 'bruit', 'renchérie' / 'divers', 'affaires', 'ouverts', 'guères') suggests his assertive nature. This is indicated in the English in Mercury's teasing repetition of the label 'Bawd', though it gives Dryden's Mercury a more bullying tone than that of Molière. Night is eventually persuaded to oblige Mercury and his master, and the sense of resignation is conveyed in her final heptasyllabic line: 'Je vais faire une station'. The *rimes croisées* shared between Molière's characters at the end of their discussion suggest they have reached a compromise. A similar sense of shared responsibility is apparent in the balance of alliteration in Mercury's final lines of Dryden's translation of the exchange (while Night is to put a 'Spoke' into her wheels, and to delay 'the Seven Stars', Mercury will dress as a 'Serving-man', a 'false Sosia'). In the English version, however, it is Mercury who issues these instructions; the dense alliteration again serves to indicate his aggressive persuasiveness. The sound-patterning in Dryden's prose that replaces the modulating rhyme-patterning of Molière's verse casts Mercury as a more insistent rhetorician than the wily Mercure in the French play.[9]

Masculine and Feminine Rhymes

In French and English versification there are so-called masculine and feminine rhymes, though the definitions of such rhymes are different in the two languages. In French, a masculine rhyme includes words that do not end in a mute 'e' (an example from the extract of *Amphitryon* above is 'Nuit'/'bruit'), whereas those in a feminine rhyme do end in a mute 'e' (an example from the extract above is 'Mercure'/'figure'). In a feminine rhyme the mute 'e' is not counted in scansion, but it has the effect of lengthening the preceding stressed vowel and was pronounced in declamation. Masculine rhymes can end on a consonant or a stressed vowel sound, and can therefore sound more clipped. From the sixteenth century onwards it became convention in French versification to alternate these two types of rhyme throughout a section of verse (*alternance des rimes*).

In English, a masculine rhyme is a rhyme in which only the stressed final syllable is matched (for example 'success'/'happiness'), whereas a feminine rhyme occurs when two or more syllables match and the final syllable or syllables are unstressed (for example 'fully'/ 'Cully'). Masculine rhyme is much more common than feminine rhyme in English verse, because the latter is more difficult to construct. It is a common feature of the English 'hudibrastic' verse form, named after Samuel Butler's *Hudibras* (1663–78), a form of mock heroic narrative poem written in couplets of iambic tetrameter. Owing to its apparent affectedness, feminine rhyme has become associated with comedy and satire.

Given the different definitions and values attributed to masculine and feminine rhyme in French and English, how were the effects of the rhyme gender in one language to be conveyed in the other? Clearly the few seventeenth-century translators who did use rhyme had to tackle the problem. This difficulty perhaps offered a source of justification for those translators who avoided putting Molière into rhyme at all. A fundamental question to address is whether the use of masculine and feminine rhyme in French verse can be considered to have any semantic significance or whether it is a tool by which a dramatist can enhance the presentation of character interaction. If the *alternance des rimes* had become a tradition by the sixteenth century, was the dramatist simply a slave to convention? Scott argues that the tension between rhyme gender and grammatical gender in French contributes to the presentation of gender politics in *Les Femmes savantes* (1672), though it is certainly debatable whether one type of gender really has an impact on the other:

> Even as the *femmes savantes* exploit their rights to feminine power and education provided by the [grammatical] femininity of words like 'puissance' and 'philosophie', their enterprise is undermined by the fact that rhyme so frequently endorses the prejudices of sexual discrimination. (p. 204)

Such interpretations might seem convincing in a play that explores gender stereotypes, but does rhyme gender play a significant role in other areas of Molière's *œuvre* and if so how is it conveyed in translation?

Amphitryon demonstrates how rhyme gender can work in a rhetorical mode. Like Mercury, Jupiter is a character who cannot only change his bodily form; he is also adept at manipulating his language to infiltrate and to serve his own ends. At the conclusion of the play, when Jupiter returns on a cloud to reveal his trick, he speaks in carefully-constructed verse (I have marked the rhyme patterns to show their intricacy):

Regarde, Amphitryon, quel est ton imposteur;	A
Et sous tes propres traits, vois Jupiter paraître.	B
À ces marques, tu peux aisément le connaître;	B
Et c'est assez, je crois, pour remettre ton cœur	A
Dans l'état auquel il doit être,	B
Et rétablir chez toi, la paix, et la douceur.	A
Mon nom, qu'incessamment toute la terre adore,	C
Étouffe ici les bruits, qui pouvaient éclater.	D
Un partage avec Jupiter,	D

N'a rien du tout, qui déshonore:	C
Et sans doute, il ne peut être que glorieux,	E
De se voir le rival du souverain des Dieux.	E
Je n'y vois, pour ta flamme, aucun lieu de murmure;	F
Et c'est moi, dans cette aventure,	F
Qui tout dieu que je suis, dois être le jaloux.	G
Alcmène est toute à toi, quelque soin qu'on emploie;	H
Et ce doit à tes feux être un objet bien doux,	G
De voir, que pour lui plaire, il n'est point d'autre voie,	H
Que de paraître son époux:	G
Que Jupiter, orné de sa gloire immortelle,	I
Par lui-même, n'a pu triompher de sa foi;	J
Et que ce qu'il a reçu d'elle,	I
N'a, par son cœur ardent, été donné qu'à toi.	J

(III.10.1890–12; *OC*, I, 933)

The octosyllabic lines interspersed with alexandrines summarize Jupiter's argument, and thereby his most controversial points. Jupiter's reasoning that Amphitryon need not worry about cuckoldry because 'Un partage avec Jupiter | N'a rien du tout, qui déshonore' is presented succinctly and in a comically matter-of-fact way that contrasts with the verbose introduction of the interloper in the opening of the speech. The lingering surprise at the revelation of the 'imposteur' is dissipated in the phonetic echo in the more positive rhymes 'cœur' and 'douceur'. The introduction of a couplet (or *rimes plates*) with curt masculine rhymes in the following lines emphasizes the bluntness with which Jupiter justifies his behaviour ('Et sans doute, il ne peut être que glorieux | De se voir le rival du souverain des Dieux'). Although he suggests that Amphitryon can consider it glorious to be victim to Jupiter the cuckolder, the rhyme really hints at the god's sense of his own glory. Jupiter apparently revels in the ease with which he has carried off the trick, and the ease of this rhyme supports this interpretation.

The audience is invited either to be impressed by Jupiter's rhetoric and power, or to question the validity of his lines of reasoning. Molière employs several prosodic techniques to make it difficult for a clear-cut assessment to be made. Even within the intricate and complex blending of different rhyme patterns, Molière observes the rules of *alternance des rimes*, alternating masculine rhymes with feminine ones. Towards the beginning of the speech the feminine rhymes do not carry the most semantic weight ('paraître', 'connaître', 'être'), but from the line in which Jupiter claims he himself should be 'le jaloux', the feminine rhymes work to present Alcmène as the faithful wife who was wholly unaware that she was involved in cuckoldry. As Jupiter explains that there was no alternative course of action but to disguise himself as her husband, the feminine rhymes help to shift the focus from his intrusion to Alcmène's fidelity. The associations that might be made between 'jaloux', 'doux', and 'époux' to conjure up the image of the jealous husband and the successes of the cuckolder are turned on their head by the suggestion that the steady constancy of the wife demanded the assumption of the disguise.

It might be argued that the gender of the rhyme is nothing more than the result of convention here, but the patterning bears out the idea that Molière works with the rule of *alternance* for rhetorical ends. The feminine rhyme between the alexandrine that ends in 'immortelle' and the octosyllabic line that ends in 'd'elle', for example, emphasizes the figure of faithful Alcmène. The use of *rimes croisées* throughout the description of Jupiter's submission to Alcmène's attitude serves to suggest the struggle between the god's desires and the internal emotional fidelity of the wife.

However true it may be that Alcmène is a faithful wife, the rhymes serve Jupiter's rhetoric in which he seeks, perhaps sardonically, to exonerate himself. Audiences are left wondering if it is Alcmène's loyalty that triumphs over the god, or the god's rhetoric that triumphs over Amphitryon's anger. The ambiguity is a deliberate comic feature, as Amphitryon's servant Sosie corroborates in his line following Jupiter's speech: 'Ce Seigneur sait dorer la pilule'. Sosie can see that the rhetoric is artifice and the audience is invited to consider the rhyme scheme as part of the pill-gilding process.

Masculine and feminine rhymes in English are different from masculine and feminine rhymes in French. No argument can be made for symmetry or tension between grammatical gender and rhyming gender in English, not only because of the difference in rhyme types, but also because of the ungendered status of most inanimate nouns. English masculine rhyme is much more common than English feminine rhyme and is the form in which Dryden translates Jupiter's final speech. In the main action of the play Dryden's Jupiter mostly speaks in blank verse, particularly in response to Alcmena's loving verses, though at the end of Act I Dryden adds in a series of rhyming couplets in which Jupiter revels in his scheme. Jupiter's malleable form and persona are conveyed in Dryden's version when he switches from verse to prose as the 'two Amphitryons' are called on to prove their authenticity in Act V. At the end of the play, however, Jupiter returns to his normal form and re-adopts the ostentatious rhyming verse that appears on occasion in his asides in Act I. The rarity of sustained rhyme in Dryden's sections translated from Molière emphasizes the significance of Jupiter's ironic speech and signals the conclusion of the play:

> Look up, *Amphitryon*, and behold above,
> Th'Impostour God, the Rival of thy Love:
> In thy own shape, see *Jupiter* appear,
> And let that sight, secure thy jealous fear.
> Disgrace and Infamy, are turn'd to boast:
> No Fame, in *Jove's* Concurrence can be lost:
> What he enjoys, he sanctifies from Vice;
> And by partaking, stamps into a price.
> 'Tis I, who ought to murmur at my Fate;
> Forc'd by my Love, my Godhead to translate;
> When on no other terms I could possess,
> But by thy form, thy features, and thy dress;
> To thee were giv'n, the Blessings that I sought,
> Which else, not all the bribes of Heav'n had bought.
> Then take into thy Armes thy envy'd Love;
> And, in his own despight, triumph over *Jove*. (pp. 56–57)

At first glance this appears to be a close translation of Molière. The rhetorical effect of Jupiter's illeism in the original French is retained in the English and facilitated by the synonymous name 'Jove'. The patterning of *rimes embrassées*, *rimes croisées*, and *rimes plates* in the French is converted into familiar rhyming couplets, most of which are in iambic pentameter in the English. The regular rhyming couplets of Dryden's translation tease out the argument over several lines, rather than emphasizing key points with shorter metrical segments, but the rhyming couplets stress and betray Jupiter's key rhetorical technique: they present the apparent negative viewpoint and offer the positive 'spin'. Thus 'boast' is paired with 'lost' and 'Vice' is paired with 'price' (prize) to suggest that Jupiter has read Amphitryon's thoughts and offered a reinterpretation of his situation. Though the rhyming could be interpreted as working in the god's favour, its artificiality also emphasizes the pairings of the words in order to call into question the legitimacy of Jupiter's arguments. Dryden's Mercury notes the bewilderment of the married couple: 'both stand mute, and know not how to take it'. His Sosia, like Molière's, is more assertive: 'Our Sovereign Lord *Jupiter* is a sly Companion; he knows how to gild a bitter Pill' (p. 57).

But where in Dryden's translation is Alcmena? The only references to her are 'thy Love', 'my Love', and 'thy envy'd Love'. Whereas her faithfulness is described at length in Molière's alternating French masculine and feminine rhymes, in Dryden the epithet 'Love' is all that indicates her good qualities, and its main purpose is to facilitate rhymes with 'above' and 'Jove'. In the English version she is presented as an object to be possessed rather than as an assertively faithful wife. Jupiter's comment, 'Forc'd by my Love, my Godhead to translate; | When on no other terms I could possess', does suggest Alcmena's fidelity, but it is not explored rhetorically as it is in Molière's version. This may be because Dryden does not alternate masculine and feminine rhymes or think about the gender of certain terms. Instead, he uses a series of punchy English masculine rhymes that leave the married couple bemused. While in Molière's play Sosia concludes the drama with the observation that 'Sur telles affaires, toujours, le meilleur est de ne rien dire', and audiences are thus invited to keep thinking about how successful Jupiter's rhyming rhetoric has been, in Dryden's translation, a firmer conclusion is drawn by Sosia:

> Tis true, the Lady has enough in store,
> To satisfie these two, and eke, two more:
> In fine, the Man, who weighs the matter fully,
> Wou'd rather be the Cuckold than the Cully. (p. 57)

The final two lines of the play include a rare English feminine rhyme that ends the drama on a note of satirical frivolity. The audience is invited to weigh Mercury's words fully and to discern the irony of his comment (the opposition set up between 'Cuckold' and 'Cully' invites the initial reading of Amphitryon as fortunate cuckold and Jupiter as less fortunate cully (meaning a companion). But 'cully' more commonly means 'fool' or 'dupe' so the contrast between 'cuckold' and 'cully' is tenuous. There is a deliberate circularity to Mercury's remark that is reinforced by the repetitive syllables of the feminine rhyme.

This is not to state that the use of masculine and feminine rhymes in the English translation mirrors the interaction between male and female characters in the play, but rather to state that the absence of the need to alternate masculine and feminine rhymes in the English allows Dryden to offer a translation that emphasizes the lustful aims of Jupiter and downplays the fidelity of Amphitryon's wife for a different comic effect. The intensified bawdiness that emerges at the end of Dryden's *Amphitryon* complements the scene between Mercury and Night, in which Mercury makes repeated reference to the Night's status as a 'Bawd' in contrast to Mercure's more delicate appeals to the 'jeune Déesse' in Molière.

Thus, the different definitions and uses of masculine and feminine rhymes in French and English provide a challenge to translators of Molière's verse, but also an opportunity to vary the tone of the comedy without straying far from the words of the source-text. Rhyming provides an ironic frame of reference that can be employed and manipulated by dramatists in order to show the rhetorical prowess of scheming characters, but also to betray their negative features. Dryden's Jupiter may claim that 'What he enjoys he sanctifies from Vice | And by partaking, stamps into a price', but by partaking in rhyme, his vices, like his form, are disguised only to be revealed.

Song

Although this chapter has shown that certain translators did transfer elements of versification from Molière's comedies in order to use English metrical and rhyming patterns to contribute to the presentation of character, sustained complementing of French verse with English verse was rare in translations of the period 1663–1732. Material translated from plays such as *L'École des maris*, *L'École des femmes*, *L'Étourdi*, and *Les Fâcheux* was converted from alexandrines into prose. The only common trends amongst translators and adaptors were to include rhyming couplets at the end of acts that were otherwise composed of lines of prose, and to frame translated texts with newly invented rhymed prologues and epilogues.

One form of metrical composition which consistently escaped suppression in the first translations of Molière's work, however, was song. The plays that were designed to be combined with other entertainments such as music and dance, generally known nowadays as *comédies-ballets*, were an innovative form of theatre that interested the Francophile British court of the late seventeenth and early eighteenth centuries. *Comédies-ballets* also suited the English theatrical taste for variety. So where there is a song in a Molière play, there is usually an equivalent song in its early English translation. A musicological exploration of the English translations of the songs in Molière's plays is beyond the scope of this study, but it is worth noting how the translation and adaptation of song contributed to the 'Englishing' of Molière's plays both on stage and in print.

The Citizen Turn'd Gentleman (1672) by Edward Ravenscroft is a hybrid of translations of *Monsieur de Pourceaugnac* (1669) and *Le Bourgeois gentilhomme* (1670) and includes all of the songs from the latter play, set to new music by English composers.[10] The commitment to the translation of the songs is perhaps the result of the recognition that the songs in *Le Bourgeois gentilhomme* are a crucial element of the satire. In other *comédies-ballets* by Molière the musical elements are not always as vital to the progress of the action of the play. *George Dandin* (1668), for example, included musical *intermèdes*, or interludes, that related to each other but could stand alone as a pastoral opera and were not printed as parts of the comedy. A comparison of the first song in *Le Bourgeois gentilhomme* with its translation in the Ravenscroft adaptation demonstrates a certain level of fidelity to the original, with added comic overtones. When Monsieur Jourdain objects to the solemnity of a music student's rendition of a song, he offers an alternative, disregarding the advice of the music master:

MUSICIEN, *chantant*	Je languis nuit et jour, et mon mal est extrême,
	Depuis qu'à vos rigueurs vos beaux yeux m'ont soumis:
	Si vous traitez ainsi, belle Iris, qui vous aime,
	Hélas! que pourriez-vous faire à vos ennemis?
MONSIEUR JOURDAIN	Cette chanson me semble un peu lugubre, elle endort, et je voudrais que vous la pussiez un peu ragaillardir par-ci, par là.
MAÎTRE DE MUSIQUE	Il faut, Monsieur, que l'Air soit accommodé aux Paroles.
MONSIEUR JOURDAIN	On m'en apprit un tout à fait joli il y a quelque temps. Attendez... Là... comment est-ce qu'il dit?
MAÎTRE À DANSER	Par ma foi, je ne sais.
MONSIEUR JOURDAIN	Il y a du Mouton dedans.
MAÎTRE À DANSER	Du Mouton?
MONSIEUR JOURDAIN	Oui. Ah.

Monsieur Jourdain chante.

> Je croyais Janneton
> Aussi douce que belle;
> Je croyais Janneton
> Plus douce qu'un Mouton:
> Hélas! hélas!
> Elle est cent fois, mille fois plus cruelle,
> Que n'est le Tigre aux Bois. (1.2; OC, II, 269)

The translation of this exchange in *The Citizen Turn'd Gentleman* reads as follows:

> SONG
> I sigh all the night, and I languish all day,
>   And much to be pitty'd I am:
> E'er since your bright eyes, my heart did surprise
>   I could not extinguish the flame:
> But you, since y'ave known my heart was your own,
> Tho' before you was kind, now scornful are grown:
>   If so cruel you prove
>   To the man that does love;
> Ah Phyllis! Ah! Phyllis, what fate
> Have you in reserve for the wretch that you hate?

DANCING MASTER, MUSIC MASTER	Very well.
JORDEN	But me thinks this Song is a little too doleful, and enough to put a woman into the dumps, if she have any kindness for me.
MUSIC MASTER	'Tis a delicate air, and the words are not amiss.
JORDEN	I learnt a very pretty one t'other day of a friend; stay, how begins it?
MUSIC MASTER	Nay, I know not:

JORDEN	There is something of Mutton in it.
DANCING MASTER	Mutton?
JORDEN	Yes, — oh, no, no, no, 'twas Lamb — ah — I have it. [*He sings*

>   SONG
> *My Mistress is as kind as fair,*
> *My Mistress is as kind as fair,*
> *And as gentle as Lambs are;*
> *And yet alass, alass, ah lass,*
>   *Sometimes to me*
>   *She'l as cruel be,*
> *As in the wood fierce Wolves and Tygers are.*[11]

Jorden's musings that the song he tries to recall has 'something of Mutton in it' is a literal translation of Monsieur Jourdain's use of the French partitive article ('du') with 'mouton', and serves the comic purpose of making audiences think of lamb as food rather than as the stock pastoral image of the lamb. There are similar variations in metre in the English as in the French, though the hackneyed line 'Hélas, hélas' is lengthened to add the pun on the equivalent English term. This switch from 'mistress' to the colloquial term 'lass' precipitates the bathetic ending to the song. Just as the music master remarks that 'the air must fit the lyrics', so too must the English versification match the English lyrics, and in the case of the translation the English lyrics should complement the sense of the French. The unequal metre of the lines of the song in both the French and the English contributes to the presentation of Jourdain as an inept musician, particularly when compared with the music master's composition of measured recitative in the French and its more intricate adaptation in the English.

The music master's composition is extended slightly in the English translation to include reference to 'Phyllis', a name commonly used in both French and English pastoral songs of the period. The early 1670s saw a spate of printed song collections in England. The music master's song from *The Citizen Turn'd Gentleman* was reprinted along with its melody in John Playford's *Choice Songs and Ayres for One Voyce to Sing to a Theorbo-lute or Bass-viol*.[12] This work was first published in 1673, and expanded in the second edition of 1675 and the third edition of 1676, and the title page advertised the 'newest Ayres and Songs' performed at the 'Publick Theatres'. The music master's song in *The Citizen Turn'd Gentleman* is unattributed in Playford's text, but other songs translated from *Le Bourgeois gentilhomme* are also included. The *dialogue en musique* in Act I, scene 2, for example, is printed alongside its new English melody under the name of the musician Robert Smith (pp. 82–83), so the preceding song may also be his work as the two share a pastoral theme. Playford's collection also includes a translation of the second of two *chansons à boire* from Act IV, scene 1, of *Le Bourgeois gentilhomme* ('Buvons, chers amis, buvons'). The melody to the song 'Let's drink dear Friends lets drink' that features in *The Citizen Turn'd Gentleman* (p. 38) is attributed to the composer Thomas Farmer, thereby demonstrating the collaborative nature of the translation of the *comédie-ballet* for the English stage, just as the production of the French play involved the input of several creators, including the court composer Jean-Baptiste Lully.

Several translators of Molière chose to put their own stamp on the adaptations of the French plays by including new songs that have no model in the French sources. In Playford's *Choice Songs and Ayres,* for example, there were songs from Shadwell's *The Miser* (1672), a loose translation of *L'Avare* (1668). The melodies to the songs are attributed to Robert Smith in the musical collection (pp. 36, 40). The inclusion of the songs in *The Miser* helped to justify Shadwell's claim that 'more than half of this play' is 'his own' (A3), even if a certain level of collaboration was required to set them to music. Amongst the group of translators who added new songs to their versions of Molière's plays was John Dryden. In *Sir Martin Mar-all; or, The Feign'd Innocence* (1667), an adaptation of a translation of *L'Étourdi* (1653) with elements of Philippe Quinault's *L'Amant indiscret* (1656), the French influence extends beyond the content of the play to the songs themselves. The second of two songs in *Sir Martin Mar-all* is adapted from a song by the French poet Vincent Voiture.[13] Although the lyrics of the songs were printed in the main body of the play in its first edition, they were also printed in collections such as *Westminster-drollery; or, A Choice Collection of the Newest Songs & Poems both at Court and Theatres* (1671) or *The New Academy of Complements* (1671), which includes '*an exact collection of the newest and choicest songs à la mode*'. So songs included in translated or partially translated works had an afterlife of their own that reminded the reader of their original theatrical context while also allowing them to exist as pieces of poetry in their own right.

Dryden also added songs to his version of *Amphitryon* (1690). While the lyrics appeared in standard form in the main body of the play in the first printed editions, they were also published alongside the melodies at the end of the playbooks. They included a separate title page announcing *The Songs of Amphitryon, with the Musick. Composed by Mr. Henry Purcel[l]*. Purcell's collaboration contributed to the commercial success of the play both on stage and in print, but drawing attention to the songs also provided a way of emphasizing the novel additions made to Molière's model, which included metrical variations but no songs. As has been demonstrated, Dryden matched Molière's experimentation in French verse with experimentation in prose, in verse, and, as an added extra, in English song.

Plays by Molière that included sustained intermingling of verse and song received more prosodic attention in translation than verse comedies without musical elements. Thus, Thomas Shadwell's version of *Psyche* (1674/5), a translation and adaptation of the *tragédie-ballet Psyché* by Molière, Corneille, and Quinault, included octosyllabic and decasyllabic verse, couplets, and songs to correspond with the various verse forms in the French.[14] The music was composed by Matthew Locke and the performance contributed to the introduction of opera in England. Several decades later John Ozell also chose to translate *Psyché* into verse, even though his *Works of Monsieur de Molière* (1714) was mostly a collection of prose translations intended for reading rather than performance. Ozell took the same approach when translating the verses and songs that were performed on the first day of the lavish court entertainments at Versailles known as *Les Plaisirs de l'île enchantée* (*Works*, III). Owing to time pressures, Molière wrote the second day's play *La Princesse d'Élide* partly in verse and mostly in prose. Ozell reverts to prose translation for his *Princess of Elis* but the fact that he versifies his translations of the most music-laden of Molière's works shows that even in printed translations of Molière there were efforts to point to the auditory appeal of the original performances.

Although the translators of the 1732 *Select Comedies* explain their distaste for rhyme in their preface to their parallel prose translations, they do allow themselves the liberty of translating the songs absorbed into the action of Molière's plays into jaunty rhyming couplets. Their bourgeois gentleman's inexpert song, for example, is comically rendered as:

> *I thought my dear* Namby
> *As Gentle as Fair-o:*
> *I thought my dear* Namby
> *As mild as a Lamb-y.*
> *Oh Dear, Oh Dear, O Dear-o!*
> *For now the sad Scold, is a thousand times told,*
> *More fierce than a Tiger or Bear-o.* (II, 17)

Mr Jordan's fifth line might well echo the reader's reaction to the verse itself, but if so it is in such a way that the doggerel achieves its comic effect. The translators betray their pleasure in rhyme and to some extent contradict their claim in the preface that rhyme is 'a villainous practice', not least because it has proved 'a Clog' in their translating process (A9ʳ). The versifying required in transposing songs, however, proves to have quite the opposite result and offers a reminder of the vocal performance of the plays that the translators seek to preserve in print.

The varied and disparate prosodic elements of Molière's *œuvre* clearly posed challenges to his first translators for the English stage and page. While the prevalence of prose translations of Molière in the period 1663–1732 would indicate that many did not 'take up the gauntlet', the relatively rare moments of engagement with prosody show an understanding of the ways that rhythm, rhyme, and song could contribute to a comical or satirical presentation of Molière's characters.

The relative flexibility and looseness of dramatic dialogue in English compared to French alexandrines allowed translators such as Rawlins to convey the miscommunication of characters in a range of ways, including variations in syllable-count, stress, repetition, and juxtaposition with prose. The English wariness of rhyme in drama makes those translators who make occasional use of rhyme stand out. While it had been an English dramatic tradition to end scenes or acts with rhyming couplets to draw audience attention to the progression of plot, other uses of rhyme tended to be self-conscious or employed to emphasize the affected behaviour of characters. Given the different rhyming conventions in French and English, it is worth considering what is lost and what is gained when Molière's rhymed lines are transformed into English verse. The alternation of so-called masculine and feminine rhymes in French, along with the gendered nature of the language, often contributed to semantic resonance in French that could not be transferred into the structures of English rhymed verse. So the very act of rhyming in the target language could result in rhetorical effects that diverge from those in Molière.

Even translators who claimed to be firmly committed to the merits of translating

Molière in prose could not ignore the metrical compositions required in presenting musical elements of the texts. Indeed, the translation of songs into English verse was a means by which translators for print could conjure an image of the *performance* of Molière's plays. The first translations of Molière's plays survive through their print editions, but their metrical traces offer insights into the translator's perceptions of how the comedies were voiced on the French stage to elicit emotional responses from the audience, and how they should or could be voiced on the English stage to achieve a similar impact.

Notes to Chapter 3

1. Pepys was a great fan of Dryden's *Sir Martin Mar-all; or, The Feign'd Innocence* (1667), an adaptation of a translation of *L'Étourdi* (1653) combined with Quinault's *L'Amant indiscret* (1656). In the entry for 1 January 1668 the diarist wrote that the play was 'the fullest of proper matter for mirth that ever was writ' (Pepys, *The Diary*, IX, 2. See Chapter 1, n. 14, for Pepys's negative review of 'The Ladys à la mode', presumably Flecknoe's *The Damoiselles à la mode*.
2. Thomas Shadwell, for example, well known for his cavalier attitude to translating, adapted Molière's *Les Fâcheux* (1661) into the prose play *The Sullen Lovers; or, The Impertinents* (1668). Yet the prose in the printed version of the text is set out in lines that look like blank verse, even though there is no sustained metre.
3. Thomas Rawlins (c.1620–70) was principally an engraver, but became a playwright with the publication of *The Rebellion* (1640). Rawlins made medals during the civil wars until he seemingly fled to France. After the Restoration he was made chief royal engraver. It is uncertain when *Tom Essence* was written as it was licensed and published after his death.
4. Thomas Rawlins, *Tom Essence: or, The Modish Wife* (London: printed by T. M. for W. Cademan, 1677). Further references to this edition are given after quotations in the text.
5. Sir Robert Howard, *Four New Plays* (London: printed for Henry Herringman, 1655), a3^v–a4^r.
6. Miles, 'The Original of the Non-juror', p. 197.
7. Clive Scott, *The Riches of Rhyme: Studies in French Verse* (Oxford: Clarendon Press, 1988), p. 158.
8. For a detailed discussion of the various interpretations of Molière's *raisonneurs* see Michael Hawcroft, *Molière: Reasoning with Fools* (Oxford: Oxford University Press, 2007).
9. For detailed comparison of the power relations in Molière's *Amphitryon* and Dryden's *Amphitryon* see J. Douglas Canfield, *Tricksters and Estates: On the Ideology of Restoration Comedy* (Lexington: University Press of Kentucky, 1997), pp. 241–48.
10. Edward Ravenscroft (c.1654–1697) joined Inns of Court, but spent more time writing drama than studying law. His first play was *The Citizen Turn'd Gentleman* (1672), which audaciously mocked the *citizens* on whom theatres depended during the Anglo-Dutch Wars. He purportedly had trouble persuading actors to perform French farce in *Scaramouch a Philosopher* (1677), but continued to produce a wide range of plays throughout his career. Like Shadwell, Ravenscroft sustained a literary dispute with Dryden.
11. Edward Ravenscroft, *The Citizen Turn'd Gentleman* (London: printed for Thomas Dring, 1672), p. 3. Further references are given after quotations in the text.
12. John Playford, *Choice Songs and Ayres for One Voyce to Sing to a Theorbo-lute or Bass-viol* (London: printed by William Godbid, 1676), pp. 26–27. Further references are given after quotations in the text.
13. John Dryden, *The Poems of John Dryden: Volume 1, 1649–1681*, ed. by Paul Hammond (London: Longman, 1995), pp. 203–04.
14. Thomas Shadwell, *Psyche: A Tragedy* (London: printed by T. N. for Henry Herringman, 1675).

PART II

Lexical Choices and Recontextualizations

CHAPTER 4

Cuckoldry and Gallantry

In John Dryden's *Marriage à la mode* (1673) Melantha asks her maid to teach her French words so that she can appear fashionable in society. The servant obliges by reeling off some expressions. Amongst them is *double entendre*. This is the first recorded usage of the term in the *OED*, although in this context it is not really being used in English. In late seventeenth-century England there was a strong French influence at court and many French words and phrases were carried over into English without modification.[1] Their new linguistic and social context, however, meant that they carried a different meaning in English than they did in French. *Double entendre* is an example. It is a corruption of the French adverbial phrase *à double entente* meaning 'with a double meaning', though it is obsolete in modern French, in which *à double sens* is the more common expression. Yet in English the term 'double entendre' often specifically refers to a double meaning with suggestive innuendo. It is therefore often used in the comic domain of coupling and marriage.

In this chapter, Molière's treatment of marriage and its reconfiguration in late seventeenth- and early eighteenth-century English dramatic settings will be explored by analysing translations of *Sganarelle ou le Cocu imaginaire* (1660), *L'École des femmes* (1662), *La Critique de L'École des femmes* (1663), and *George Dandin, ou Le Mari confondu* (1668). The focus of the analysis will be the translation of terms used to describe cuckoldry and gallantry (*le cocuage* and *la galanterie*). These themes are common in Molière's representation of marriage and the language used to describe them is rich in metaphor, imagery, and double meanings. Much of the figurative language was established in European literary tradition, so English translators could preserve some of the imagery. Thanks to the fashion for lexical borrowing from French into English, they also had some French terminology at their disposal. The following analysis will demonstrate that the translators' mixture of traditional tropes and vocabulary from France enabled them to convey Molière's portrayal of the relationship between language and social behaviour.

Le Cocu

In modern French the word *cocu* or *cocue* describes a man or a woman whose partner has been unfaithful. The word originated from the Old French *coucou*, or 'cuckoo'. The females of some species of cuckoo lay their eggs in others birds' nests and leave their offspring in the care of the other birds. The equivalent term in English, 'cuckold', which likewise derives from 'cuckoo', has a more specific meaning: it refers to a husband whose wife has committed adultery.[2] 'Cuckold' is now considered an archaic term in English and does not have the same intensity of derogatory charge as it did prior to the twentieth century. But in seventeenth- and eighteenth-century Europe the theme of cuckoldry formed the dramatic axis of many comedies. In *Fashioning Adultery: Gender, Sex and Civility in England, 1660–1740* David Turner explains that comedy about cuckoldry 'thrived on its ability to adapt familiar themes and tropes to contemporary concerns'.[3] Turner also points out that familiarity was part of the appeal:

> On the one hand, early modern humour worked through the constant retelling, adaptation and appropriation of stock characters, themes and plots — many of which had a heritage traceable to classical literature and medieval fables. Repetition served the purpose of recognition essential to generating a comic register and conditioning a human response to marital discord. Language also played an important role in this respect. Cuckoldry determined its own terminology for adultery and its victims [...]. On the other hand, cuckoldry, like other topics of humour, also depended on [...] topical allusions to social life which contributed significantly to its interpretation. (p. 95)

It is surprising that Turner does not refer to the influence of Molière on comedy about cuckoldry, especially given that the historical reach of his work covers the remarkable proliferation of English translations of Molière. Nevertheless, his assertion is especially pertinent to the analysis of the ways in which the terminology of cuckoldry in Molière's comedy was reworked by translators to suit English social dramatic contexts. The following analysis of the language of *cocuage*/cuckoldry will demonstrate that the 'impurity' of the translations was key to making them resonate comically and satirically in England.

The theme of cuckoldry is fundamental to Molière's *Sganarelle ou le Cocu imaginaire*. The plot centres on a misunderstanding that leads Sganarelle to believe that he is being cuckolded, and this false belief leads to more confusion. Célie, a young woman whose father is preventing her desired marriage to Lélie, falls into a swoon. Sganarelle comes to her aid, but his wife sees and misinterprets the situation. His wife also finds a picture of Lélie that Célie had dropped when she fainted. When Sganarelle sees his wife with this portrait he believes she is cheating on him. He obtains the picture and comes across Lélie. He accuses him of having a relationship with his wife, and when Lélie hears that Sganarelle obtained the portrait from his wife, he believes that Célie had married Sganarelle during his recent absence. Several further misunderstandings occur, until Célie's maid resolves the situation by asking direct questions.

Le Cocu imaginaire was the first of Molière's plays to be translated into English. The translation made up one act of William D'Avenant's *The Playhouse to be Let*, first performed in London in 1663. The play and its author are not mentioned explicitly by title, but the piece is described as a new farce from France. The translation, though contracted in places, keeps the main focus on Sganarelle's false belief that he is being cuckolded. Parts of the *Le Cocu imaginaire* were also translated in Thomas Rawlins's 1677 play *Tom Essence; or, The Modish Wife* (see Chapter 3). Another version of the play by John Vanbrugh was performed at the Haymarket Theatre in 1706, though the full text of his *The Cuckold in Conceit* is not extant. Complete English translations of the play emerged in collected works: *The Imaginary Cuckold* is published in the second volume of Ozell's *Works of Monsieur de Molière* (1714), and *The Cuckold in Conceit* is published in the first volume of *Select Comedies of Mr de Molière* (1732). Perhaps the title in the *Select Comedies* was inspired by Vanbrugh's play, or perhaps it is Vanbrugh's play itself, since the *Select Comedies* also contains other pre-existing translations of Molière's works. The lexical choices in the latter translations of *Le Cocu imaginaire* differ considerably from D'Avenant's seventeenth-century rendition, though efforts are still made to maintain the wordplay that is so crucial to conveying social anxiety about cuckoldry. Indeed, the variations in lexical choice demonstrate changes in social attitudes towards marital discord from the mid-seventeenth to the early eighteenth centuries in England.

Molière took up the themes of *Le Cocu imaginaire* and reconfigured them in *L'École des femmes* (first performed 1662, first published 1663). Arnolphe differs from Sganarelle in that he is not married, but he still fears the potential for cuckoldry. He guards his young ward Agnès with a mind to marrying her, but despite her apparent innocence she manages to pursue a relationship with the young Horace. Arnolphe's friend Chrysalde is on hand to reason with his friend and to try to temper his obsessive fear of cuckoldry. *L'École des femmes* was adapted frequently in the seventeenth century: as we saw in Chapter 1 parts of it were woven into the hybrid plot of Richard Flecknoe's *The Damoiselles à la mode* (1667); and it formed the basis of the plot of John Caryl's *Sir Salomon; or, The Cautious Coxcomb* (1671). *L'École des femmes* also inspired parts of Wycherley's *The Country Wife* (1674/5) and the centrality of the theme of cuckoldry in Molière's play was identified and exploited in Edward Ravenscroft's adaptation, *The London Cuckolds* (1681). The first full translations of *L'École des femmes* emerged in the collected works of the early eighteenth century. A translation entitled *A School for Women* is included in the second volume of Ozell's *Works of Monsieur de Molière* and a translation called *The School for Wives* appears in the fourth volume of *Select Comedies of Mr de Molière*. The lexical choices made in these translations form a helpful comparison with the vocabulary of cuckoldry that appears in the various translations of *Le Cocu imaginaire*. Chrysalde's attempts to reason with Arnolphe are particularly useful in analysing the ways in which the language of cuckoldry can be construed in different ways. It often includes double meanings, but it can lead to multiple interpretations that are at once anxiety-inducing to 'imaginary cuckolds' and comic to audiences. The translators sought to keep this constantly in mind when rendering comedy about cuckoldry into English.

The Language of Cuckoldry

In parts of southern Europe today the 'sign of the horns', a gesture made by extending the index finger and the little finger, is still used as a harsh insult because it carries connotations of cuckoldry.[4] The trope of the cuckold having or wearing real or imaginary animal horns goes back to ancient times and exists in numerous European languages. It is suggestive not only of bestial stupidity, but of ignorance.

As a beast cannot see its own horns, a cuckold does not (at least initially) know that his wife is having an affair. A sense of public shame is indicated in the idea that others can see 'the horns'. The popularity of the trope in European literature, particularly in comedy, is also due to its phallic connotations and the wordplay that can derive from it. Though the 'sign of the horns' is no longer used with this meaning in either France or England, references to both the gesture and the image it evokes are widespread in the nations' seventeenth- and eighteenth-century comic drama. Direct reference is made to the gesture in Molière's *Le Cocu imaginaire*:

> Faut-il que désormais à deux doigts on te montre,
> Qu'on te mette en chansons, et qu'en toute rencontre,
> On te rejette au nez le scandaleux affront
> Qu'une femme mal née imprime sur ton front? (9.261–64; *OC*, I, 55)

This passage is translated closely in the English versions of the texts. In the *Select Comedies* of 1732, for example, the neighbours are imagined as having their 'Fingers set out like Horns' (I, 35). This demonstrates that the gesture was easily recognizable and significant in both early modern France and early modern England. However, whereas the gesture may have had a universal meaning, its associated wordplay did not, so translators had to be more inventive in carrying it across in their versions.

The image of a horned beast in relation to cuckoldry is used for comic effect elsewhere in *Le Cocu imaginaire*. When Sganarelle falsely believes that his wife is having an affair with Lélie, she naturally professes ignorance of the situation. Sganarelle responds thus:

> Tu ne m'entends que trop Madame la carogne,
> Sganarelle est un nom qu'on ne me dira plus,
> Et l'on va m'appeler Monsieur Corneillius.
> J'en suis pour mon honneur [...]. (6.190–93; *OC*, I, 50)

Georges Forestier notes in the Pléiade edition of Molière's works that the wordplay linking cuckoldry with the Roman name Cornelius (derived from the word for 'horn') had been adopted in ancient Latin literature. Forestier also notes that the essayist François de La Mothe Le Vayer had taken up the pun in his dialogue *Du mariage*, and that it had appeared in plays performed by the Italian actors who shared the Palais Royal with Molière in the 1660s (*OC*, I, 1244). The spelling of the name as shown above follows the 1660 and 1662 editions of *Le Cocu imaginaire* and points to additional wordplay on the name of the best-known dramatist in Paris at the time, Pierre Corneille. It may also evoke his younger brother Thomas Corneille whom Molière mocked more pointedly in *L'École des femmes*.[5] This orthography may also allow for wordplay involving the term *corneille* and its meaning of 'crow'. Cuckoos often lay their eggs in crows' nests. This interpretation leads us back to the designation '*cocu*'. So within one imagined name there are numerous comic connotations related to the context in which the play is performed. The translators of the English versions, therefore, had to choose phrases that could highlight the comic force of the situation.

D'Avenant's 1663 text is written in French-accented English, designed for comic effect. We are to understand that the actors playing the characters are part of a French acting troupe. The passage cited above is translated with this in mind in the English version when Sganarelle complains that his name will become 'mi lore Cuckol' (p. 79). In this version, reference to the name Cornelius and its association with horns is absent. Instead, there is a comic combination of registers that conveys the essential thrust of the complaint; Sganarelle will be called a cuckold by his neighbours, or so he imagines. Sganarelle's self-identification as 'Monsieur Sganarelle' indicates that we are to understand him as a French comic character, but the phrase *'mi lore'*, more usually spelled *milord*, has a particular significance in both French and English. Randle Cotgrave notes that *milort* means 'My Lord; or, as Monseigneur (*a word borrowed of, and imployed on, us*)'.[6] So this is a French term derived from the English words 'my lord', which was then reappropriated in English, often with a satirical edge. It is supposedly a title of respect, but linked to the title 'Cuckold' it becomes bathetic. The imagined change in title also gestures towards D'Avenant's translation process itself. The French Monsieur imagines himself recast as an English lordly cuckold.

The wordplay involving names and titles also conveys the bourgeois preoccupation with status that is central to Molière's comedy (see Chapter 7). Sganarelle is less concerned with his wife's supposed affair than with his public reputation. In the version printed in Ozell's 1714 *Works of Monsieur de Molière*, Sganarelle's preoccupation with honour is emphasized through ironic politeness. Mrs Sganarelle expresses her surprise at her husband's accusation by supposing that he must be drunk or mad. Sganarelle takes umbrage: 'Horn-mad, Mrs. Carrion, thank you that make me so. *Sganarelle* is now my Name no longer. I shall henceforth be saluted, *Signior Cornuto*. You have Honour'd me (II, 9). This translation is closer to Molière's original French, though there is a possible additional pun if 'honour'd me' is read as 'horn-er'd me' or even 'horn-ear'd me'.[7] In calling his wife an insulting name Sganarelle is also insulting himself, hence the structural symmetry in 'Madame la carogne' and 'Monsieur Corneillius', or in Ozell translations, 'Mrs Carrion' and 'Signior Cornuto'. David Turner recalls Ephesians 5: 23 in emphasizing that in marriage in early modern Europe 'men and women were imagined as comprising a single corporeal entity, with the husband as its head and the wife as the body. In this process, the wife became an extension of her husband's being' (p. 55). This idea may elucidate the horned cuckold trope, given that the wife's use of her body could determine what was imagined to grow on the husband's head. This image is clearly evoked in the adjective 'horn-mad', which has several shades of meaning.[8] At the simplest level it means that Sganarelle is so angry that he is like a horned beast about to charge. It more specifically means that he is enraged with the belief that he is a cuckold. There is a third possible suggestion of sexual jealousy and rage in the phallic connotations of the image.

The pun on the name 'Cornelius' in Molière's play is changed to the joke Italian name 'Signor Cornuto' in Ozell's translation. The switch in language could suggest discomfort on the part of Sganarelle in that he does not want to call himself a cuckold outright, although since the fifteenth century the word *cornuto* had occasionally been used in English as an alternative to 'cuckold'. The noun *cornuto* features in Ozell's translation of *L'École des femmes* which appeared in the same volume as his version of *Le Cocu imaginaire*. In Ozell's *A School for Women* Arnolphus mocks the type of husband who allows his wife to bestow riches on 'those that take care to make him Cornuto' (*Works*, II, 108). This is a close translation of Molière's 'ceux qui prennent soin de le faire Cornard' (1.1.26; *OC*, I, 400). The term *cornard* is an occasional alternative to *cocu* in Molière's plays and demonstrates the prevalence of the trope of horns. *L'École des femmes* also includes the term 'becque cornu', a French transposition of the Italian *becco cornuto* meaning 'a horned billy-goat'. *Becco* was occasionally used in English to refer to a cuckold (*OED*), so 'becque cornu' is rendered as 'becco cornuto' in the 1732 *Select Comedies*.[9] The image of a horned beast was absorbed in numerous ways into the vocabulary of cuckoldry in both French and English, often via Latin and by extension Italian.

The translation of *Le Cocu imaginaire* in the 1732 *Select Comedies* is the most literal of the three English versions. The translators have emphasized that their text is as close as possible to the original French. This text does not, therefore, include as much alternative wordplay as the other translations and has a slightly more 'sanitized' tone. Thus, the 1732 translation of the passage quoted above is similar to Ozell's version, though Sganarelle is written as 'Sganarell' and the manner in which he addresses his wife is softened slightly: 'You know but too well, Mrs. *Impudence*. My Name no longer will be *Sganarell* [*sic*]; Every Body now will give me the Title of Mr. *Cuckold*: I am so to my Honour' (*Select Comedies*, IV, 27). Ozell does not translate the meaning of 'j'en suis pour mon honneur', which is 'I have lost my honour'. This could be an error, or it could allow for a pun whereby 'honour' is read as 'horner', a term for a horn-maker, a cuckold-maker. Nevertheless, the rendition emphasizes that Sganarelle's main concerns are his name, honour, and reputation in society. This attitude is also demonstrated in the character of Arnolphe in Molière's *L'École des femmes*. Arnolphe worries constantly about the possibility of becoming a cuckold if he were to marry Agnès and indeed treats her flirtations with the young Horace as if they were acts of adultery. Arnolphe's friend Chrysalde takes him to task for holding the belief that 'On est homme d'honneur quand on n'est point cocu' (IV.8.1235). The translators of the versions in both the 1714 and the 1732 collected works choose fidelity here, though there is an additional echo of the term 'horner' which could suggest the pervasiveness of Arnolphe's fear of cuckoldry: 'he's a Man of Honour if he's not a Cuckold' (*Works*, II, 141; *Select Comedies*, IV, 117). This statement epitomizes the way in which Sganarelle and Arnolphe believe that cuckoldry threatens their social identity.

Given his anger, we might wonder why Sganarelle 'dresses up' his accusations with imagined designations such as 'Mr Cuckold'. This is undoubtedly for the comic effect of contrasting a term of respect with a disrespectful name. But Sganarelle is also aping the surface politeness that was a feature of behaviour known in the seventeenth and eighteenth centuries as 'gallantry'. The 'imaginary cuckold' worries that the elegant language cultivated by such behaviour might help to cast a veil over acts of cuckoldry, but he adopts it in his attempt to extract a confession from his wife.

A Taste for Gallantry

The social practice and ideology of *la galanterie* underpinned much literary writing of seventeenth- and eighteenth-century France.[10] In 'Molière et le langage galant' Alain Viala asserts that there is a great deal of *galanterie* in Molière's works.[11] By tracing the word *galanterie* and its cognates in Molière's last four works, *Les Fourberies de Scapin*, *La Comtesse d'Escarbagnas*, *Les Femmes savantes*, and *Le Malade imaginaire*, Viala illustrates the two main and contradictory meanings of the term. On the one hand, according to Viala, the most common early modern definition is: 'l'art des belles manières, en particulier l'art et la manière d'être agréable aux dames de la belle société. C'est l'art qui distingue les gens du beau monde et du bon goût' (p. 100). So according to Viala the positive meaning is the art of conducting oneself in a pleasant and cultivated manner in high society. But he goes on to point out that:

> Face à ce sens positif, laudatif, le corpus offre d'autres sens contrastés. Le Chrysalde des *Femmes savantes* dit que dans sa jeunesse il a été un 'vert galant' (II, 2, v. 345). Argante, dans *Les Fourberies*, dit lui aussi que dans sa jeunesse il a pratiqué la 'galanterie', lutiné les femmes les plus 'galantes' (I, 4). Et, toujours aux *Fourberies*, Scapin se flatte de ses 'galanteries ingénieuses', terme qu'il explicite par celui de 'ruse galante' (I, 2).
>
> Cette série d'occurrences renvoie à un sémantisme alors vieillissant de 'galant'. (pp. 100–01)

Here Viala explains that a *vert galant* was originally a term used to describe a forest highwayman, but by extension came to refer to a seducer of women, someone with 'le goût de séduire'. The words *galanterie* and *galant* derived from the old verb *galer* meaning 'to play' or 'to trick'. So *galant* could, in informal and popular contexts, mean a 'seducer' or 'cheat'. Viala argues that the discrepancy between the contemporary form and understanding of gallantry and the popular connotations of the words used to describe it reveal the characters' pretentions. Their ambitions are undercut by audiences' knowledge of the original meanings of their language.

The different meanings of *galant* are illustrated in the following passage from *L'École des femmes*, when Chrysalde is trying to convince Arnolphe that his honour does not depend on whether or not he will be cuckolded:

> Mettez-vous dans l'esprit qu'on peut du cocuage,
> Se faire en galant homme une plus douce image
> [...]
> Il y faut comme en tout fuir les extrémités,
> N'imiter pas ces gens un peu trop débonnaires,
> Qui tirent vanité de ces sortes d'affaires;
> De leurs femmes toujours vont citant les galants,
> En font partout l'éloge, et prônent leurs talents,
> Témoignent avec eux d'étroites sympathies [...].
> (IV.8.1244–56; *OC*, I, 457)

When the adjective *galant* precedes a noun, as in *galant homme*, it tends to carry the positive connotation of an honourable man. Thus in the first complete English translations of *L'École des femmes* 'galant homme' as it appears in the passage above is rendered as 'Man of Honour' (*Works*, II, 142; *Select Comedies,* IV, 117). When the adjective *galant* follows a noun, or when it stands alone as a noun, it carries connotations of amorous intrigue. Thus, when Chrysalde talks of foolish husbands who welcome and praise their 'Wives' Gallants', Ozell's version glosses the comment with the observation that they 'pretend to a sympathy with their cuckold-makers' (*Works*, II, 142). This emphasis demonstrates that the different meanings of *galant* could not be translated into English with the help of grammatical customs; the position of the adjective does not change in standard spoken English and the sense of the noun 'gallant' can only be understood from its context.

Just as there is a discrepancy between the uses of the term *galanterie* and its cognates in French, there is also discrepancy in the uses of the term 'gallantry' and its cognates in English. In Edward Phillips's *The New World of English Words* (1658) the term is associated with its French origin and given a seemingly positive definition referring initially to perfection in behaviour: '(French) compleatnesse, accomplishment, or a bold confident way of courtship. *Artam*'.[12] Yet even this entry hints at potentially illicit courtship in its reference to boldness, thereby inviting a suggestion of 'overboldness' which Phillips uses to define 'impudence'. In 1702 the term 'over-gallantly' features in John Kersey the younger's *A New English Dictionary*,[13] and in 1735 the dubious sense of the word precedes other definitions of 'gallantness, gallantry' in Benjamin Norton Defoe's *A New English Dictionary*: 'Intrigue, or Amour, courteous Behaviour, Gentleness, Bravery, Valour'.[14] The early translators of Molière demonstrate an understanding of the different shades of meaning both in the original French and in the English that borrowed from the French.

The different connotations of 'gallantry' are illustrated in a passage from *George Dandin, ou le Mari confondu* (1668) and its first translation into English in Thomas Betterton's *The Amorous Widow; or, The Wanton Wife* (1670?).[15] George Dandin has married a woman of higher social class and has just discovered that she is maintaining a correspondence with a gentleman. Dandin complains to his in-laws, who initially claim they will help him, only to be taken in by their daughter and her suitor later in the play.

> GEORGE DANDIN Tout ce que je vous puis dire, c'est qu'il y a ici un certain Courtisan que vous avez vu, qui est amoureux d'elle à ma barbe [...]
> M. DE SOTENVILLE Corbleu, je lui passerais mon épée au travers du corps, à elle et au galant, si elle avait forfait à son honneur. (1.4; OC, I, 982)

Betterton translates this passage quite closely, but makes a pointed use of the term 'gallant' to describe the 'Courtisan' (meaning 'courtier' as in a man who attends court; the double meaning associated with the feminine form does not apply to men). By the end of the seventeenth century, however, the potential duplicity of a 'gallant' in English was defined in *A New Dictionary of the Terms Ancient and Modern of the Canting Crew* (essentially an early dictionary of slang) as: 'a very fine Man; also a Man of Metal, or a brave Fellow; also one that Courts or keeps, or is Kept by a Mistress'.[16] Betterton changes Dandin's name to the apposite 'Barnaby Brittle', and by using the French-derived term 'Gallant' he highlights the character's double concern at the gallant gentleman's high social status and his threat as a prospective cuckold-maker. Brittle appeals to his father-in-law Sir Peter Pride:

> BRITT. Why, she has just now receiv'd a Letter from her Gallant, and made an Appointment to meet him this Evening; and judge how small a time a Pair of Horns are agrafting.
> [...]
> SIR PET. Nay, if it be, this good Sword, (never yet drawn in vain) shall do you Right. Where is she Son-in-Law?
> BRITT. Within I'll warrant, studying what Excuse to make to get abroad and meet her Gallant.[17]

Throughout the translation Brittle frets that the gallant is already turning him into a cuckold. It is worth noting that not every instance of the term *galant* is translated by 'gallant' in early translations of Molière, even though the ambiguities of the term are frequently tested out within them. An alternative English word that became increasingly prevalent as a synonym for 'gallant' in the late seventeenth and early eighteenth centuries was 'spark'.[18] Its exact etymology is uncertain, but it is likely to be a figurative association with the light and beauty of a spark, as well as the idea of a sudden yet ephemeral appearance. It could be applied positively to females to evoke beauty and wit, but was usually used in a derogatory sense when applied to men. As with the term 'gallant', the attractive qualities associated with a 'spark' could signal his potential to cuckold and thus lead to a depreciatory use of the name. When George Dandin once again tries to convince his in-laws of his wife's guilt, he decides to try to show the supposedly adulterous pair together: 'Mais vous, que pourrez-vous dire, si je vous fais voir maintenant que le galant est avec elle?' (II.7; *OC*, I, 997). In both Ozell's 1714 *Works of Monsieur de Molière* and Baker, Miller, and Clare's 1732 *Select Comedies of Mr de Molière* the reference to the *galant* is rendered with the term 'spark' (*Works*, IV, 88; *Select Comedies*, V, 73), indicating through this use of a disparaging label Dandin's increasing agitation.

Where *George Dandin* differs from the earlier play *Le Cocu imaginaire* is in the legitimacy of the grounds for suspicion. In both plays there is a close intertwining of anxiety about gallantry and anxiety about cuckoldry, but in *Le Cocu imaginaire* the apprehension is born out of misinterpreted signs. Sganarelle's fears come to the fore in the confrontation with his wife:

> Bref en tout et partout ma personne charmante,
> N'est donc pas un morceau dont vous soyez contente,
> Et pour rassasier votre appétit gourmand,
> Il faut à son Mari le ragoût d'un galant. (6.169–72; *OC*, I, 49)[19]

In the Pléiade edition, Forestier notes that the term *ragoût* had often been used in opposition to the term *dégoût* in regard to marital relations. In the abbé de Pure's novel *La Prétieuse* (1656–58) there is a chapter called 'Des ragoûts pour les dégoûtés de mariage'.[20] It explains that marriages require 'spicing up' from time to time. Indeed the etymology of the word *ragoût* relates to the stimulation of appetite, Pierre Richelet's 1680 dictionary noting that it is a highly seasoned dish while also recording a secondary meaning: a pleasure that incites the senses.[21] Antoine

Furetière's 1690 dictionary explains that *ragoût* is a dish given to revive the appetite of those who have lost it owing to illness or gluttony.[22] Given its associations with domesticity and pleasure, it is unsurprising that it became a euphemistic term related to female sexuality and the marital bed. In his barbed comment, Sganarelle echoes contemporary idiom as recorded in French literature of the time. His linking of the term with the word *galant* reveals his concern for the type of gallantry that leads to cuckoldry.

Cuckoldry is frequently explored in early modern comedy through metaphors that refer to appetite and eating. In *L'École des femmes* Molière takes up the imagery again when Arnolphe's servant, Alain, likens a wife to a bowl of soup that one wants to guard from those who might dip their fingers into it:

> Dis-moi, n'est-il pas vrai, quand tu tiens ton potage,
> Que si quelque affamé venait pour en manger,
> Tu serais en colère, et voudrais le charger?
> [...]
> La femme est en effet le potage de l'homme;
> Et quand un homme voit d'autres hommes parfois
> Qui veulent dans sa soupe aller tremper leurs doigts,
> Il en montre aussitôt une colère extrême. (II.4.432–39; OC, I, 420)

Like the *becque cornu*, this image of illicit 'finger dunking' has an Italian connection. It is based on an element of *commedia dell'arte*, the *lazzo*, a stock comic routine or set of gestures, in which a comedian would join the thumb and index finger in a ring-shape and slip the index finger of the opposite hand into the gap, while referring verbally to the soup metaphor it represents. As Bénédicte Louvat-Molozay points out, it is not unreasonable to suppose that Alain might enact this gesture as he speaks.[23] William D'Avenant adapts this metaphor and absorbs it into his translation of *Le Cocu imaginaire* in *The Playhouse to be Let*. In what is otherwise a close translation of Molière's earlier play, D'Avenant's Sganarelle declares that his supposed rival has stolen away 'To eate de good pottage to make him abel [*sic*] | To make me more Cuckold' (p. 82). In early modern England 'pottage' bore a greater resemblance to porridge, stew, or ragoût than to soup, and there is literary precedent for using the term with sexual connotations.[24]

'Le ragoût d'un galant' as described in *Le Cocu imaginaire*, was more difficult to render in English, but translators' attempts to preserve Molière's pun demonstrate that the borrowing of French words in English was not an expedient that simplified translations, but a means of enriching them. The term *ragoût* (also spelled *ragout, ragoust,* and *ragoo*) was also used in England from the early seventeenth century, but generally in the culinary domain. D'Avenant therefore turns to a term that was etymologically and thematically related to *ragoût*:

> Is not min morsell sufficiant to
> Stay your stomach, but must you taste de
> Haut gout of a Gallant. (p. 79)

Whereas the word *ragoût* was used in English to refer to a spicy stew, *haut goût* (spelled variously as *haut gout, hogough, hogoo*) was used in English from the late sixteenth century to mean a seasoning or relish.[25] It thereby gives the heightened sense that the 'gallant' is an addition to the marital mix. Its usage in relation to sexuality also had some literary precedent which adds an extra comic edge to this English version. The euphemistic use of 'seasoning' to mean a dose of venereal disease had long been in use in comedy. Thomas Killigrew over-labours the pun in *The Parson's Wedding* (1663). A wit imagines a night with a young girl: 'We'll worke ourselves into such a sauce [...] so poynant and yet no hogough; Take heed of a hogough [...] shook together by an English cook (for your French seasoning spoils many a woman)'.[26] In typical English comic fashion, the French derivation of the term is exploited. Yet D'Avenant's choice plays not only on the pun, but also on the context of his play involving the French actors. There is additional humour in the idea that the French player may not realize the full comic potential of what he is uttering in an English context.[27] So, like Molière, D'Avenant manages to achieve a range of resonances that draws on both contemporary parlance and literature in England.

D'Avenant's use of the term *haut gout* and his orthographical choice draw attention to the separate words *haut* and *gout*. *Haut* in English could mean 'haughty' or 'lofty' and therefore forms a semantic link with the idea of gallantry as well-mannered behaviour seen in high society. As Viala explains, *galanterie* in its seventeenth-century connotation was related to *bon goût*, good taste. With the increasing influence of French fashions and behaviour in English society came an increasing concern in England about what the language of *galanterie* might hide. Turner notes that:

> The influence of French ideas of 'politesse' increased greatly during later decades of the seventeenth century. This shift owed something to the French influence on the culture of the exiled Royalists during the Interregnum, to an explosion of courtesy literature in France during the latter part of the century and its subsequent translation into English, and to the growing popularity of France as a destination on the gentleman's grand tour after the Restoration. One important aspect of the influence of French models of polished expression was the translation and publication of growing number of romances and books of compliments which promoted a more general refinement of the language of love. (p. 37)

Moreover, the translation of French comedy was a means of probing and laughing at the emerging anxiety surrounding the new modes of expression. In Ozell's 1714 version of the *Le Cocu imaginaire* Sganarelle ironically adopts the discourse of *politesse* to accuse his wife: 'our Person is thought too coarse a Morsel for your Ladyship's Stomach. You must have the *Ragoo* of a Gallant, to make the Husband go down' (p. 8). The sense of the palliative use of *ragoût* is suggested here, the husband being portrayed as an irritating cause of indigestion. The metaphor is modified slightly in the version in the 1732 *Select Comedies*. The husband there is described as the 'standing Dish', the 'staple fare' (p. 25). The overriding concern (unfounded and therefore comic in Sganarelle's case) is that cuckoldry may have become commonplace, part of society's 'diet'. More worrying still to the character is that the new language used to describe extra-marital intrigue may suggest that such behaviour is consistent with the behaviour of upper classes and therefore pursued enthusiastically by his wife.

The Theatricality of Gallantry

The pervasiveness of the language of gallantry is evident when Sganarelle once again adopts it to confront his suspected rival. He is of course trying to provoke a response from Lélie, and he does so by using the gallant technique of obsequiousness that he believes Lélie has been using on his wife. He says, in reference to his spouse, and with a double meaning: 'Je ne sais pas si j'ai dans sa galanterie | L'honneur d'être connu de votre Seigneurie' (IX.285–86; OC, I, 56). The translation in the 1732 English version is: 'I can't tell whether I've the honour to be known to your Worship in this Piece of Gallantry' (p. 37). In the early eighteenth century the phrase 'piece of gallantry' became synonymous with an act of adultery, as demonstrated in a 1729 tract *Hell Upon Earth*, in which the writer admonishes 'Folks of Fashion' for describing extra-marital relations as 'taking a Wench' on the part of a man and 'only a Piece of Gallantry' on the part of married ladies.[28] The term 'piece of gallantry' points to something planned, composed, and possibly performed in a theatrical way.[29]

The idea of gallantry as a performance or game features in *George Dandin, ou le Mari confondu*. In Act II, scene 2, Dandin upbraids his wife for encouraging admiration from other men:

GEORGE DANDIN	Je veux que vous y fassiez ce que fait une femme qui ne veut plaire qu'à son mari. Quoi qu'on en puisse dire, les Galants n'obsèdent jamais que quand on le veut bien, il y a un certain air doucereux qui les attire ainsi que le miel fait les mouches, et les honnêtes femmes ont des manières qui les savent chasser d'abord.
ANGÉLIQUE	Moi les chasser? Et par quelle raison, je ne me scandalise point qu'on me trouve bien faite, et cela me fait du plaisir.
GEORGE DANDIN	Oui. Mais quel personnage voulez-vous que joue un mari pendant cette galanterie ?
ANGÉLIQUE	Le personnage d'un honnête homme qui est bien aise de voir sa femme considérée.

The 1732 *Select Comedies* translates the language relating to roles and acting most clearly out of the first three English translations of the play: 'But what Part would you have a Husband act in this Galantry?' (v, 57). The irony of the exchange above is that even as the couple speak, Clitandre, Angélique's suitor, is onstage with them. In the first English translation of the play Betterton contracts this passage but what he omits in verbal exchange he replaces with extra dramatic gestures. Act II, scene 2, of the first edition of *George Dandin* includes only one stage direction for Clitandre: '*derrière Angélique, sans être aperçu de Dandin*' (II.2; OC, I, 992); though in the 1682 French collected works more stage directions were added to match the interaction between Angélique and Clitandre that is signalled by Dandin's bemused remarks on his wife's curtseying, shoulder movements, and nodding (all of which, unbeknownst to the husband, are directed at the suitor). Betterton, however, escalates the gestural comedy of this section in *The Amorous Widow; or, The Wanton Wife*:

> [*She takes* Brittle *round the Neck, and beckons* Lovemore, *who comes and kisses her Hand over her Husbands Shoulders all the while*
> You know, I love you dearly, by this I do.   [*kisses him*
> Why will you not be satisfy'd? Had I the World to give, it cou'd not make me more happy than this Minute   [Lovemore *still kisses her Hand.*
> (p. 41)

So Betterton answers Dandin's question of which role he should play in his wife's gallantry by enhancing the stage directions to emphasize his function as dupe. The ambiguity of gallantry is on physical display, because gestures of supposedly chivalrous regard are shown to encroach on the feigned marital intimacy.[30]

Betterton also includes an additional scene in *The Amorous Widow* to demonstrate where the young wife has learnt her skills in gallantry. In Act II Mrs Brittle tells her husband:

> I'll to the Play [...] where one is entertain'd with [...] fine Gallants, which ogle, sigh, and talk the prettiest things in the World. Methinks 'tis rare to hear a young brisk Fellow court a handsome young Lass, and she all the while making such pretty dumb Signs: first turns aside to see who observés, then spreads her Fan before her Face [...] she, blushing, Curtesies low I am not wedded to my Grave. (pp. 22–23)

The wife's remark works as a metatheatrical joke, and also foreshadows the scene in which she interacts with her husband and her suitor at the same time. But the speech also conjures an image of the blurring of boundaries between theatre and reality; is Mrs Brittle dreaming about these acts of gallantry on stage or amongst the audience? It is not farfetched to imagine the uneasy laughter of spectating spouses in the actual audience of this performed translation of *George Dandin*.

At the end of Molière's earlier play, *Le Cocu imaginaire*, Sganarelle is disabused and it is discovered that he has misconstrued the situation completely. Célie's servant suspects that something is awry before figuring out the confusion: 'Ma foi je ne sais pas | Quand on verra finir ce galimatias' (2.571–72; *OC*, I, 76). The word *galimatias*, meaning nonsense or gibberish, is supposed to have derived from the garbled statement of a lawyer in court, but Viala wonders whether it also relates to *galanterie* in terms of its connotations of ruses and games.[31] D'Avenant translates this word as 'Galantries' [*sic*] in his version (p. 84). On the one hand, the servant could be commenting ironically given that the characters are all insulting each other. On the other, she may be referring to the further meaning of gallantries — amorous intrigues. But she may also be pointing to the idea that the characters are seemingly playing parts because of the language they use. She has to see through the gallantries to sort out the confusion. The later translators choose 'Tale of a Tub' (*Works*, II, 20) and 'perplexities' (*Select Comedies*, II, 67) for *galimatias*. 'Gallant' discourse is perplexing to the characters in *Le Cocu imaginaire* because it is a style of language constructed so that people can play parts in society. The innate theatricality of the language allows Sganarelle's imagination to run wild and to fabricate the plot of his own comedy. In *L'École des femmes*, however, Arnolphe is too attuned to the theatricality of gallantry and seeks to prevent Agnès from becoming exposed to it.

His constant imaginary projection of a cuckoldry plot hinders rather than helps his cause.

Onstage Gallantry Under Review

The linguistic techniques that draw Molière's dupes into an obsessive fear of gallantry and its role in relation to cuckoldry led to some disapproval from spectators. Molière responded to critics of *L'École des femmes* by writing the one-act play *La Critique de L'École des femmes* in 1663. In the years following its first appearance it was often performed as a companion piece to *L'École des femmes*. *La Critique de L'École des femmes* begins with a conversation between the characters Uranie and Élise who anticipate the arrival of some visitors, one of whom is 'un extravagant', an affected marquis who uses language à la mode. Élise gives an example of this kind of language and indicates her displeasure with it through sarcasm:

> La belle chose de faire entrer aux conversations du Louvre de vieilles équivoques ramassées parmi les boues des Halles et de la place Maubert! [...] qu'un homme montre d'esprit lorsqu'il vient vous dire; *Madame, vous êtes dans la place Royale, et tout le monde vous voit de trois lieues de Paris, car chacun vous voit de bon œil, à cause que Boneuil est un village à trois lieues d'ici*. Cela n'est-il pas bien galant [...]? (1; *OC*, I, 488)

This section appears in Ozell's collected works translated as follows:

> 'Tis a fine thing indeed to bring into the Conversation of the *Louvre* old Conundrums pick'd out from amongst the Fishmarket Rhetorick! [...] a Man shews a mighty deal of Wit when he comes and tells you, Madam, you are in the Royal Square, and every body sees you three Leagues from *Paris* for each beholds you *de bonœil*, [with a good Eye] because Bon œil is a Village three Leagues off. Is not this gallant and witty? (*Works*, II, 164)

Ozell delocalizes and therefore simplifies the references to the market places of Paris in his translation. Ozell's uninspiring translation work in his inclusion of square-brackets is perhaps indicative of the laboured nature of the wordplay in French. Élise's mocking imitation of 'un extravagant' touches on all the shades of meaning of 'gallant' language. On the surface, the extravagant remark would be intended to flatter a lady. It can, however, be interpreted as an amorous advance and so hints at the more disreputable aspects of gallantry. It points to the links between gallantry and games in referring to the act of wordplay. This section also foreshadows the ensuing discussion about the propriety of *L'École des femmes*, which, within the timeframe of the drama, is being performed at the Palais-Royal. The critical debate centres on the *équivoques*, the ambiguous puns found in the play.[32]

When the prudish Climène arrives to denounce the play as indecent, the other women question her as to which parts offended her. Climène is reluctant to explain the full significance of the wordplay for fear of being accused of having indecent thoughts herself, and thus Molière deploys the argument that innuendo is as much in the mind of a spectator or reader as it is in the author's linguistic creation. This is why the concept of gallantry, and the language used to describe it, is such a powerful tool in comedy and why translators of Molière's texts made efforts to ensure that it was conveyed as ambiguously in English as it was in French. Taken at face value, it could be polite discourse, but its undertones and subtext could be read quite conversely.

The first complete translation of *La Critique de L'École des femmes* was Ozell's version in his collected works translation, but the exchange between the women forms the basis of a scene in William Wycherley's *The Plain Dealer* (1676/7), modelled for the most part on *Le Misanthrope* (1666). The scene in question relates to Wycherley's earlier and highly successful play *The Country Wife* (1674/5).[33] The faux prude Olivia criticizes a certain Miss Trifle for having been seen watching *The Country Wife* without blushing. The following exchange, which adapts sections of *La Critique de L'École des femmes*, demonstrates the cognitive leaps that are triggered by the types of vocabulary already explored in this chapter:

ELIZA   Why, what is there of ill in't, say you?
OLIVIA Oh fie, fie, fie, would you put me to blush anew? [...] first, the clandestine obscenity in the very name of Horner.
ELIZA   Truly, 'tis so hidden I cannot find it out I confess.
OLIVIA Oh horrid! Does it not give you the rank conception, or image, of a goat, a town-bull, or satyr? [...]
ELIZA   What then? I can think of a goat, a bull, or satyr, without any hurt.
OLIVIA Ay, but, cousin, one cannot stop there.
ELIZA   I can, cousin.
OLIVIA Oh no — for when you have those filthy creatures in your head once, the next thing you think, is what they do: as their defiling of honest men's beds and couches, rapes upon sleeping and waking country virgins, under hedges and on haycocks. Nay further —
ELIZA   Nay, no further, cousin.[34]

The simultaneous fear and allure of a young gallant such as the cuckold-maker Horner in *The Country Wife* is evoked in Olivia's railing.[35] The women even go so far as to compare 'the world' with 'a constant keeping gallant, whom we fail not to quarrel with, when anything crosses us, yet cannot part with't for our hearts' (p. 308). Olivia responds to this with the comment that 'if the world is a gallant, 'tis such an one as is my aversion'. Olivia expresses her 'aversion' to many pursuits. The term 'aversion' was another recent borrowing from French and Olivia peppers her conversation with the word. The actual weakness of her aversion to gallantry is revealed, however, when she becomes infatuated with a manservant, who, it is later revealed, is an heiress in disguise. There is comic irony in Eliza's comment that their age is one of 'plain dealing'. The English language of the time was far from plain given the influx of French vocabulary as well as French literature in both original and adapted forms.

The scene from *The Plain Dealer* represents an adaptation of parts of *La Critique de L'École des femmes* rather than a translation such as Ozell's *School for Women Criticised* in the 1714 collected edition. Though *La Critique* was omitted from Baker, Miller, and Clare's 1732 *Select Comedies*, it was included in the expanded version of this text in 1739. A reading of Élise's distaste for gallant discourse in this version demonstrates the way that French vocabulary had been increasingly absorbed and distorted in English: 'A pretty thing indeed to bring into the conversation of the *Louvre* your double Entendres, rak'd together from the Kennels [gutters] of *Halles* and *Place Maubert!*'.³⁶ This comment includes a metaphor for the movement of vocabulary from one place to another, albeit in this case the distance is not great in terms of geography, even if it is considered great in terms of sophistication or propriety. The comment as it appears in this translation also enacts the metaphor by including the term 'double entendre'. The spirited Élise harbours some of her disgust in jest. Her witty teasing of those characters against Molière's play indicates that she appreciates the better-crafted double entendres that underpin its comic force.

The various translations of *Le Cocu imaginaire*, *L'École des femmes*, and *La Critique de L'École des femmes* allowed for a satirical exploration of the effects of gallant language and its association with fears of cuckoldry. The translations of the vocabulary of cuckoldry largely rely on the bank of images and allusions that had been built up in the romance languages. The lexical choices relating to cuckoldry point to old traditions and etymologies and demonstrate that *le cocu* was a well-established figure in comedy. The familiarity of the images of horned beasts contributes in part to their comic force, but the references to them in Molière's plays and in their translations meant that they were reinvigorated with new satirical double meanings.

The translation of the language of gallantry from French to English, however, points to the novelty of such language. The translators' retention of French words was not an exercise in expediency, but represented both a challenge and an opportunity to demonstrate that they were attuned to the way in which the recontextualization of the vocabulary would lead to its adoption of different meanings and resonances. The translators' self-conscious inclusion of French terms in translations of Molière's French comedies created an extra level of comic irony with which they could comment on the effects of French fashions, behaviours, and language on areas of English society. The translators played a part in essentially re-coining the pre-existing French expressions so that they could have a high comic value in an English dramatic context. Audiences were intended to recognize the novelty of the terms and to reflect on the intriguing ambiguities they held within the world of the comedy, but also within the society outside the theatre.

Notes to Chapter 4

1. See Nevalainen, 'Early Modern English Lexis and Semantics', pp. 368–70.
2. The term 'cuckquene' was coined to describe a woman whose husband had been unfaithful, though it was used rarely.
3. David Turner, *Fashioning Adultery, Gender, Sex and Civility in England, 1660–1740* (Cambridge: Cambridge University Press, 2002), p. 95.
4. The so called 'V' sign in England could convey the same meaning. See Jacqueline Simpson and Steve Round, 'V-sign', in *A Dictionary of English Folklore* (Oxford: Oxford University Press, 2000), p. 376. See also the 'sign of the horns' as enacted by Sganarelle on the cover image of this book. William Hogarth's representation of scene 6 of *Sganarelle, ou Le Cocu imaginaire / The Cuckold in Conceit* for *Select Comedies of Mr de Molière* demonstrates artistic licence insofar as in the printed editions of the play in French there are no stage directions explicitly instructing Sganarelle to make this gesture as he misinterprets the sight of his wife admiring a portrait of

Lélie. In the first unauthorized French edition of *Sganarelle ou le Cocu imaginaire*, however, an *argument* supposedly written by an appreciative spectator notes that 'il est à propos de vous dire, qu'il ne s'est jamais rien vu de si agréable que les postures de Sganarelle, quand il est derrière sa femme, son visage et ses gestes expriment si bien la jalousie, qu'il ne serait pas nécessaire qu'il parlât pour paraître le plus jaloux de tous les hommes' (*OC*, I, 47).

5. CHRYSALDE: 'Je sais un Paysan qu'on appelait gros Pierre | Qui n'ayant pour tout bien qu'un seul quartier de terre, | Y fit tout à l'entour faire un fossé bourbeux, | Et de Monsieur de l'Ile en prit le nom pompeux. (1.179–82; *OC*, I, 405). In seventeenth-century Paris it was well known that Thomas Corneille had taken to calling himself 'le sieur de l'Île', 'Monsieur de l'Île', or 'Monsieur Corneille de l'Île'.

6. Randle Cotgrave, 'Milort', in *A Dictionarie of the French and English Tongues* (London: printed by Adam Islip, 1611).

7. See Florio, 'Cornáro', in *Queen Anna's New World of Words*, p. 124. Florio uses the term 'horner' as a translation of the Italian *cornáro*. His entry for this term is preceded by a definition of the verb *cornáre* which makes a clear link with cuckoldry: 'to horn, or set horns upon ones head, to cuckold'. The definition is curious in that it blurs the distinction between a cuckold-maker and a cuckold. The question of who is culpable is at the forefront of comedies exploring cuckoldry.

8. It is important to recall that adjectives such as 'horn-mad' were not new in the period; Shakespeare had made extended use of horn imagery in numerous plays. See Nathalie Vienne-Geurrin, 'Horn', in *Shakespeare's Insults: A Pragmatic Dictionary* (London: Bloomsbury, 2016), pp. 236–38. Vienne-Guerrin notes that Randle Cotgrave draws a link between 'horn' and 'scorn' via *escorner*: 'To unhorne, dishorne, or deprive of hornes [...] to ruine, deface, disgrace any thing'.

9. See also William Thomas, 'Becco', in *Principal Rules of the Italian Grammar* (London: printed by Thomas Berthelet, 1550): 'the poinct or beeke, and it signifieth also a Goate, and many tymes it is taken for a cuckolde, that knoweth him selfe and will not'.

10. See Alain Viala, *La France galante* (Paris: Presses universitaires de France, 2008), and Delphine Denis, *Le Parnasse galant: institution d'une catégorie littéraire au XVIIe siècle* (Paris : Champion, 2001).

11. Alain Viala, 'Molière et le langage galant' in '*Car demeure l'amitié': mélanges offerts à Claude Abraham*, ed. by Francis Assaf and Andrew H. Wallis (Paris, Seattle, & Tübingen: Biblio 17, 1997), pp. 99–109 (p. 99). Further references are given after quotations in the text.

12. Phillips, 'Gallantry', in *The New World of English Words*. Note that the reference to '*Artam.*' relates to Madeleine de Scudéry's novel sequence *Artamènes, ou Le Grand Cyrus* (1649–53, translated into English 1653–55), indicating that the term 'gallantry' in this sense is a relatively new usage, and demonstrating how translation of French texts contributed to the absorption of new terms.

13. Kersey, 'Over-gallantly', in *A New English Dictionary*.

14. Benjamin Norton Defoe, 'Gallantness, Gallantry', in *A New English Dictionary* (Westminster: printed for John Brindley, Olive Payne, John Jolliffe, Alexander Lyon, Charles Corbett, and Richard Wellington, 1735).

15. This is actually a hybridized translation of Thomas Corneille's *Le Baron d'Albikrac* (1667) and Molière's *George Dandin, ou Le Mari confondu* (1668). Thomas Betterton (c. 1635–1710) was a leading actor of the Restoration period. After the reopening of the theatres Betterton was hired by the Duke's Company, and when the rival King's Company collapsed he became the artistic director of the merged troupes. Following a dispute with the manager Christopher Rich, Betterton led a breakaway group of older actors at Lincoln's Inn Fields and later at the new Haymarket Theatre.

16. B. E., 'Gallant', in *A New Dictionary of the Terms Ancient and Modern of the Canting Crew* (London: printed for W. Hawes, 1699).

17. Thomas Betterton, *The Amorous Widow; or, The Wanton Wife* (London: printed for W. Turner, 1706), p. 29. Further references are given after quotations in the text.

18. See John Wilkins, 'Spark: "Gallant (person)"', in the dictionary table appended to *An Essay towards a Real Character and a Philosophical Language* (London: printed for Sa: Gellibrand and John Martyn, 1668).

19. The last line reads as 'Il faut joindre au mari le ragoût d'un Galand' in the 1682 collected works edition.

20. See Michel de Pure, *La Prétieuse, ou Le Mystère des ruelles*, ed. by Émile Magne, 2 vols (Paris: E. Droz, 1938–39).
21. See Pierre Richelet, 'Ragoût', in *Dictionnaire françois*, 2 vols (Geneva: Jean Herman Widerhold, 1680), II, 251.
22. See Furetière, 'Ragoust', in *Dictionnaire universel*, III, 295.
23. Bénédicte Louvat-Molozay, drawing on the work of Claude Bourqui and Claudio Vinti in *Molière à l'école italienne: le 'lazzo' dans la création moliéresque* (Turin, Paris: L'Harmattan Italia, 2003), offers a detailed explanation of the 'soup *lazzo*' by recalling Bourqui's observation that it is mentioned in Rabelais (*Tiers Livre*, Chapter 12) and by drawing attention to its presence in the Dutch painting by Frans Hals, *Merrymakers at Shrovetide* (c. 1616–17). Bénédicte Louvat-Molozay, 'L'Obscénité: du texte à la scène', in *Mettre en scène(s) 'L'École des femmes' selon les sources historiques / Staging 'L'École des femmes' According to Historical Sources*, special issue of *Arrêt sur scène / Scene Focus*, 5 (2016), 101–10 (p. 109). This special issue of an online journal is an invaluable source for understanding the stagecraft of the first performances of *L'École des femmes*, < http://www.ircl.cnrs.fr/productions%20electroniques/arret_scene/arret_scene_focus_5_2016.htm> [accessed 20 September 2019].
24. Gordon Williams, 'Porridge, or pottage', in *A Dictionary of Sexual Language and Imagery in Shakespearean and Stuart Literature*, 3 vols (London: Athlone Press, 1994), III, 1072–73.
25. Guy Miège, 'Hogoo' and 'Viande', in *A New Dictionary, French and English, with Another English and French* (London: printed by Thomas Dawks, 1677) (*viande de haut goût*, 'a hightasted meat').
26. *Six Caroline Plays*, ed. by A. S. Knowland (Oxford: Oxford University Press, 1962), p. 490.
27. The mixing of French within English for euphemistic purposes was common in Restoration writings. Samuel Pepys, for example, often reverts to French to relate his extra-marital escapades. David Turner accounts for this as a possible act of prudishness, supposing that Pepys might feel more ashamed if he used plain English. He also conjectures that it might work as an amorous secret code (pp. 30–31). It is more likely that the use of French is a way of constructing a comic, bragging narrative discourse.
28. [Anon.], *Hell Upon Earth; or, The Town in an Uproar* (London: printed for J. Roberts and A. Dodd, 1729), p. 14.
29. It should be noted that in French the term *pièce galante* relates to short pieces of writing in the literary style of *la galanterie* (not *pièces de théâtre*). Though the language of *galanterie* was viewed with curiosity, it did not develop as a literary category in England, whereas in France the *œuvre galante* was a disparate group of writings that reflected the predominantly upper-class social codes that guided conversation and behaviour. In *Le Parnasse galant* Delphine Denis demonstrates the complexity and instability of the French literary category by exploring the ways in which it emerged while the very definitions of *la galanterie* were being discussed and debated in both the social and literary spheres of seventeenth-century France. The conflation of the forms of behaviour and the literary category of *la galanterie* is evident in the titles given to *galant* writings, and the translation of such works into English led to the unusual use of the term 'piece of gallantry' in a literary context. In the 1670s a number of French works of fiction were translated into English: René le Pay's *Zélotyde, histoire galante* (1666) was translated as *The Drudge; or, The Jealous Extravagant: A Piece of Gallantry* (1673); Gabriel de Brémond's *L'Amoureux africain, nouvelle galanterie* (1671) was translated as *The Fair One of Tunis; or, The Generous Mistres* [sic]: *A New Piece of Gallantry* (1674); and Sébastien Brémond's *Le Pelerin, nouvelle* [1678(?)] was translated as *The Pilgrim: A Pleasant Piece of Gallantry* (1680). These subtitular uses of the term 'piece of gallantry' in English are rare, but they do signal the translators' understanding of the ways that the French literary labels were adapted according to social practices. The use of the term 'piece of gallantry' in English, then, relates obliquely to the role of literature and fiction in the development of the concept of *galanterie* in France, but it is not a literary designation that acts as a direct equivalent to *pièce galante* in French.
30. Derek Hughes claims that Betterton's translation is indicative of a move in late seventeenth-century British theatre to present gallantry and the lure of cuckoldry as an understandable path for a young woman pushed into marriage: 'As Aphra Behn was to do in adapting *Le Malade imaginaire* as *Sir Patient Fancy*, Betterton modifies Molière so as to concentrate upon the young

wife's plight and viewpoint. Brittle is an aged boor, with none of the semi-tragic status that Dandin acquires, and Mrs Brittle is a young and lively beauty who has been sacrificed by her parents' greed. Whereas Dandin ends his play abjectly humiliated and on an inexorable course towards cuckoldom, Mrs Brittle learns the dangers of playing with fire and Brittle the dangers of jealous oppressiveness, and there is some hope that the bourgeois and the gentlewoman will live in tolerable peace. In *George Dandin*, rigidities of class attitude create a situation which progresses with mechanical inexorability, whereas here it is the specific dispositions of husband and wife that first mar and then mend the marriage. Adultery is not endorsed, but the temptation is treated with understanding, and this is a sign of the direction in which drama was moving' (Derek Hughes, *English Drama 1660–1700* (Oxford: Clarendon Press, 1996), p. 120. For more on Aphra Behn's presentation of women within the framework of medical satire in *Sir Patient Fancy* (1678) see the section 'Milady Malady: Translation and Gender' in Chapter 6.
31. Viala, *La France galante*, p. 55.
32. See Richard Parish, 'How (and Why) not to Take Molière too Seriously', in *The Cambridge Companion to Molière*, ed. by David Bradby and Andrew Calder (Cambridge: Cambridge University Press, 2006), pp. 71–82.
33. Wycherley's sources for *The Country-wife* include Molière's *L'École des maris* (1661) and *L'École des femmes* (1662).
34. William Wycherley, *The Plain Dealer*, in *The Country Wife and Other Plays*, ed. by Peter Dixon (Oxford: Oxford University Press, 2008), pp. 283–399 (p. 318). Further references are given after quotations in the text.
35. See n. 7 for the significance of the name 'Horner' in relation to cuckoldry.
36. Molière, *The Works of Mr. de Molière, French and English*, trans. by Henry Baker, James Miller, and Martin Clare, 10 vols (London: printed for J. Watts, 1739), III, p. 35.

CHAPTER 5

Zealotry and Hypocrisy

Religion was at the centre of national politics in both France and England in the seventeenth century. By the 1660s Catholicism was the national religion of France, whereas across the Channel the status of the Protestant Church of England was being redefined in the aftermath of the civil wars, Cromwell's republican government, and the restoration of the monarchy. In 1662 the Act of Uniformity set down the authorized form of public worship in England, requiring adherence to a new edition of the Book of Common Prayer and episcopal ordination for ministers. The aim of the act was to restore the features of the Church of England that Puritans had removed during the interregnum. The Puritans advocated a more intense form of Protestantism that had not been accommodated by the Church of England's 'middle-way' compromise between Rome and Reformation. By the end of the seventeenth century considerable numbers of Puritans had moved to the New World, but their influence was still felt in English society and national politics, particularly in the parliamentary 'Country Party', soon to be named the 'Whigs', which was sympathetic to Puritan non-conformists.

Given that the religious situation in late seventeenth-century France was relatively settled compared with the religious climate in England (state wariness of the Jansenists and Huguenots apart), and that the former was officially Catholic and the latter Anglican, it might be expected that few analogies were drawn between the nations' religious affairs. Following the alleged Whig plot to assassinate Charles II and his Catholic brother in 1683 (the 'Rye House Plot'), however, England's king turned to French history in his response to the rebellion. Charles's relationship with France was close, not least because he had been exiled there and was first cousin to Catholic Louis XIV; this fact itself was of concern to the Puritans in England and was a significant factor in the 1683 plot. Charles asked the then royal historiographer, John Dryden, to translate Louis de Maimbourg's *Histoire de la Ligue* (1683), a historical account of the Catholic League that had attempted to usurp Henri III in the French Wars of Religion (1562–98). Dryden provides extra explanatory material to render the historical example relevant to his contemporary environment.

It is in his 'Postscript of the Translator' in *The History of the French League* (1684) that he demonstrates his propagandist aims by forcing the analogy between the Catholic League and the Whig anti-royalist rebels both before and after the Restoration:

> I will briefly take notice of some few particulars, wherein our late Associators and Conspirators have made a Third Copy of the *League,* For the Original of their first Politiques was certainly no other than the *French:* This was first copied by the Rebels in Forty One, and since recopyed within these late years by some of those who are lately dead, and by too many others yet alive, and still drawing after the same design. Our *English* are not generally commended for Invention; but these were Merchants of small Wares; very Pedlers in Policy: they must like our Taylors have all their Fashions from the *French*: and study the *French League* for every Alteration, as our Snippers go over once a year into *France,* to bring back the newest Mode, and to learn to cut and shape it.[1]

Dryden himself attempts to cut and shape his translation of Maimbourg's French history, seeking to fashion the text as a fitting analogy for the 1683 plot; instead, it reads as if it were cut and pasted from a pamphlet. The postscript of *The History of the League*, relates less to the translation than to an earlier dramatic work. In 1682 Dryden collaborated with Nathaniel Lee in the tragedy *The Duke of Guise* (1682), which likened the French leader of the Catholic League to the Duke of Monmouth, Charles's illegitimate son and pretender to the English throne. As Barbara Shapiro notes:

> The French civil wars [...] provided ample material for Restoration dramatists. [...] While pre-civil war plays dealing with the French civil wars tended to laud Protestants and condemned the Guises and the Holy League, Restoration efforts were more likely to castigate both the French and English.[2]

Most significantly, Restoration writers sought to explore contemporary religious and political events through the lens of another country's history. Given Charles II's personal history and the close Anglo-French relations that this established, it is unsurprising that this country should have been France.

In the 'Postscript of the Translator' Dryden outlines the characteristics of the civil-war rebels and those involved in the 1683 plot against the monarch:

> But for those Sectaries and Commonwealths-men of 41 [...] generally they were a sowr sort of thinking men, grim and surly Hypocrites; such as coud cover their Vices, with an appearance of great Devotion and austerity of Manners: neither Profaneness, nor Luxury, were encouraged by them, nor practisd publickly, which gave them a great opinion of Sanctity amongst the Multitude [...] but these new Reformers, who ought in prudence to have trodden in their steps, because their End was the same, to gull the People by an outside of Devotion, never us'd the means of insinuating themselves into the opinion of the Multitude. [...] they were never esteem'd by the Zealots of their Faction. (p. 404)

Dryden's description of the 'sectaries and Commonwealths-men' is typical of anti-Puritan satire that had been dominant at the beginning of the seventeenth century.[3] His anti-Whig and associated anti-Puritan stance is evident in the derogatory references to hypocrisy, concealment of vices, and 'opinion of Sanctity' amongst the earlier rebels. He emphasizes the ineptitude of the later rebels of 1683 by explaining that they did not even feign godliness as their predecessors did, thereby criticizing both groups. This postscript then, attached to a translation of an episode in French history, makes it clear that the text as a whole is intended to comment on religious affairs in England.

Post-Restoration dramatists, as well as post-Restoration propagandists, turned to the translation of contemporary French texts in order to reflect on the religious climate of England. Late seventeenth-century France had her own 'grim and surly Hypocrites' and false zealots with an 'appearance of great devotion'. The best theatrical examples of the 1660s were Molière's Tartuffe and Dom Juan. These characters were remodelled by translators in order to comment on the various forms of perceived zealotry and hypocrisy to be found in the complex religious environment of post-Restoration England. This was not achieved by means of lengthy expositional material such as Dryden's 'Postscript of the Translator' in his translation of Maimbourg. Instead, the themes of zealotry and hypocrisy were explored by means of particular vocabulary choices that related to each other within the new semantic fields of the translations.

This chapter will demonstrate this re-casting by examining Matthew Medbourne's *Tartuffe; or, The French Puritan* (1670). Close analysis of the terms 'zeal' and 'saint' in this translation will be followed by discussion of John Ozell's later translation of *Le Tartuffe* (in *The Works of Monsieur de Molière*, 1714) and Martin Clare's translation (in the *Select Comedies of Mr. de Molière*, 1732). This comparison will demonstrate the singular status of Medbourne's version of the play, in which vocabulary that does not necessarily stray far from the source-text resonates in a specifically anglicized dramatic frame. The chapter will then explore the language of hypocrisy and religious libertinism in Molière's *Dom Juan, ou le Festin de pierre* (first performed in 1665 and first published in 1682). This analysis will draw on John Ozell's 1714 English translation of the play and will show that differences in religious practice in France and England did not present a barrier to translation. The disparity, in fact, encouraged translators to consider the social significance of the theme of religion in the French plays in order to choose language for them that would resonate in England.

Zèle

Dryden's description of the 'Sectaries and Commonwealths-men' in his postscript to *The History of the League* is reminiscent of the characterization of the falsely zealous hypocrite in Molière's *Le Tartuffe*, albeit in the French play the titular character is nominally Catholic. It is not clear, however, exactly which type of Catholic Molière's Tartuffe is intended to represent; this has long been a topic of debate amongst critics. Many conclude that Tartuffe is a composite figure made up of features reminiscent of several branches of French Catholicism. Julia Prest, for example, notes that:

> Via a single character, Molière not only portrays the generic religious hypocrite but also mocks the extremism of the self-mortifiers, the interfering zealotry of the type associated with the Company of the Holy Sacrament, and the casuistical laxism of some Jesuits.[4]

Given the fluid nature of Tartuffe's identity, it is unsurprising that he has undergone many transformations in translation and that the first translation of the play into English should have moulded him into a Puritan.

Since the beginning of the seventeenth century the Puritan had been portrayed in English drama and satire as a religious hypocrite. Medbourne's recasting of Tartuffe as a Puritan was to a certain degree outmoded, but it was topical in 1670 insofar as Puritan influence was still strong in the growing Whig faction in parliament. Medbourne was also motivated by his own religious identity as a Catholic. According to Gerard Langbaine's 1691 *Account of the English Dramatick Poets*, Medbourne was an actor 'whose good parts deserv'd a better fate than to die in Prison, as he did in the time of the late *Popish-Plot*, thro' a too forward and indiscreet Zeal for a mistaken Religion'.[5] The Popish Plot was an invented conspiracy against Charles II, devised by the perjurer Titus Oates in order to attack Jesuits and other Catholic orders in England and to stoke anti-Catholic sentiment. Excess of zeal in any non-conventional religious practice was dangerous, and printed commentary on religious matters was rarely neutral. For all Medbourne may have tried to mask his anti-Puritan satire by designating Tartuffe a *French* Puritan, his bias is evident and was possibly a contributing factor in his personal downfall.[6] Langbaine's reference to Medbourne's 'indiscreet Zeal' refers to the actor's strong Catholic faith. Medbourne himself, however, uses the term 'zeal' and its cognates to criticize the rival religion within his satirically charged translation.

In Molière's play and its translations, Tartuffe's main means of fooling Orgon and Madame Pernelle into believing that he is a devout man is through the ostentatious demonstration of his zeal. Orgon tries to defend Tartuffe to his brother-in-law by illustrating this: 'Mais vous ne croiriez point jusqu'où monte son zèle; | Il s'impute à péché la moindre bagatelle' (1.5.305–06; OC, II, 111). Dramatic irony lies in the audience's realization that this zeal is ridiculously excessive, whereas Orgon believes that Tartuffe's abundance of zeal is a sign of great virtue. The fundamental meaning of 'zeal', or *zèle*, is innocuous: it means ardent affection or regard. But in seventeenth-century definitions it is additionally associated with excess. For example, in Richelet's *Dictionnaire français* (1680), the term *un zéle [sic] discret* is listed alongside 'un zéle [sic] indiscret, fatal, aveugle, ardent, brulant, grand, violent'.[7] The servant Dorine's assessment of Tartuffe demonstrates the negative associations of *zèle* and its adjectival cognate *zélé*:

> S'il le faut écouter, et croire à ces Maximes,
> On ne peut faire rien, qu'on ne fasse des crimes,
> Car il contrôle tout, ce Critique zélé. (1.1.49–51; OC, II, 101)

Here, Dorine associates a zealous person with someone who criticizes others. Julia Prest notes in her exploration of the definitions of the zealous in seventeenth-century France that:

> Often the zealot is controlling and highly critical [...]. Owing to his tendency to concern himself with the [...] salvation of others, the zealot naturally leaves himself open to the accusation of the type of hypocrisy that is more concerned with the speck in another's eye than with the beam in his own. (pp. 75–76)

Intrusion in the life of the members of the household is the main charge levelled against Tartuffe at the beginning of the play, and though this is a result of his zeal, whether feigned or otherwise, it is not necessarily indicative of his lack of religious sincerity at this point.

Puritan Zeal

Definitions of 'zeal' in seventeenth-century English dictionaries are less detailed than definitions of *zèle* in seventeenth-century French dictionaries. In John Wilkin's *Essay Towards a Real Character, and Philosophical Language* (1668), readers of the dictionary section are directed to the entry for 'zeal' in his 'Universal Philosophy' section. This consists of classificatory tables that function more like a thesaurus than a dictionary. The entry for 'zeal' in a chapter entitled 'Spiritual Action' includes 'ardent, Devotion, earnest, fervent, hot, warm intent, eager, Zelot'.[8] Henry Preston's *Brief Directions for True-spelling* (1674) offers an unsurprisingly concise definition of the term as 'great love, ardent affection'.[9] More frequent and detailed definitions are offered for the synonymous terms 'zealot', 'zelot', or 'zelor'. In Thomas Blount's *Glossographia* (1656), for example, 'zelors' (or 'zelotes') are defined in relation to the words' Greek etymology and their contemporary usage meaning 'they that have fear lest the thing they love should be common to another, they that envy at one, or assay to follow another in living; but most used, for those that are zealous or fervent in matters religious'.[10] This dictionary, however, does not offer a definition of 'zeal' or 'zealous'.

Seventeenth-century monolingual dictionaries in English were relatively new and still being developed. Bilingual dictionaries often provided more cognates. Guy Miège's *A New Dictionary French and English* (1677) lists 'zeal' alongside 'zealot', 'zealous', and 'zealously' and their French equivalents. The entry for 'zeal' also points to the religious application as described in Blount's dictionary by including the example 'to burn with zeal for the Service of God'.[11] Amongst seventeenth-century English dictionaries, an anomalous suggestion of negativity in relation to zeal is found in Wilkins's *Essay*, in which a 'zealot' is defined as a person who is especially 'corruptive'.

The required brevity of seventeenth-century dictionary entries meant that not all contexts of word-usage could be described. In the first translation of *Le Tartuffe*, the term 'zeal' functions in a specific satirical context in which the significance of the word is determined by its relation to other concepts. Whereas *zèle* and its cognates appear nineteen times in Molière's *Le Tartuffe*, the equivalent terms in English appear twenty-eight times in Matthew Medbourne's *Tartuffe; or, The French Puritan*. This discrepancy is due in part to the additional material that Medbourne added in adapting the play's plot, but it does not account for all the repetitions of the term. In his translation of Orgon's initial portrait of Tartuffe, there is a deliberate repetition of the word 'zeal' within the same speech. Tartuffe is described as:

> Darting his Prayers to Heav'n with such a Zeal
> It did attract the Eyes of all the Church
> [...]
> You can't imagine how his Zeal aspires,
> Each frivolous Action he accounts a Sin. (pp. 8–9)

Here Medbourne translates 'l'ardeur dont au Ciel il poussait sa prière' with reference to 'such a Zeal' rather than to 'ardour'. Elsewhere in the text Medbourne replaces the term 'forfanterie' (III.2.857; *OC*, II, 142), meaning 'roguery', with 'blind zeal' (p. 28) and 'cagoterie' (III.4.1038; *OC*, II, 150), meaning 'hypocrisy', with 'pretended Zeal' (p. 33). Though the word *zèle* is repeated and pejoratively charged in Molière's *Le Tartuffe*, Medbourne finds numerous additional opportunities to increase the frequency of the use of the word 'zeal' in his derogatory charges levelled at Tartuffe. This proliferation of the term is due to Medbourne's satirical portrayal of stereotypical Puritan behaviour and language.

The notion of zeal was not limited to Puritan worship and contexts, but it was a characteristic that was identified and often mocked by non-Puritans. As Charles Laurence Barber notes:

> The puritan movement developed some language usages of their own [...]. It was [...] the puritan vocabulary that attracted the most attention. In many cases, the favourite puritan words existed in the general vocabulary of the language, but the puritans used them much more frequently than other people, or used them in different contexts.[12]

Barber then goes on to list some of the vocabulary often used by Puritans; amongst them is the word 'zeal'. Medbourne was also drawing on previous dramatic representations of Puritans that had been prevalent at the beginning of the seventeenth century. Ben Jonson's *Bartholomew Fair* (1614), for example, includes a character called Zeal-of-the-Land Busy and a prologue addressed to James I alluding to 'the zealous noise | Of your land's faction'.[13] Despite its early seventeenth-century topicality, Jonson's play was revived by the King's Company at the Theatre Royal in 1668.[14] It is worth mentioning here the alternative running title for Medbourne's *Tartuffe; or, The French Puritan*, which is *Tartuffe; or, The French Zealot*; the latter title is printed above Act 1, scene 1, in all editions of the text. In the satirical context of the play, therefore, 'Puritan', 'zealot', and their various cognates are closely linked. Medbourne thus increases the references to zeal in Molière's text in order to alter the semantic resonance of the equivalent term in English.

Medbourne also makes small changes in the vocabulary that characters use to express their judgements of what religious zeal should be. In response to Orgon's evident blindness to Tartuffe's hypocrisy, Cléante tries to explain, at length, the differences between true and false zeal, concluding: 'C'est de fort bonne foi que vous vantez son zèle, | Mais par un faux éclat je vous crois ébloui'. Orgon replies in an exasperated tone: 'Monsieur mon cher Beau-frère, avez-vous tout dit?' (1.5.406–08; *OC*, II, 114). This section is translated closely in Medbourne's version, but certain vocabulary choices nevertheless lend it an extra ironic edge:

> CLEANTHES   But your strong faith does Idolize his Zeal
>   'Tis a false Light that dazzles thus your Eyes.
> ORGON   O Providence! How does my Patience reel? (p. 11)

Medbourne translates Cléante's reference to 'de fort bonne foi', meaning 'in the utmost good faith', as 'strong faith' and makes it the subject of the sentence. He therefore alters a phrase that is most often used in a secular sense to a phrase that has a much more direct religious significance. Puritans placed a heavy emphasis on justification by faith, but that faith had to be actively nurtured. They acknowledged that faith could be weak and that over-confidence in one's faith was wrong.[15] The application of the term 'strong faith' to the 'worship' of Tartuffe thereby serves to emphasize Orgon's misguided behaviour.

Medbourne continues to put an anti-Puritan 'spin' on the language he uses by making word-choices that could be considered straightforward translation on the surface, but that have special significance. Thus, Medbourne translates Cléante's observation that Orgon extols Tartuffe's zeal ('vous vantez son zèle') with the verb 'to idolize'. This is another deliberate choice, because the Puritans were notoriously averse to idolatry, which they associated with 'popery', Catholic practices of worship. The criticism therefore suggests that the nature of Orgon's religious practice is confused. The fact that it is Tartuffe's zeal that Orgon idolizes is also vaguely blasphemous. Medbourne's Cleanthes goes on to point out that Orgon is dazzled by a 'false Light'. Puritans believed that they had an inner spiritual light that would guide them in their faith.[16] Here, though, the exterior light is blinding Orgon, and echoes the earlier reference to 'blind Zeal'.

Orgon's exasperated response to the conclusion of his brother-in-law's argument is made to be facetious in Molière's play, but is charged with more satirical meaning in Medbourne's version with the addition of Orgon's exclamation 'O Providence! How does my Patience reel?' (p. 11). Charles Barber notes in *Early Modern English* that: 'the cultivation of mild asseverations like "in good sooth" may be a sign of puritan influence, for the puritans deplored swearing' (p. 24). Yet the exclamation 'O Providence' is not mild within a Puritan context. Puritans believed firmly in divine providence and its power to pre-elect the human souls that would be saved. In *Providence in Early Modern England* Alexandra Walsham points out that:

> 'Providence' is a word and a concept that many readers [...] may associate instinctively with zealous Protestantism. This is not surprising: the bulk of specialized research on early modern providentialism has focused upon the mentality of those 'godly people' whom hostile contemporaries labelled puritans. [...] Certainly 'providence' is an all too familiar ingredient of the daily vocabulary of that select and cliquish company of sixteenth- and seventeenth-century Englishmen and women who called themselves the 'saints'. It was a learned technical term for an elaborate theological doctrine which they used as an evocative shorthand for the powerful spiritual presence they detected within and around them.[17]

This chapter will return to consider the Puritans' self-designation as 'saints'. Here it is worth noting that Orgon's reference to providence offers no suggestion of its being a 'learned technical term'. He is, rather, taking the term 'providence' in vain, thereby highlighting his dubious credentials to be a Puritan. Patience too was a crucial aspect of the Puritan practice of internal reflection, so again Medbourne's Orgon is comically made to undermine the faith he claims to admire with his seemingly casual reference to his reeling patience.[18] The fact that 'reel' rhymes with 'Zeal' serves to throw attention back onto the operative term at play in this section.

Though Medbourne capitalizes on the Puritan connotations of the term 'zeal', the use of the word *zèle* in Molière's text already has satirical significance. When Tartuffe describes his zeal for Elmire, for example, there is a deliberate blending of religious and amorous vocabulary:

TARTUFFE	Et je ne veux aussi, pour grâce singulière,
	Que montrer à vos yeux mon âme tout entière;
	Et vous faire serment, que les bruits que j'ai faits,
	Des visites qu'ici reçoivent vos attraits,
	Ne sont pas envers vous, l'effet d'aucune haine,
	Mais plutôt d'un transport de zèle qui m'entraîne,
	Et d'un pur mouvement ...
ELMIRE	Je le prends bien aussi,
	Et crois que mon salut vous donne ce souci.
	Il lui serre les bouts des doigts.
TARTUFFE	Oui, Madame, sans doute; et ma ferveur est telle...
ELMIRE	Ouf, vous me serrez trop.
TARTUFFE	C'est par excès de zèle. (III.3.905–14; *OC*, II, 145)

This section is translated closely in Medbourne's text so the emphasis on the Puritan connotations of zeal is not so pronounced; the comedy here lies in the amorous zeal disguised as religious zeal. Medbourne, for example, translates 'pour grâce singulière' as 'since I have the occasion' (p. 30), thereby missing the chance for potential wordplay with the more literal rendition 'by a singular grace'. In French, the term *grâce singulière* was used in Catholic theological contexts to refer to the grace of God. Puritan doctrine placed even greater weight on the power of the grace of God in relation to the selection of souls to be saved. In this section of Medbourne's translation, however, the worldly, sexual nature of Tartuffe's 'excess of Zeal' is at the forefront. This part of the translation focuses on the universal comic effect of a scene in which a supposedly devout man is expressing his carnal devotion to a married woman.

Saint

When Cléante tries to make Orgon see sense, he explains his distaste for people who flaunt their religious devotion while actually being far from truly devout:

> Aussi ne vois-je rien qui soit plus odieux,
> Que le dehors plâtré d'un zèle spécieux;
> Que ces francs Charlatans, que ces Dévots de Place
> De qui la sacrilège et trompeuse grimace
> Abuse impunément, et se joue à leur gré,
> De ceux qu'ont les Mortels de plus saint, et sacré.
> (I.5.359–64; *OC*, II, 113)

In modern French, *saint* and *sacré* tend to be used synonymously with the general sense of 'holy'. In specifically religious contexts they are slightly different: *saint* relates to sanctity, the state of being holy because of association with divinity; *sacré* relates to sacredness, the state of inspiring spiritual awe. Thus, 'sacrilège', meaning 'sacrilege' or 'sacrilegious', relates to the profanation of anything held sacred.

Orgon initially describes Tartuffe as 'une sainte Personne' (III.7.1141; *OC*, II, 155), meaning a person devoted to the worship of God. In its alternative substantive sense in French, *saint* means either a canonized person or an extremely devout person. Dorine accuses Madame Pernelle of mistaking Tartuffe for 'un Saint' (I.1.69; *OC*, II, 102). She uses the title for ironic effect; she is well aware that Tartuffe is neither of these, but that the way Madame Pernelle and Orgon idolize him renders him a false saint-figure.

Unlike Cléante, the translators of *Le Tartuffe* do not distinguish between *saint* and *sacré*. Cléante's reasoning is translated thus in Medbourne's text, as he explains that falsely devout people are:

> Mere Mountebanks of Piety, devout in Publick;
> Whose seeming holy and deceitful Faces
> Do take the Freedom boldly to abuse
> What amongst Mortals is most Sacred held. (p. 10)

Medbourne conflates the words *saint* and *sacré* in the term 'sacred', but he does gesture to the meaning of *saint* in describing the 'seeming holy' faces. When Molière uses *saint* as an adjective Medbourne usually translates the word as *holy*. Thus 'la sainte ferveur d'un véritable zèle' becomes 'the holy fervour of a sincere Zeal' (p. 9) and 'Qui d'une sainte vie embrasse l'innocence' (II.2.497; *OC*, II, 121) becomes 'Whoe'er pretends an Innocent Holy Life' (p. 16). But the noun 'saint' is frequently used in Medbourne's text, and functions like the term 'zeal', in a semantic context relating to Puritanism.

The episode in which Dorine accuses Madame Pernelle of falsely believing that Tartuffe is 'un Saint' is translated closely in Medbourne's version: 'He passes for a Saint in your esteem, | But you will find he is all Hypocrite' (p. 3). Later translators of *Le Tartuffe* were to choose 'The Hypocrite' as the subtitle for the play.[19] Medbourne's subtitle, however, is 'the French Puritan', and this comment from Dorine is fitting for the Puritan designation. The noun 'saint' can mean, in biblical use, one of God's chosen people. In the New Testament it designates one of the 'Elect', those predestined for Heaven, hence Puritanical sects called themselves 'saints', or collectively 'the sainthood'. Medbourne adds sections to the text to make it clear that Madame Pernelle is a radical Puritan; she talks of singing hymns with the 'Brethren', another collective term for Puritans (p. 39). Membership of the 'Brethren' depended on whether or not an individual demonstrated that he or she was a 'visible saint', as John Spurr notes, 'In practice the godly [Puritans] [...] judged those who seemed to be saints to be their brethren. [...] Visible godliness, zeal, piety, a life without sin, a fulsome profession of faith, were evidence enough of membership of the godly community'.[20] So the idea that Tartuffe 'passes for a Saint' according to Madame Pernelle, may point to the manner in which Puritan sects admitted members to their church: the outward demonstration of a particular type of worship was required, and Tartuffe is shown to be playing on this knowledge.

Medbourne emphasizes the Puritan context by adding a comment from the servant Dorina in response to Madame Pernelle's praise of Tartuffe. The forthright maid sarcastically wishes that the 'two Saints' (Tartuffe and Madame Pernelle) 'were bound to live together' (p. 4). This comment is particularly noticeable in the printed text because Medbourne marks it with a manicule as one of his own 'considerable additionals', as mentioned in the preface. Dorina's remark relates to Madame Pernelle's allusions to the Puritan collective, the 'Brethren'. There are several other instances in which Medbourne's additions refer to the Puritan sainthood. Tartuffe's servant Laurence, for example, renounces his master's 'Saints' in favour of his own amorously elected 'Saint', Dorina (p. 13). The passages Medbourne has added within his translation of Molière's play serve to emphasize the satirical references to 'saints' in the body of lines translated directly from the French.

Medbourne sometimes makes unusual vocabulary choices. The following section of *Le Tartuffe*, in which Dorine argues with Orgon's decision to marry off his daughter Mariane to Tartuffe, alludes to religious hypocrisy in the use of the word *bigot*:

> Votre Fille n'est point l'affaire d'un Bigot.
> Il a d'autres emplois auxquels il faut qu'il pense;
> Et puis, que vous apporte une telle alliance?
> A quel sujet aller, avec tout votre bien,
> Choisir un Gendre gueux [...]. (II.2.480–84; *OC*, II, 120)

In French *bigot* can mean both a person who holds rigid partisan ideas and a person who is overly zealous or hypocritical in religious matters. Both meanings existed in seventeenth-century English, as the word had passed from French into English usage in the middle of the century. In Thomas Blount's *Glossographia*, 'Bigot (Fr.)' is defined as 'an hypocrite, or one that seems much more holy, then he is, also a scrupulous or Superstitious fellow'.[21] Similarly, Edward Phillips's entry for 'bigot' in *The New World of English Words* (1658) reads: '(French) a scrupulous superstitious fellow'.[22] In these cases, 'superstitious' means overscrupulous or excessive, and thereby has a close association with 'zealot'. The compilers of both of these dictionaries claim that they are recording 'hard words', some of which were new to the English language, but subsequent seventeenth-century dictionary appearances of the term 'bigot' suggest it had passed into common usage. Given that 'bigot' seems an apt descriptor for the character of Tartuffe in late seventeenth-century French and English, it is telling that Medbourne replaces it with 'saint' in his translation (albeit he pays more attention to vocabulary than to regular prosody):

> Your Daughter Sir's not fit for such a Saint,
> He has Employments proper for his Thoughts;
> Did Providence thus amply bless you, Sir;
> And make you Master of such large Revenues
> To choose a Beggar for your Son-in-law? (pp. 15–16)

Medbourne repeats the designation 'saint' to emphasize the fact that Tartuffe is posing as a godly Puritan: he should not be thinking of marrying a young woman in order to wrest away her family's wealth. Elsewhere in the text Tartuffe's Puritanism is related to his acquisitiveness.[23] Dorina's reference to Providence is another satirical attack on the Puritan providentialist doctrine concerning the Elect, though Dorina is using it as a rhetorical technique to get Orgon to rethink his plan.

Molière's Dorine uses further rhetorical strategies in the following scene when she tries to use reverse-psychology as Mariane contemplates marriage with Tartuffe:

> MARIANE Mon Dieu ...
> DORINE   Quelle allégresse aurez-vous dans votre âme,
>   Quand d'un Époux si beau vous vous verrez la Femme!
>   (II.3.649–50; OC, II, 129)

Knowing that Mariane is concerned with physical appearance, Dorine ironically describes Tartuffe as a handsome man in order to force Mariane to consider the reality. Medbourne alters the focus to his satire:

> MARIANA Oh Heaven!
> DORINA   What joy will then possess your Soul,
>   To see yourself the Wife of such a Saint? (p. 20)

The association of ideas between 'heaven', 'soul', and 'Saint' serve to reinforce the vision of what Mariana's life will be as the wife of a Puritan saint. Medbourne's Dorina is dissuading Mariana because Tartuffe is an imposter, not because he is a Puritan; the comments she makes serve as anti-Puritan satire.

In Molière's play, despite Mariane's request that Dorine stop teasing her, the servant persists in deliberately misrepresenting her mistress's potential future life by referring to the entertainment she might enjoy as a married lady:

> Vous irez visiter, pour votre bienvenue,
> Madame la Baillive et Madame l'Élue,
> Qui d'un Siège pliant vous feront honorer.
> Là, dans le Carnaval, vous pourrez espérer
> Le Bal et la Grand'bande, à savoir, deux Musettes,
> Et, parfois, Fagotin, et les Marionnettes. (II.2.661–66; OC, II, 129)

At first glance, it may seem that these entertainments would contribute to marital felicity, but 'la baillive' is understood as the wife of a low-level magistrate and 'Madame l'élue' is the spouse of a middling town official. The 'great band', a term usually used to describe the King's twenty-four-strong group of violinists, here consists of two bagpipes. At some point, if she is lucky, Mariane may see Fagotin the performing monkey, or a puppet-show. Dorine is being highly ironic. Here is how Medbourne renders this section into English:

> And you shall be visited at your first Coming,
> By Mrs. Mayor, and Mrs. Constable;
> Nay more, be honour'd with a groaning-Chair
> And in the Holy-days be nobly treated
> With charming Bag-Pipes, and the Morris dancers;
> And at the Countrey Fairs with Puppet-shows. (p. 20)

There is a different type of irony being used here. At first, it works in much the same way as in the French text. The middle-class status of the women may point to Puritan circles; anti-Puritan satire often linked the religious group with the middle classes.[24] Puritans treated 'Holy-days' as solemn periods and frowned upon pagan-style festivities that might include much folk-music and dancing. Puppet-shows were supposedly another entertainment of which Puritans disapproved; Ben Jonson's Zeal-of-the-Land Busy unsuccessfully attempts to shut down the puppet-show in *Bartholomew Fair* (Act IV, scene 5). The small vocabulary changes made in Medbourne's translation, then, offer Mariana a vision, albeit an exaggerated image, of a Puritan lifestyle that would not suit here in the slightest, thereby aiming to make her stand up to her father and refuse his request that she marry Tartuffe.

It should be noted that by 1670 satirical representations of Puritan life were outmoded and less topical once Puritan influence had been curbed by the Restoration. Medbourne was looking back to the satirical dramas of the early seventeenth century. His lexical choices and new associations of ideas, however, show that he aimed to make *Le Tartuffe* relevant to English audiences who had been familiar with the earlier satire.

Zealous Saints in Context

Beyond the first English translation of *Le Tartuffe*, Molière's play has endured in numerous contexts and languages. By the early eighteenth century England's religious settlement had been more firmly established, though it did not please all parties. When William and Mary began their reign in 1689 they passed the Toleration Act. This granted freedom of worship to Protestant nonconformists, groups that had been identified as Puritans for much of the seventeenth century. In 1701 the Act of Settlement carefully managed the succession so that the following monarchs, Queen Anne (r. 1702–14) and George I (r. 1714–27), were Protestant. These changes triggered anti-Catholic satire, as Catholics had not been included in the Toleration Act. Thus, in 1689 John Crowne produced *The English Frier*, an anti-Catholic loose imitation of *Le Tartuffe* in which 'Father Finical' is exposed as a grasping fraud. This version of the Tartuffe character was based on Father Petre, a Jesuit adviser to James II who was made Privy Councillor, and his dupes were representative of the court Papists.

The changes under William and Mary also caused protests and rebellion. After William III deposed Catholic James II in 1688, the Anglican clergy were obliged to swear an oath of allegiance to William and Mary, recognizing them as the monarchs of England. Those who felt duty bound to James II refused and became known as 'Nonjurors'. The Nonjuring schism existed beyond the reign of William and Mary, and was particularly prevalent in Scotland, where Presbyterianism had been reintroduced to replace the Episcopalian Church. Nonjurors became associated with the more general Jacobite movement which rebelled in 1715 and 1745 in attempts to reinstate James II and his heirs, though many Nonjurors did not support the uprisings. Another imitation of *Le Tartuffe* was produced in response to this situation. Colley Cibber's *The Non-juror* was first performed in December 1717, and proved a great success. Tartuffe is recast as Doctor Wolf, a Nonjuror, and, as it emerges at the end of the play, a 'Priest in *Popish* Orders'.[25] Despite their topicality, the reincarnations of Tartuffe that feature in the plays by Crowne and Cibber are not comparable with the effects of Medbourne's version because they do not use the French play as a close textual model. In order to gauge the way in which the vocabulary in Medbourne's *Tartuffe* functions at a particular time and in a particular satirical tradition, it is more helpful to read it in relation to the next more direct translations of the play, *Tartuffe; or, The Hypocrite* in *Works* (1714) and *The Imposter* in *Select Comedies* (1732).

In the early eighteenth-century translations of *Le Tartuffe* the notional religious identity of the protagonist is left unclear, as is also the case in Molière's final and only extant 1669 version of the play. The lack of specific satirical context in these versions is in part due to the change in England's religious identity and in part because these translations were designed to preserve Molière's plays in English. Medbourne's translation was produced just after the final version of Molière's *Le Tartuffe* had been authorized, and looked back to an earlier tradition of anti-Puritan satire that still lingered in the decades following the Civil War. The translators of the early eighteenth-century collected works, however, sought to retain the text for the future and so did not reframe *Le Tartuffe* within a particular historical context.

The versions in the collected works of 1714 and 1732 are close translations. Where Molière's text includes the term *zèle*, the eighteenth-century translations include the word 'zeal'. Without an anti-Puritan frame, the term does not take on any further significance than excessive fervour, supposedly religious. As mentioned, however, the use of the term still works towards satirizing a religious hypocrite. At the start of Molière's play, the references to Tartuffe's zeal contribute to the suspicions that his ostentatious religious practice is merely an act. The references to zeal take on an ironically amorous connotation during Tartuffe's exchange with Elmire and in the discussions following his exposure as a carnally-motivated individual. Madame Pernelle herself uses the term ironically, though it is unwitting on her part. Orgon has great trouble in persuading his mother that Tartuffe has been trying to seduce his wife. In Molière's play, Madame Pernelle responds with initial disbelief to Orgon's attempts to convince her of Tartuffe's guilt:

> Enfin d'un trop pur zèle on voit son âme éprise,
> Et je ne puis du tout me mettre dans l'esprit,
> Qu'il ait voulu tenter les choses que l'on dit.
> (v.3.1690–92; *OC*, II, 178)

According to Pierre Richelet's 1680 French dictionary, *épris* or *éprise* means: 'saisi, pris, enflammé' and gives the example 'il est pris d'amour pour la belle Cloris'.[26] The adjective is associated with amorous feelings, though Madame Pernelle applies it to the supposedly pure religious fervour in Tartuffe's soul. Medbourne translates Madame Pernelle's reference as 'too pure a Zeal had charm'd his Soul' (p. 55). There is perhaps some irony in the idea that a Puritan should have been bewitched or enchanted. In John Ozell's less satirically charged translation, however, the amorous connotations are emphasized in his rendition: 'his Soul is smitten with too pure a Zeal' (*Works*, IV, 167). The term 'smitten' had long been used in English, but it was only recorded in its amorous contexts at the end of the seventeenth century. Guy Miège's *The Royal Dictionary* records the figurative term 'to be smitten with a woman (to be passionately in love with her)'. In the entry for *épris* the term 'smitten' is included. Although Ozell's translation does not have a specific satirical context, his use of contemporary language shows his awareness of the comic irony of the concept of zeal. While Medbourne conceives Tartuffe's zeal as a 'Puritan zeal', Ozell emphasizes the irony of his 'pure zeal' and retains the comic drive of Molière's lines.

Ozell likewise uses the term 'saint' in a generally ironic context rather than a specific satirical framework. In his translation the term signifies a 'holy man'. In two lines Ozell chooses this noun to replace Molière's use of *homme de bien* meaning 'good man' in its most literal sense. Julia Prest notes that 'by Molière's time, *homme de bien* was more commonly used to designate an individual in Christian rather than in *mondain* or humanist terms [...] But a degree of ambiguity inevitably remained' (p. 108). Ozell removes this ambiguity in his rendition of the term *homme de bien* as 'saint'. When Orgon has been disabused he ironically calls Tartuffe 'l'homme de bien' in confronting him about the attempted seduction of his wife. Ozell translates the exclamation 'Ah, ah, l'homme de bien, vous m'en voulez donner!' as 'Ah, ha, my Saint, you'd hornify me, wou'd you?' (p. 163). The possessive pronoun is both aggressive and indicative of Orgon's foolish reverence of Tartuffe. Whereas the repetition of the term 'saint' evokes a Puritan collective in Medbourne's text, Ozell's use of the term relates to the foolish characters' idolization of Tartuffe; Dorine criticizes Madame Pernelle for believing that he is 'a Saint' (p. 123), and when Tartuffe is being disingenuously self-critical he states that everybody takes him for 'a Saint' when he is really a devil (p. 151). It would be too arbitrary to read these comments as anti-Popish references to idolatry. Ozell's use of the term 'saint' serves to highlight the foolish behaviour of the dupes and Orgon's ironic use of the term is indicative of his cold awakening.

Martin Clare takes a similar approach to Ozell in translating *Le Tartuffe* in 1726. In this version, published in the *Select Comedies* of 1732, the term *saint* is used only infrequently in relation to Tartuffe's religious 'stage properties' (e.g. a Saint's picture) and as a wholly ironic title for someone who behaves in a far from saintly manner. There is, however, a possible vestige of the anti-Puritan satire of the previous century. Clare added a prologue and an epilogue, both of which make reference to Tartuffe's appearance as a 'saint'. Clare's epilogue is an address from Madame Pernelle:

> *This Man* [Tartuffe] *has put me into such a Fright,*
> *I scarce shall be myself again to-night*
> *Who would have thought that such a Saint forsooth,*
> *Should have so sweet and liquorish a Tooth?* (*Select Comedies*, v, 178)

The reference to 'such a Saint' does not necessarily point to Puritan tendencies. The surprise that Tartuffe should have a taste for the sweeter things in life does at least suggest Madame Pernelle had initially supposed he was a strictly religious man who shunned pleasure. The prologue, however, echoes anti-Puritan satire more strongly:

> *From this Original* [Molière's Tartuffe] *to-night, we paint,*
> *The real Villain in the seeming Saint,*
> *To let you see that with prepostr'ous Care,*
> *Some seem more godly than they really are.* (π6ʳ)

The language of the prologue bears comparison, however, with a section of a work by Richard Baxter, a Puritan church leader. In *Church-history of the Government of Bishops and their Councils Abbreviated* (1680) Baxter criticizes the coercion of men to join the Church by violence or threat of imprisonment because:

> Every visible member of the Church being a seeming saint, should be loved with the special Love which belongeth to Saints [...]. But who that is not out of his wits can by any obedience to the Church, be brought to Love all those as *seeming Saints*, who will choose a Sacrament before a jaile?[27]

Clare's prologue may not suggest that Tartuffe is feigning Puritanism, but it is reflecting Puritan ideology to warn that religious hypocrites can be difficult to uncover, particularly when they use language to convey religious concepts that draw in followers. On the other hand, such hypocrites can be exposed so long as there are individuals who can understand and criticize the imposters' manipulation of language. A religious hypocrite's language is tailored to an audience — Medbourne conceived of Tartuffe's audience as one that had witnessed Puritan religious practice, Ozell and Clare followed Molière in keeping the religious context more general — but the ambiguities of the meanings and associations of religious terms are put to satirical effect in all the English translations, as they are in the original French play.

Hypocrite

The term *tartuffe* has become synonymous with *hypocrite*. The character's behaviour throughout Molière's play denotes his hypocrisy and his detractors mention it directly (I.1.70, I.5.332, III.4.1026; *OC*, II, 102, 112, & 149). In late seventeenth-century France the term *hypocrite*, used as an adjective or as a noun, referred specifically to someone who feigns religious piety.[28] Likewise, in English, the noun 'hypocrite' most often referred to someone who dissembles religious devotion. Thus, the title of John Ozell's translation, *Tartuffe; or, The Hypocrite* (1714), is instantly indicative of the false piety presented in the play. Choosing this title also allows Ozell to draw attention to a term that functions as a keyword elsewhere in Molière's corpus.

Although central to the plot of *Le Tartuffe*, an exploration of the semantic resonances of the term *hypocrite* in both French and English can be more fruitfully conducted with reference to Molière's *Dom Juan ou le Festin de pierre* and its first translation into English.[29] *Le Tartuffe* and *Dom Juan* often share critical attention, because of their explicit and inflammatory treatment of the topic of religion. Moreover, one play makes reference to the other. The story of Dom Juan had already been disseminated widely before Molière adapted it. In Molière's version, Dom Juan, the famous womanizer who flouts all moral and social codes, initially conducts his exploits with ease. He disregards the warnings that he receives from other characters, and the omen provided by an animate statue of a commander whom he has recently killed. Arrogantly, he invites the statue to dinner and his guest invites him to a return dinner the following day. Instead of heeding his servant's warning that the animate statue is a sign of Heaven's wrath, he decides to become a religious hypocrite in order to achieve his dissolute aims 'undercover'. When Dom Juan visits the statue, however, he is swallowed up by the flames of Hell.

Molière's *Dom Juan* was first performed in 1665 but was soon withdrawn, probably because critics were concerned by the way in which the main character revels in his profanity. It was first published posthumously in Molière's collected works of 1682. The book's printing process was interrupted for censorship, resulting in a surviving non-censored text as well as the final censored version in the collected works.[30] A further extant edition of the play called *Le Festin de Pierre* was published in Amsterdam in 1683.[31] The 1683 edition claims that it is different from previous editions and is more strident in its description of Dom Juan's heresy. It is believed that this edition was based on the original acting version. The first English translators of the text worked on the censored collected works edition, in which the more controversial religious references are absent. Nevertheless, Dom Juan's conscious assumption of religious hypocrisy is explored in depth even in the collected works edition of the play.

Before his ultimate demise, Dom Juan tricks his father into believing that he is reformed. Both the censored and non-censored 1682 editions include the stage direction '*faisant l'hypocrite*' (p. 1664) ahead of his lying assertion that he has mended his ways.[32] The hypocrite is represented as an actor playing a part and comedy lies in his obvious theatricality and the blindness of the dupe. John Ozell was the first to translate *Dom Juan*. The version that appears in his 1714 *Works* includes the stage direction above which is translated as '*Playing the Hypocrite*' (*Works*, VI, 47). Ozell had chosen *The Hypocrite* as the subtitle for his translation of *Le Tartuffe*, so this section of *Dom John; or, The Libertine* forms a semantic link with the content of *Le Tartuffe*, also published in *The Works*. As Ozell's Don John reasons in Act V, scene 2 (as does Molière's Dom Juan in all editions of the play): 'Hypocrisie is a fashionable Vice, and all fashionable Vices pass for Virtues: The Profession of an Hypocrite has wonderful Advantages' (p. 48). The term 'hypocrisie' was starting to be used beyond its religious context; its meaning was moving towards the modern one of the false appearance of virtue.[33] Don John's association of hypocrisy with fashion is indicative of this change in usage, but the religious context in which the action is played still lends a religious significance to the term.

Dom Juan's theatrical hypocrisy is emphasized further in the stage directions in the censored and non-censored 1682 collected works. When Don Carlos approaches the supposedly reformed protagonist in order to persuade him to acknowledge his sister as his wife, Dom Juan replies '*d'un ton hypocrite*' (*OC*, II, 1664). Ozell takes a slightly less literal approach in translating this stage direction. His Don John speaks '*In a canting Tone*' (p. 50). 'Canting' is an extremely versatile adjective and suits the character's hypocritical stance on several levels. Firstly, it can mean speaking in a sing-song or whining tone. The high-flown language of Don John's response, in which he claims that although he wishes to oblige he has been inspired to 'quit entirely all wordly things', would suit either sing-song or whining. A 'canting tone' had also become a key term in theatre. Peter Holland records features of late seventeenth-century tragic acting: 'The vocal technique owed much to the style of preaching and canting. The voice was used musically with a whining, nasal tone that must have risked droning monotony. The canting tone was frequently mocked in comedies'.[34] Don John's theatricality is emphasized by Ozell's use of a stage direction with specific resonances in English theatre. An example of the mocking of the canting tone is found in George Etherege's *The Comical Revenge; or, Love in a Tub* (1664). A widow is wooed by a nobleman who addresses her in rhyme 'in a canting tone'. The widow declares that 'A godly book would become that tone a great deal better', and that he could earn a living reading 'some pious exhortation at the corner of a street'.[35] The link between a canting tone and a preaching tone is linked to the fact that 'cant', or 'canting', could refer pejoratively to the language of religious sects. In Medbourne's *Tartuffe*, for example, the eponymous character is called 'his canting Worship' (p. 2). This is not to say that Ozell conceives of Don John as a faux Puritan, but his word-choice is reminiscent of traditional representations of religious hypocrisy from the seventeenth century. Owing to its associations with jargon, 'canting' also came to refer to the affected and hypocritical use of religious language. At the end of the seventeenth century the term's usage was expanded further when it was a linked with a specific Presbyterian minister. The third edition of Thomas Blount's *Glossographia* (1670) included the addition of this definition of canting:

> An affected peculiar kinde of speech used by some people, whereby they may understand themselves, yet not be understood by others, and is said to have taken origin from *Mr Andrew Cant*, a noted Presbyterish Minister of *Scotland*, who lived the last Age.[36]

Don John adopts the canting tone in order to fool those around him; he understands that his religious language is designed to conceal his true motives, but his victims do not. The various meanings of 'canting' demonstrate that words relating to hypocrisy were slippery terms, not least because hypocrisy is a form of behaviour based on duplicity.

Molière's Dom Juan claims that hypocrisy is a vice of the age and has become so widespread that it may as well become a social practice: 'Combien crois-tu que j'en connaisse, qui, par ce stratagème, ont rhabillé adroitement les désordres de leur jeunesse, et, sous un dehors respecté, ont la permission d'être les méchants hommes du monde? (v.2; *OC*, II, 897).[37] John Ozell translates this observation thus:

> How many are there, who by this Stratagem have cunningly to my Knowledge made up for the Disorders of their Youth, and under a respectful Outside, have Liberty to be the wicked'st Fellows in the World? (p. 49)

Ozell translates closely from the French, but his rendition of 'ont la permission' as 'have Liberty' points to another term that was undergoing a transition from a religious to a secular context. Dom Juan not only 'plays the hypocrite', he also plays the libertine.

Hypocrite as Libertine

Ozell's translation of *Dom Juan* bears the full title *Don John; or, The Libertine*. In choosing this title, which has a comparable format with his *Tartuffe; or, The Hypocrite*, Ozell capitalizes upon the tremendous success of Thomas Shadwell's 1676 play *The Libertine*. In his preface Shadwell claims that although the characters have been borrowed, the plot is largely new. He does acknowledge, however, that 'Four several French plays were made upon the Story' of Don John. He refers to the plays by Dorimon (1658), Villiers (1659), Molière (1665), and Rosimond (1669). Owing to the suppression of Molière's play, Shadwell adapts Rosimond's play, which was inspired by the latter. This is not to say that Shadwell did not capitalize on the controversy of Molière's version; in turn, Ozell was probably aware of Shadwell's success when entitling his translation *Don John; or, The Libertine*.

Towards the end of the seventeenth century the concept and behaviour of 'the libertine' was as topical in England as it was in France. As Gustav Ungerer notes:

> Libertinism and its controversy about free will and unrestrained freedom of religious and moral conduct was a European phenomenon fostered, in France, by the rationalism of Descartes and, in England, by the materialism of Thomas Hobbes. [...] the emergence of the libertine or rake was one of the most remarkable social and cultural phenomena of the Restoration. The English rake was bred in the hothouse of the Carolean court. The King himself set an example, which was emulated by the Court Wits.[38]

The character of Dom Juan embodies both the moral and the sexual libertine. When Ozell published the first full translation of Molière's *Dom Juan* in 1714, he looked back to the restoration libertine to define the focus of the work. Thus, he translates the servant Sganarelle's observation in Act I, scene I, that Dom Juan is 'le plus grand scélérat que la terre ait jamais porté' as 'the greatest Libertine that the Earth ever bore' (p. 7). Deborah Payne Fisk explains that:

> By the early seventeenth century 'libertine', both in France and England, connoted a freethinker, someone who held 'loose' opinions about religion. Concurrent with this meaning is Shakespeare's use of the word to describe someone of dissolute, licentious character. This latter meaning is the one that made its way into popular literature, eventually, by the end of the seventeenth century, extinguishing all prior religious and philosophical associations.[39]

Though this distinction of the uses of the term 'libertine' in English are helpful, it is wrong to state that the religious and philosophical links had disappeared by the end of the seventeenth century. As the first full translation of *Dom Juan* in English attests, both meanings of 'libertine' were still in play at the beginning of the eighteenth century.

In all editions of Molière's *Dom Juan* the term *libertin* functions in its anti-religious sense, but the heretical connotation is emphasized in the 1682 censored collected works. In the non-censored 1682 version and the 1683 edition Sganarelle confronts Dom Juan with this exclamatory question: 'Quoi? Vous ne croyez rien du tout, et vous voulez cependant vous ériger en homme de bien?' (v.2; *OC*, II, 896). In the censored version, however, Sganarelle asks: 'Quoi? Toujours libertin et débauché, vous voulez cependant vous ériger en homme de bien?'[40] It is this latter comment that Ozell translates, and though it less shocking, it does allow him to make a distinction between the older meaning of *libertin/libertine* and the definition that was becoming more prevalent in England at the beginning of the eighteenth century. Thus, the Ozell version reads: 'What! Still a Libertine and Debauchee, and yet pretend to Godliness?' (p. 48). In late seventeenth-century French *débauché* could be synonymous with *libertin*. According to Richelet it meant: 'Libertin, qui aime la débauche, qui est dans le déréglement'.[41] So it related not only to philosophical libertinism, but also to dissolute living. In English, however, only the latter sense applied to the borrowed term. In Ozell's translation, therefore, a clearer distinction is drawn between 'libertine' (rejecter of religion) and 'debauchee' (sexual hedonist). Ozell also intensifies Don John's heresy by translating 'vous ériger en homme de bien', meaning 'you set yourself up as an honourable man', as 'you pretend to Godliness' (p. 48). Ozell, having designated Don John a libertine in the title, emphasizes the anti-religious connotations of the term so that the resonances of Molière's play are preserved and not overshadowed by an emphasis on the newer carnal sense of 'libertine'.

Ozell's attempt to maintain the theme of religious libertinism is aided by Molière's use of a term that could be used as a synonym of *libertin*. In Act I, scene 2, of the censored 1682 version, Sganarelle, exculpating himself from speaking ill of his master, claims he is addressing a fictional libertine when he says 'si vous êtes libertin vous avez vos raisons; mais il y a de certains petits impertinents dans le monde qui le sont sans savoir pourquoi, qui font les esprits forts, parce qu'ils croient que cela leur sied bien' (I.2; *OC*, II, 854).[42] In the censorship process this sentence was reworked to omit the words 'vous ne croyez rien'. A similar phrase escaped censorship at the end of Act III, however, where in all editions Sganarelle declares 'Voilà les esprits forts, qui ne croient rien', translated by Ozell as 'These are your Free-thinkers, that will believe nothing' (p. 36). According to Furetière's 1690 dictionary, *esprit fort* (meaning literally 'strong mind') 'est une espèce d'injure qu'on dit à ces libertins et incrédules qui se mettent au-dessus des croyances et des opinions populaires'.[43] 'Free-thinker', Ozell's equivalent in English, was a more specific term used to refer to the rationalists who rejected Christianity on the grounds of reason.

The rationalists of the early eighteenth century were inspired by French philosophers such as Descartes. In this context, Sganarelle's comment 'si vous êtes libertin vous avez vos raisons' becomes more semantically charged when it appears in translation in Ozell's text: 'if you are a Libertine, you have your Reasons for't, but there are some impertinent People in the World, who are so, without knowing why, who pretend to be Free-thinkers, because they imagine it sits well upon 'em' (p. 10). This is not to say that Molière did not play similarly upon the word *raison* in his original version, but that the linked terms 'free-thinker' and 'reason' were immediately topical when Ozell's translation was published. Jonathan Swift's essay *Sentiments of a Church of England Man*, published in 1711, includes a reference to the term: 'the Atheists, Libertines, Despisers of Religion and Revelation in general, that is to say all those that usually pass under the name of Free-Thinkers'.[44] Detractors of ideological libertines could use the term 'free-thinker' as a synonymous insult. Yet it was also used as a name for a group of learned intellectuals, albeit a controversial group. *Dom Juan* was such a controversial play because the protagonist's cold reasoning, contrasted with Sganarelle's confused opposing arguments, could be persuasive. It would have been considered a much more dangerous play in both

France and England had it not been for its ending in which Dom Juan is consumed by the flames of Hell, giving it at least the appearance of a moral ending.[45]

In an era in which religious affairs were heavily bound up with state and social affairs, the first English translators of Molière recontextualized the plays so that they were meaningful to audiences or readers in England. Matthew Medbourne undertook the heaviest recontextualization by making additions and alterations to Molière's *Le Tartuffe*. This chapter has demonstrated, however, that the adaptations were supported by the manipulation of vocabulary in the extended sections that were translated directly from French. The words *zèle* and *saint*, present in Molière's text, were made to fit the anti-Puritan satirical frame that Medbourne gave to his translation. The early eighteenth-century translators of Molière sought to keep their translations closer to the original French in order to preserve the satirical impact of the French playwright's works. Owing to evolutions in the meaning of the words 'hypocrite' and 'libertine' in English (concurrent with changes in French), Ozell made vocabulary choices and semantic links that maintained Molière's exploration of Dom Juan's controversial attitude towards religion.

Writing about John Dryden's translation of Louis de Maimbourg's *Histoire de la Ligue*, Alan Roper and Vinton Dearing draw a comparison between the translator's propagandist use of a French historical event and his translation theory and practice. They elucidate Dryden's explanation of paraphrase as a translation method in which 'the Author is kept in View by the Translator, but his Words are not so strictly follow'd as his sense, and that too is admitted to be amplyfied, but not alter'd':[46]

> Topical amplification will be occasional and discontinuous, in no sense trying to force a complete allegory for the present out of the whole original. But some details in the original may suggest an analogy for contemporary events, and the translators can realize the suggestion by choosing terms of contemporary significance. By doing so, he frees, however briefly, one particular in the original from its proper context, its circumstances, for association with events or issues contemporary to the translator.[47]

In late seventeenth- and early eighteenth-century France and England few issues were more topical than religion and its relationship to national politics. Thus, the first translators of Molière's most controversial plays 'amplified' key vocabulary relating to religion in order to create an analogy between the play's original impact in France and its subsequent significance in English contexts.

Notes to Chapter 5

1. John Dryden, *Prose: The History of the League, 1684*, ed. by Alan Roper and Vinton A. Dearing, The Works of John Dryden, 18 (London: University of California Press, 1974), p. 409. Further references are given after quotations in the text.
2. Barbara Shapiro, *Political Communication and Political Culture in England, 1558–1668* (Stanford, CA: Stanford University Press, 2012), p. 124.
3. One of the most well-known figures associated with puritanism on the early seventeenth-century English stage is Malvolio in Shakespeare's *Twelfth Night* (1601–02). Maria describes Malvolio as 'a kind of puritan' (Act II, scene 3). See J. L. Simmons, 'A Source for Shakespeare's Malvolio: The Elizabethan Controversy with the Puritans', *Huntingdon Library Quarterly*, 36.3 (May

1973), 181–201. David Bevington draws a link between early seventeenth-century portrayals of Puritans and Molière's Tartuffe: 'Puritanism was a hot-button issue when Shakespeare wrote *Twelfth Night* around 1600–02. [...] Playwrights like Ben Jonson and Thomas Dekker were soon to spice up their plays with openly satirical sketches of puritan hypocrites, anticipating some of the points that Molière would caricature later in seventeenth-century France in his *Tartuffe*. Shakespeare, with characteristic tact, avoids any wholesale indictment of Puritanism. At the same time, he sounds a warning that has a direct bearing on the world of theatre. If Malvolio is hostile to the liberation of the human spirit that theatre can help celebrate and enhance, then there is no room for him in the concluding harmonies of this play' (*Shakespeare: The Seven Ages of Human Experience*, 2nd edn (Malden, MA: Wiley-Blackwell, 2005), p. 227).

4. Julia Prest, *Controversy in French Drama: Tartuffe and the Struggle for Influence* (New York: Palgrave, 2014), p. 76.
5. Langbaine, *An Account of the English Dramatick Poets*, p. 366.
6. This title led to confusion in Gerard Langbaine's *An Account of the English Dramatick Poets*, in which it is wrongly stated that Molière's *Tartuffe* was 'design'd as a *Satyr* against the *French Hugonots*' (p. 367). Molière's is a satire on Catholic religious hypocrites, and Medbourne's translation, despite its misleading title, is a satire on English Puritans.
7. Richelet, 'Zèle', in *Dictionnaire françois*, II, 559.
8. Wilkins, 'Zeal', in the dictionary table appended to *Essay Towards a Real Character, and Philosophical Language*.
9. Henry Preston, 'Zeal', in *Brief Directions for True-spelling: 1674* (Menston: Scolar Press, 1968), p. 58.
10. Thomas Blount, 'Zelors', in *Glossographia; or, A Dictionary, Interpreting the Hard Words of Whatsoever Language, Now Used in Our Refined English Tongue* (London: printed by Thomas Newcomb, 1656).
11. Miège, 'Zeal', in *A New Dictionary, French and English, with Another English and French*.
12. Charles Laurence Barber, *Early Modern English*, 2nd edn (Edinburgh: Edinburgh University Press, 1997), pp. 24–25.
13. Ben Jonson, *Bartholomew Fair*, ed. by Suzanne Gossett (Manchester: Manchester University Press, 2000), p. 33. Further references are included after quotations in the text.
14. Samuel Pepys notes in a diary entry on 4 September 1668 that though this revival was entertaining, the anti-Puritan satire was becoming hackneyed: 'only the business of abusing the puritans begins to grow stale, and of no use, they being the people that, at last, will be found the wisest' (*The Diary*, IX, 299).
15. The term 'strong faith' in relation to 'weak faith' recurs in Puritan texts. See *The Spirituality of the Later English Puritans: An Anthology*, ed. by Dewey D. Wallace (Macon, GA: Mercer University Press, 1989), pp. 18, 199.
16. See *The Cambridge Companion to Puritanism*, ed. by John Coffey and Paul C. H. Lim (Cambridge: Cambridge University Press, 2008), p. 159.
17. Alexandra Walsham, *Providence in Early Modern England* (Oxford: Oxford University Press, 1999), p. 2.
18. Aphra Behn's Sir Patient Fancy has Puritan leanings. See Chapter 6.
19. The first use of this subtitle is John Ozell's version (*Works*, 1714).
20. John Spurr, *English Puritanism 1603–1689* (Basingstoke: Macmillan, 1998), p. 44.
21. Blount, 'Bigot', in *Glossographia*.
22. Phillips, 'Bigot', in *The New World of English Words*.
23. See Barbeau Gardiner, 'Medbourne's *Tartuffe* (1670)'.
24. See William P. Holden, *Anti-Puritan Satire 1572–1642* (New Haven, CT: Yale University Press, 1954).
25. Colley Cibber, *The Non-juror, a Comedy* (London: printed for T. J., 1718), p. 106.
26. Richelet, 'Épris', in *Dictionnaire françois*, I, 298.
27. Richard Baxter, *Church-history of the Government of Bishops and their Councils Abbreviated* (London: printed for Thomas Simmons, 1680), p. 196.
28. Furetière, 'Hypocrite', in *Dictionnaire universel*, II, 291.

29. The typical seventeenth-century French spelling of the latter play-title is *Dom Juan*, which is usually retained in modern editions. In the edition used in the Pléaide *Œuvres complètes*, *Le Festin de Pierre*, the character's name is spelled 'Don Juan'.
30. See Georges Forestier and Alain Riffaud, 'Note sur le texte', in *OC*, II, 1648–50.
31. This version is published in *OC*, II, 845–907. The variations in the 1682 censored and non-censored version are included in the notes on the text.
32. See notes to *Le Festin de pierre* in *OC*, II, 1664.
33. See *OC*, II, 1665.
34. Holland, *The Ornament of Action*, p. 60.
35. George Etherege, *The Comical Revenge; or, Love in a Tub* (London: printed for Henry Herringman, 1664), p. 33.
36. Thomas Blount, 'Canting', in *Glossographia*, 3rd edn (London: printed by Thomas Newcomb, 1670).
37. The quotation follows the censored 1682 version, from which Ozell translated. The contraction is indicated in Variant 'l' for Act V: *OC*, II, 1664.
38. Gustave Ungerer, 'Thomas Shadwell's *The Libertine* (1675): A Forgotten Restoration Don Juan Play', in *SEDERI: Yearbook of the Spanish and Portuguese Society for English Renaissance Studies*, 1 (1990), 222–40 (p. 222).
39. Deborah Payne Fisk, 'Introduction', in *Four Restoration Libertine Plays*, ed. by Deborah Payne Fisk (Oxford: Oxford University Press, 2005), p. XVII.
40. The contraction is indicated in Variant 'g' for Act V: *OC*, II, 1664.
41. Richelet, 'Débauché', in *Dictionnaire françois*, I, 211.
42. The censored elements are given in Variants 'o' and 'p' for Act I: *OC*, II, 1651.
43. Furetière, 'Esprit fort', in *Dictionnaire universel*, I, 1010.
44. Jonathan Swift, *Miscellanies in Prose and Verse* (London: printed for John Morphew, 1711), p. 100.
45. Molière's ending is a parody of a moral conclusion because in the uncensored version Don John's punishment is undermined by Sganarelle's complaint that his master has not paid his wages.
46. Preface to *Ovid's Epistles* in Dryden, *Poems, 1649–80*, p. 114.
47. Dryden, *Prose: History of the League*, p. 433.

CHAPTER 6

Malady and Quackery

Molière's medical satires provided the source-texts for ten English translations between 1672 and 1732. The French playwright's mockery of the medical profession virtually became a genre in itself. In *Le Malade imaginaire*, in the 1682 *Œuvres*, the hypochondriac's brother expresses the wish to take the invalid to see one of Molière's comedies in order to divert him, and, by extension, to dissuade him from depending on a dubious doctor. There is also the implicit suggestion that watching a comedy at the theatre might have greater healing powers than following the doctor's orders. Argan's reaction is less than enthusiastic:

> ARGAN   C'est un bon impertinent que votre Molière avec ses Comédies, et je le trouve bien plaisant d'aller jouer d'honnêtes gens comme les Médecins.
> BÉRALDE Ce ne sont point les Médecins qu'il joue, mais le ridicule de la Médecine.
> ARGAN   C'est bien à lui à faire de se mêler de contrôler la Médecine; voilà un bon nigaud, un bon impertinent, de se moquer des consultations et des ordonnances, de s'attaquer au Corps des Médecins, et d'aller mettre sur son Théâtre des personnes vénérables comme ces Messieurs-là. (III.3; *OC*, II, 727)

Béralde's response is disingenuous if the body of 'la médecine' were to be understood as the collective group of 'médecins', as opposed to the practice of medicine. The first published close translation of the *Le Malade imaginaire* appeared as *The Hypochondriack* in the 1709 periodical *The Monthly Amusement*, edited by John Hughes and John Ozell.[1] This translation was reprinted in Ozell's *The Works of Monsieur de Molière* (1714).[2] In this version Béralde's comment reads: 'He [Molière] does not expose Physicians, but the ridiculousness of Physick' (p. 184). The tautological element is even starker in translation because 'Physick', as well as referring to the practice of medicine, could be used in English to refer to physicians collectively, or to personify the medical profession. So the concept of medicine and the people who practise it are not easily separated.

The theme of 'le ridicule de la médecine' or 'the ridiculousness of Physick' is often explored using the term 'quackery' in early modern English drama. Owen McSwiny's *The Quacks; or, Love's the Physician* (1704/5) is the only translation of Molière that includes a reference to the term in the title, but the word and its cognates appear within the main body of several translations. Béralde's comment about Molière's plays, however, cannot be translated effectively using the terms 'quacks' and 'quackery' because it would lose its comic ambiguity. Roy Porter notes at the outset of his study of quackery that 'quackery was a bad thing, as everybody in pre-modern England knew, and the quack was a wretch [...]. Nobody ever called himself a quack'.[3] Given that Molière's medical satires rely on characters who believe (often unwisely) that medicine is a good thing, as well as on characters who take on the role of *médecin* to dupe these believers, the terms 'quack' and 'quackery' had to be used carefully in translation, lest they give too much away. 'Quack' is nevertheless a useful term for exploring the careful weighing of connotations that translation of medical satire from French to English required.

This chapter will trace and analyse the lexical means by which the medical profession was satirized in the first English translations of Molière's *L'Amour médecin* (1665), *Le Médecin malgré lui* (1666), and *Le Malade imaginaire* (1673). John Lacy's *The Dumb Lady; or, The Farriar Made Physician* (*c.* 1669) is an adapted translation of *Le Médecin malgré lui*. Aphra Behn's *Sir Patient Fancy* (1677/8) is modelled on *Le Malade imaginaire* and includes sections based on a translation of an early unauthorized French edition, as well as elements from *L'Amour médecin*. Interest in the medical comedies was piqued again in the early eighteenth century when another female dramatist, Susanna Centlivre, published *Love's Contrivance; or, Le Médecin malgré lui* (1703). The following year Owen McSwiny translated *L'Amour médecin* (1665) as *The Quacks; or, Love's the Physician* (1704/5). Translations of the medical satires were included in the English collected works of Molière of 1714 and 1732 and followed by Henry Fielding's successful and enduring translation of *Le Médecin malgré lui* entitled *The Mock Doctor; or, The Dumb Lady Cur'd* (1732).

Le/La Malade and the English Patient

In order to develop the satire that he directed at physicians, Molière devised plots that included characters who needed to be cured, characters who thought they needed to be cured, and characters who believed other characters needed to be cured. In other words, he created plays in which there were real or imaginary *malades*, or patients, as well as real or imaginary doctors. The only commonly used cognate of the term *malade* that has persisted in English since the thirteenth century is 'malady'. The French noun *malade* was translated as 'patient', a term etymologically derived from Latin via French, but in seventeenth-century French was used as a noun only to refer to condemned criminals awaiting execution.[4] The different terminology relating to patienthood in French and English meant that puns and double meanings had to be transformed carefully into new linguistic contexts in translation.

In Molière's farce *Le Médecin malgré lui* the woodcutter Sganarelle is tricked by his wife and coerced into playing the role of a doctor. He is called upon to attempt to cure Géronte's daughter Lucinde, who has mysteriously become mute. It transpires that she is feigning dumbness in order to resist her father's plans for her marriage. This is hinted at in the first exchange between Géronte and Sganarelle, when the latter is pretending to diagnose the illness:

GÉRONTE	Elle est devenue muette, sans que jusques ici, on en ait pu savoir la cause: et c'est un Accident qui a fait reculer son mariage.
SGANARELLE	Et pourquoi?
GÉRONTE	Celui qu'elle doit épouser, veut attendre sa Guérison, pour conclure les choses.
SGANARELLE	Et qui est ce Sot-là, qui ne veut pas que sa Femme soit muette? Plût à Dieu que la mienne eût cette maladie, je me garderais bien de la vouloir guérir. (II.4; *OC*, I, 750)

Géronte's description of the effects of his daughter's ailment allows Sganarelle to make the ironic remark that he would welcome muteness in his own wife. From the beginning of this scene Lucinde is referred to as 'la malade':

SGANARELLE	Est-ce là, la malade?
GÉRONTE	Oui, je n'ai qu'elle de fille: et j'aurais tous les regrets du monde, si elle venait à mourir.
SGANARELLE	Qu'elle s'en garde bien, il ne faut pas qu'elle meure, sans l'ordonnance du médecin.
GÉRONTE	Allons, un siège.
SGANARELLE	Voilà une malade qui n'est pas tant dégoûtante: et je tiens qu'un homme bien sain s'en accommoderait assez.
GÉRONTE	Vous l'avez fait rire, Monsieur. (II.4; *OC*, I, 749)

Sganarelle begins this scene with his best attempt at an initial doctorly phrase. His calling Lucinde a 'malade' allows him to make the somewhat bawdy comment that a fit and healthy man would make do with her quite gladly. The double meaning of 'sain' as 'healthy' and 'sane' suggests that a man would be insane to refuse her even in her 'ill' state. In the context of the marriage deferral caused by Lucinde's supposed malady, Sganarelle's remark hints at the charade by drawing attention to the surprisingly attractive appearance of the invalid. This, along with the innuendo, is why she laughs in response.

In the first English translation of *Le Médecin malgré lui*, entitled *The Dumb Lady; or, The Farriar Made Physician* (c. 1669), John Lacy strays from a literal translation of Sganarelle's observation.[5] Drench the Farrier (Sganarelle) describes Olinda (Lucinde) as 'a very pretty Patient, and one a man may venture on in sickness, or in health'.[6] This works on several bawdily comic levels. In the plainest sense, it states that Olinda, whether ill or healthy, would be worth pursuing. The comment also alludes to the marriage vows as recorded in the Book of Common Prayer, 'in sickness and in health', thus suggesting that any sane available man would wish to marry her while at the same time undermining the allusion to Christian marriage through its suggestive meaning. The use of the term 'patient' to translate 'malade' also has ironic connotations. Though the most common meaning of 'patient' is 'sick person', it can additionally mean 'a person who undergoes an action, a passive recipient, as opposed to an agent'. This meaning renders Drench's sexual overtones starker than those in Sganarelle's comment in French.

The use of innuendo in Molière's *Le Médecin malgré lui*, however, is by no means subtle. Sganarelle abuses his doctoring role by making forthright amorous advances on the nurse in Géronte's household: 'Mais, comme je m'intéresse à toute votre famille, il faut que j'essaye un peu le Lait de votre Nourrice: et que je visite son Sein' (II.3; *OC*, I, 749). Unsurprisingly, the nurse's husband is alarmed by Sganarelle's behaviour, but the mock doctor responds with the threat that he will give him 'la fièvre'. In Lacy's translation this warning is supplemented by a 'diagnosis' and a 'remedy': 'I'll put thee into a Fever, and keep thee in't a year; I tell thee fellow, thy wife is not well, and I will give her a gentle gentile Glister; prethee be sick Nurse' (p. 19). A glister, or clyster (suppository), was a common phallic symbol in English comedy, so Drench's meaning is plain.[7] The adjective 'gentle' could here refer to the mildness of the 'medicine' or the mode of administration while 'gentile' may refer to gentility, a status Drench comically assumes, having been promoted from farrier to doctor. It is possible that there are also echoes of the other human-related meaning of 'gentile' as a non-Jewish (Christian) man. The nurse goes on to request the remedy, describing it as 'a gentle gentile, as you call it' and 'a gentle gentile, what d'ye call it' (p. 19). The English word 'gentile', also spelled 'gentil' and 'gentle', is a word for 'maggot' or more generally 'worm'.[8] Drench can use his expertise as a farrier to feign being a doctor, as maggots were used on both animals and humans to help cure wounds. The nurse's confusion over the term and eagerness to obtain the 'remedy' also allows for bawdiness, given the phallic associations of the zoological 'gentile'. As is a common trend in the first English translations of Molière's plays, sexual innuendo, however suggestive in the original, is made coarser in English translation.

In Lacy's translation of *Le Médecin malgré lui* the nurse is a willing patient in the sense that she is keen to be the passive recipient of Drench's advances. The nurse in Molière's original, Jacqueline, is much more resistant to both Sganarelle and her husband. When her spouse frets about his rival, she asks: 'est-ce que je ne suis pas assez grande pour me défendre moi-même, s'il me fait quelque chose, qui ne soit pas à faire? (II.3; *OC*, I, 749). The nurse in the English version is more compliant in order to allow for the extended passages of innuendo in which she becomes the unknowing participant. When Drench suggests cooling her husband's anger with medicine she encourages her spouse to take it:

> DOCT. Sir, I find you'r cholerick, but I'l give you a purge shall make you so patient, that if you saw me lye with your wife, you should not have so much gaul left, as would make an angry line in your face.
> NUR. Now good husband take Physick.
> DOCT. God a mercie Nurse. (p. 19)

The 'taking of physick' was common slang for sexual relations, with 'taking' often, though not always, an action attributed to women rather than to men.[9] This perhaps explains Drench the Doctor's response, which can be read either as praise that she is heeding him by encouraging her husband to take the 'purge', or as surprise at her choice of words, which could be interpreted as being quite another instruction. Drench himself plays on the word 'patient' when he describes the effects of his treatment. 'Patient' as adjective can mean both 'capable of enduring affliction calmly' and 'passive'. Drench aggressively conjures a scene in which the husband is totally passive and he is extremely active, and justifies his behaviour by emphasizing his role as doctor with the linguistic overtones of medicine: the patient must obey the physician.

Patience is a Virtue?

Despite her claims that she took only a 'bare hint' from Molière, Aphra Behn included significant plot elements and several scenes of *Le Malade imaginaire* in *Sir Patient Fancy*.[10] The title of the English play reflects the title of the French play, though the gender of this patient is indicated by 'Sir' rather than a definite article, and *malade* is rendered as 'patient'. It is true that Behn's play cannot be labelled a literal translation of *Le Malade imaginaire*, not least because it includes large amounts of original material combined with some elements from *L'Amour médecin*. Behn's play does, however, show how the rendering of the French word *malade* as the English word 'patient' allows for wordplay in medical satire in English.

Sir Patient Fancy's belief that he is sick is reinforced by his unfaithful wife who is looking for opportunities to cheat on him. Given his hypochondriacal tendencies he assumes the character of patient very easily and repeats variations on the phrase 'Patience, thou art a Virtue', echoing his own name. In fact, the name may relate to Sir Patience Ward, a staunchly Protestant London merchant; Sir Patient Fancy is ridiculed as a Puritan as well as an imaginary invalid. This serves to heighten the contrast between Sir Patient's patience and the frenzied plans of Lady Fancy and her lover. While Sir Patient Fancy's name evokes imagined patienthood, his wife's name brings to mind her amorous exploits with her lover Wittmore. The language chosen by the adulterous pair contributes to the ridicule of the play's eponymous character. Lady Fancy says to Wittmore: 'I am impatient till I can have less of his [Sir Patient's] Company and more of thine' (p. 14). Wittmore later declares 'I'm impatient for the Sight and Enjoyment of the fair Person I love' (p. 16). Despite the contrast, the lovers' impatience is presented as no more commendable than the cuckold's patience. In a play in which the main character is being tricked under his very nose, his patience, both in the sense of 'enduring affliction' and in the sense of 'undergoing medical treatment', is a hindrance.

Although *Sir Patient Fancy* only includes small sections translated from *Le Malade imaginaire*, repetition works in a similar way in both texts. While there is ironic effect in Sir Patient's recurrent saying 'Patience is a virtue', there is similar mockery of Molière's Argan, who constantly describes himself as 'malade'. Argan responds angrily to queries about the authenticity of his illness:

> ARGAN Comment, Coquine, si je suis malade? si je suis malade, Impudent.
> TOINETTE Hé bien oui, Monsieur, vous êtes malade, n'ayons point de querelle là-dessus. Oui, vous êtes fort malade, j'en demeure d'accord, et plus malade que vous ne pensez; voilà qui est fait. Mais votre fille doit épouser un mari pour elle; et n'étant point malade, il n'est pas nécessaire de lui donner un Médecin. (1.5; *OC*, II, 649)

The reiteration of the word *malade* is suggestive of Argan's insistence on perpetuating his invalid state. Argan's obsession with medical practice threatens his daughter's marriage plans, whereas Sir Patient's obsession facilitates his wife's trickery. In both cases, the state of being patient is ridiculed because it relates to social rather than physical maladies.

The influence of Behn's *Sir Patient Fancy* endured into the early eighteenth century. Owen McSwiny's *The Quacks; or, Love's the Physician*, a loose translation of Molière's *L'Amour médecin*, recasts Sganarelle as Sir Patient Carefull, a name clearly inspired by Behn's character. The essential plot of *The Quacks* is the same as that of *L'Amour médecin*. At the end of the first act in both plays the main character is concerned about his daughter's depressed state and calls for the doctors. As in *Le Médecin malgré lui*, the daughter is pretending to be ill in order to bide her time in the marriage market. At the beginning of Act II in *The Quacks,* however, McSwiny adds in a scene in the lodgings of 'Dr Medly', who explains how his practice has evolved:

> Five years ago I was sent only to such Slovenly Diseases, as Gripes, Headachs and Surfeits, — I never heard of the Refind disorders of the Spleen and Vapours, — Why all the Distempers, I Cure now, are only Imaginary, and the great Secret is to keep my Patients from Fancying themselves well. (p. 16)

Evidently there are echoes of Behn's *Sir Patient Fancy* and by extension *Le Malade imaginaire* in this comment. McSwiny is pointing to other medical satires for self-conscious comic effect and contextualization, evoking the spate of translations of Molière's medical satires. At the beginning of Act II, scene 3, of *L'Amour médecin* Sganarelle's doctors assemble and talk of the long journeys that their horses have to make when they visit patients (*OC*, I, 618–19). McSwiny takes inspiration from this to expand on the equestrian theme:

> TICKLE-PULSE Why really if it were not for destroying so usefull an Animal, we might make fine Experiments and improve as much as we do upon humane bodies.
>
> REFUGEE Me be against dat, for if de Physician turn de Farryer, *Morbleau* de Farryer will turn de Physician. (p. 20)

The doctor called Refugee is modelled on a Huguenot who has settled in London. This is why he speaks in cod-French language and accent, the representation of which was popular in English comedies of the time. His comments are also designed for comic effect with the reference to Lacy's translation of the *Médecin malgré lui*, one of the titles of which is *The Farriar Made Physician*. Audiences are to understand that there have been several re-imaginings of Molière's medical satires and that McSwiny's translation-adaptation is joining them.

The Hypochondriack

The ways in which *les malades* were represented in the first English translations of Molière's works continued to evolve. Although Aphra Behn was inspired by *Le Malade imaginaire* in writing *Sir Patient Fancy*, the first full translation of the French play, *The Hypocondriack*, did not appear until the early eighteenth century, in the sixth volume of the 1714 *Works*.[11] The next translation in the eighth volume of the 1732 *Select Comedies* has the same title, though with a variant spelling: *The Hypochondriack*. Subsequent English translations also carry this title, but it should be borne in mind that the early eighteenth-century definitions of 'hypochondria' differ from the common modern sense of 'excessive concern with one's health'. According to the medical dictionary *Dr Willis's Practice of Physick* (1681) 'hypochondriac' meant 'a windy Melancholy, bred in the Hypochondria [the 'forepart of the Belly and sides about the short Ribs'], from whence a black phlegm arises that infects and troubles the mind, one troubled with such melancholy'.[12] The humour of black phlegm was more often described as 'black bile' and is not to be confused with the separate humour of phlegm. So the term 'hypochondriac' meant someone afflicted with morbid thoughts rather than someone specifically concerned with their health.

The term *hypochondriaque* and its root-word *hypochondre* existed in seventeenth-century French but were not used in *Le Malade imaginaire*. The first edition of the Académie française dictionary (1694) records the following definitions:

> HYPOCHONDRE. s.m. La pluspart escrivent hypocondre la partie du ventre au dessous des costes, au costé droit, ou au costé gauche. *Les deux hypochondres. la ratte est à l'hypochondre gauche. le foye dans la region de l'hypochondre droit. il a les hypochondres enflez, tendus. les fumées des hypochondres.*
>
> HYPOCONDRIAQUE. adj. Malade des fumées de la ratte des hypochondres, causées par une bile noire, qui le rendent extremement melancolique et visionnaire. *Ne vous attachez pas à ce qu'il dit, il est hypochondriaque, c'est un hypochondriaque. la grande solitude rend les hommes hypochondriaques,* En ce sens on dit aussi qu'*Un homme est Hypochondre.*[13]

As in English, the terms as applied to people relate to susceptibility to the humour of black bile produced in the spleen, which causes melancholy. The anxiety could be directed at personal health, even if the definition encompassed more general pensive dejection. Significantly, Molière himself had been associated with the term *hypocondre*. In 1670 a satirical comedy by Le Boulanger de Chalussay, *Élomire hypocondre, ou les Médecins vengés* was published.[14] The aim of the play is clearly to lampoon Molière, and it focuses on criticizing the dramatist's character through the label *hypocondre*. Indeed the first scene shows Élomire worrying about his coughing, lack of sleep, paleness and weight, thereby associating the term *hypocondre* with the specific health anxiety that hypochondria came to signify. Other parts of the satire reflect the Académie française dictionary definition of *hypocondre* as a 'malade [...] mélancolique et visionnaire', when Élomire, for example, describes having seen a phantom in his doorway (1.3.306). How far this satirical play fed into *Le Malade imaginaire* is a question of debate. Patrick Dandrey suggests a possible link:

> *Élomire hypocondre* paraît bien avoir eu pour effet [...] de susciter une réplique de Molière sur le sujet dans lequel cette satire l'enveloppait: celui de sa maladie, considérée comme imaginaire et fantasmatique, espèce de folie hypocondriaque. Dans ce cas, *Le Malade imaginaire* [...] pourrait bien être tenu pour un autoportrait ambigu et biaisant de Molière par lui-même en réplique aux calomnies dont Chalussay l'accablait sous le pseudonyme d'Élomire.[15]

Regardless of any autobiographical influence there may have been in the production of *Le Malade imaginaire*, Molière may have sought to depart from Chalussay's depiction of a *malade imaginaire* precisely by avoiding the use of the term *hypocondre* in his play. Yet the close association of the overactive imagination of Élomire the *hypocondre* and his concern with his health presages the gradual evolution of the label in French, and its equivalent in English.

The semantic cross-currents of the expressions *malade imaginaire* and *hypocondre/hypochondriaque* help to explain why early eighteenth-century translators of *Le Malade imaginaire* titled the English versions *The Hypocondriack*. They recognized in Argan's frenzied fear of dying the symptom of someone with hypochondriacal melancholy.[16] Aphra Behn's *Sir Patient Fancy* even includes an explanation of the protagonist's affliction from a Molière-inspired 'Affected Learned Woman', Lady Knowell:

> His Disease is nothing but Imagination, a Melancholy which arises from the Liver, spleen, and Membrane call'd *Mesenterium*; the *Arabians* name the distemper *Myrathial*, and we here in *England*, *Hypochondriacal Melancholy*; I cou'd prescribe a most potent Remedy, but that I am loth to stir the Envy of the College. (p. 31)[17]

The link between hypochondria, melancholy, and imagination is reinforced in Samuel Johnson's later *Dictionary of the English Language* (1755) in which the definition of 'hypochondriack' is 'Melancholy; disordered in the imagination'.[18] The early eighteenth-century translators of *Le Malade imaginaire* essentially associated the play's title with the term 'hypochondriack'. In the lists of dramatis personae of both English versions this label is attached to Argan. Rather than the term's definition being fixed when the translators chose it, their title contributed to the development of 'hypochondriac' in English towards a generalized meaning of anxiety surrounding health. Nevertheless, it is the extreme concern of Molière's *malades*, or their relatives, which necessitates the onstage presence of doctors, a group who bear the brunt of the dramatist's satire. The terminology used to present the medical figures in translation therefore required considerable reflection in order to retain the satirical impact.

Doctor Doctor

The titles of the first English translations of Molière's medical comedies demonstrate that the term *médecin* could be rendered in several ways: *Le Médecin malgré lui* is variously translated as *The Farriar Made Physician*, *The Forced Physician*, *A Doctor and no Doctor*, and *The Mock Doctor*. *L'Amour médecin* is translated as *Love's the Physician* and *Love the Best Physician*. Though 'physician' and 'doctor' could be used interchangeably to translate *médecin*, they have different connotations depending on the contexts in which they are used. The term 'physician' rather than 'doctor' is used in the translations of *L'Amour médecin* because the medical term is being used figuratively to cast Love as a Healer of Ills, and because it hints at a distinctly concrete physical remedy to lovesickness.

In the late seventeenth and early eighteenth centuries the English term 'physician' was applied more readily to metaphorical phrases than 'doctor', not least because 'doctor' can describe a medical practitioner, a teacher, or a learned person, and is both noun and title in English. The term *docteur* existed in early modern French, but was not as widely used to refer specifically to a doctor of medicine as 'doctor' was in England. Thus, the *Dictionnaire de l'Académie françoise* gives the following definition of *docteur*:

> Qui est promeu dans une Université au plus haut degré de quelque Faculté. *Docteur en Theologie. Docteur en Droit. Docteur en Droit Civil. Docteur en Droit Canon. Docteur en Médecine. Docteur de Sorbonne, de Navarre* [...] On appelle, *Docteur Regent,* Un Docteur qui enseigne publiquement. Il se dit aussi en style familier d'un homme docte, quoy qu'il n'ait pas esté receu Docteur. *Il est fort sçavant en telle science, il y est docteur. Ce n'est pas un grand docteur.*[19]

In Molière's *Le Malade imaginaire* there are two uses of the term *docteur*. In Act II, scene 5, Monsieur Diafoirus assures Argan that his son is up to the physical job of being a husband, 'selon les règles de nos Docteurs' (*OC*, II, 676), thereby referring to doctors of medicine. But later in the play in the 1682 *Œuvres* Argan employs the term with a more ironic intention, when his brother tries to reason with him:

> BÉRALDE   Dans les discours, et dans les choses, ce sont deux sortes de personnes, que vos grands Médecins. Entendez-les parler, les plus habiles gens du monde; voyez-les faire, les plus ignorants de tous les hommes.
> ARGAN   Hoy. Vous êtes un grand Docteur, à ce que je vois, et je voudrais bien qu'il y eût ici quelqu'un de ces Messieurs pour rembarrer vos raisonnements, et rabaisser votre caquet. (II.3; *OC*, II, 727)

Here Argan sarcastically questions Béralde's reasoning, labelling him a 'grand Docteur' to mean a great learned man, and possibly someone who preaches. He sardonically wishes for the presence of 'les grands Médecins' to defeat Béralde in academic debate. The subtle differences between the French terms *médecin* and *docteur* required astute translation into English; though 'physician' could replace *médecin*, and 'doctor' could replace *docteur*, the two English terms were employed in translation with more complex ironic effects in order to carry across the satire of Molière's plays.

In *The Dumb Lady; or, The Farriar Made Physician* (c. 1669), John Lacy plays with the terms 'doctor' and 'physician' to describe the medical profession. It seems likely that the choice of 'physician' in the title was instigated by the alliterative and rhythmic parallel with 'farriar'. The title also indicates Lacy's main adaptation to Molière's play: while Sganarelle is a woodcutter, Drench is a farrier. This is perhaps a natural choice given that a seventeenth-century farrier was understood to be part-smith, part-equine vet. The definition for 'farrier' in John Wilkins's *Essay Towards a Real Understanding and a Philosophical Language* (1688) is 'Physitian for Horses', and in John Kersey's *A New English Dictionary*, 'Horse-doctor or shooer of horses'.[20] There is a telling description of the doctoring role in Robert Campbell's later work *The London Tradesman*, a compendium of trades practised in eighteenth-century London:

> He has a certain *Materia Medica* of his own adapted to the Constitution of his Patient, and administers to the Horse without consulting the Faculty of Physicians, or understanding one word of their Dispensary: He has particular Terms of Art peculiar to himself, affects Mystery in his Profession as much as the Graduate of the College; and, to do him Justice, is just as certain of Success as they are.[21]

This passage demonstrates that the translation of Molière's medical comedies was just one avenue through which writers attacked the medical profession. It also suggests that the changes Lacy made in translation were culturally relevant to the long-held views of London townspeople.

As well as changing Sganarelle's profession from woodcutter to farrier, Lacy changes his name to 'Drench'. A 'drench' is a veterinary dose of medicine; in the play, the farrier contemplates trying out his usual remedy on his new human patient (p. 14), confident that he will succeed: 'Come my Squire Softhead, never fear thy wench, | She shall be cur'd by Learned Doctor *Drench*' (p. 15). After this, Drench's title of 'Doctor' is emphasized along with his assumption of the theatrical role. In the printed version of the play the character's speech prefix changes from 'Dr.' for Drench to 'Doct.' for Doctor Drench. The *OED*'s first records of 'Dr.' as an abbreviation for 'doctor' date from the mid-seventeenth century, so this detail may be a typographical pun. Medical terminology is absorbed elsewhere in the printed text; in the dedication, for example, Lacy writes '*since you so graciously have received my Farriar, who dares say he is no Physician? When you vouchsafe to call him Doctor, he has Commenced, and from your Mouth he has taken his Degree*' (A2ʳ). The other characters in the play, however, are not easily convinced.

In the final act of *The Dumb Lady; or, The Farriar Made Physician* Lacy embellishes Molière's reunion between the mock doctor and his wife. He does so in order to emphasize the deceiving power of the title of 'Doctor'. Whereas in the French play Martine simply asks Sganarelle, 'dis-moi un peu des Nouvelles du Médecin que je vous ai donné' (III.9; *OC*, I, 765), this exchange in its first English translation is further prolonged as Drench carries on playing his new role, assisted by his patient's suitor Leander:

> ISA   Pray tell his Doctorship's worship, that here's his wife.
> [...]
> Good Doctor dog-bolt, how long have you been worshipful?
> LEA.   Prethee be gone, woman; for I assure thee Doctor *Drench* has n'er a wife.
> ISA   But there is a horse-Doctor *Drench* a Farrier that has a wife.
> DOCT. I, the Farrier *Drench* may have a wife, but I assure thee Doctor *Drench* has none, therefore be gone woman.
> ISA   [...] who made you a Doctor, but my invention and a good cudgel? I'll spoil your trade of physic, sirrah. (p. 36)

In English, the term 'doctor' can be used as a title as well as a descriptor; it is a label that can be assumed. In *Le Médecin malgré lui* Sganarelle initially thinks that Géronte is 'monsieur le médecin', and, discovering his mistake, he performs a simple ceremony: he says, beating him, 'Vous êtes Médecin, maintenant, je n'ai jamais eu d'autres Licences' (I.2; *OC*, I, 746). In Henry Fielding's translation *The Mock Doctor* this line is translated as 'Why now you're made a Doctor of Physick — I am sure 'tis all the Degrees I ever took' (p. 15). Whereas Fielding's mock doctor is called 'Doctor' (and presented as 'Doctor Lazy' by his wife), Molière's Sganarelle is addressed simply as 'Monsieur', though he is believed to be, and is described as, a 'médecin'. In English, the common appellation 'doctor' encourages translators to experiment with ironic naming.

Another way in which the term *médecin* is rendered in the first English translations of Molière's medical satires is by the term 'physician'. This word comes from the French *physicien* meaning 'medical practitioner' or, from the sixteenth century onwards, 'a natural scientist or philosopher, a physicist'. By the seventeenth century, *physicien* was reserved for natural scientists rather than medical doctors; in English, however, the term 'physician' could carry either meaning and was commonly used to describe a medical practitioner. Yet natural philosophy, or physics, is far from the minds of the physicians in the translations of Molière's works; they are even remote from the medicine they are supposed to practise. If, as the section above on *les malades* explores, the (English) patient is the 'taker of physic', the physician is the 'giver of physic'. In seventeenth- and early eighteenth-century English the adjective 'physical' could relate to medicine and medical practice, but it was not until the mid- to late eighteenth century that it came to relate to the body and sexual intimacy. Nevertheless, the physicians in the English satirical translations are interested in physical concerns of both kinds, and their privileged position and access to patients' chambers lead to copious innuendo in comedy.

By the time Molière's plays were being translated into English the term 'physician' was well established as slang for 'supplier of sexual physic'.[22] In the early translation *The Dumb Lady; or, The Farriar Made Physician*, the reasons for the nurse's interest in the 'physician' are clear enough, but Lacy chooses to embellish the translation to spell out the bawdy elements of the role. In *Le Médecin malgré lui* Sganarelle teases Léandre when he comes to seek the 'doctor's' help to woo his beloved Lucinde: 'Pour qui me prenez-vous? Comment oser vous adresser à moi, pour vous servir dans votre amour, et vouloir ravaler la dignité de médecin, à des emplois de cette nature?' (II.5; *OC*, I, 754). Lacy makes this somewhat more explicit, in Anglo-Saxon style. Upon hearing the request that the doctor 'befriend' Leander and Olinda, Drench exclaims:

> I begin to find that physic is but one part of a Doctor's trade, and I shall gain the Character of *Chaucer's* Semstriss; for says he,
>
> > *She keeps a shop for countenance;*
> > *But baudeth for her sustenance;*
> > So I shall physick give for countenance;
> > But pimping's my chief maintenance. (p. 28)

Drench offers a rather loose translation of the last two lines of Chaucer's incomplete *Cook's Tale*, in which the wife's profession is not revealed. The misquotations may be intentional insofar as it could indicate Drench's lack of learning, though other references to Chaucer's seamstress were used around the time of the play's appearance alongside lewd references to seamstresses' handling of needles.[23] In any case, Drench's comment shows an attempt on the part of Lacy the translator to establish the physician as a comic figure within an English literary context. Drench's comment can be read in several ways: on the one hand, he may follow Sganarelle's mocking tone in chastising the young man for seeking his help; on the other hand, he may be complaining that he is being called on to share his 'physick-giving' rather than being the sole privileged supplier.

An even more explicit demonstration of the connotations of the term 'physician' is provided in McSwiny's *The Quacks; or, Love's the Physician* (1704/5). The colourful content of the first epilogue to this translation of *L'Amour médecin* is indicated in its title: 'Epilogue Forbid to be Spoke'. A contracted quotation evokes its controversial nature:

> *How easily a Woman's Ails are Brib'd,*
> *When Physick by her Lover is prescrib'd?*
> *[...]*
> *He kills his Patients too, but such a way*
> *Had they nine Lives they'd loose 'em in a Day!*
> *[...]*
> *The Widows and the Orphans joys recall,*
> *For Love's the great Physician for them all.* (E6ᵛ)

It is hardly surprising that there was an alternative epilogue focusing on the other title of the play, *The Quacks*. The replacement declares that if the audience does not support the dramatist it is they 'that are the Quacks and murder him' (E7ʳ).

The innuendo-laden references to 'physicians' endured into the eighteenth century. Henry Fielding points to the origins of his translation/adaptation *The Mock Doctor* by including a scene in which the mock doctor decides to test his wife's virtue by pretending to be a French doctor:

GREG.   Come hider, Shild, leta me feela your Pulse.
DORC.   What have you to do with my Pulse?
GREG.   I am de *French* Physicion, my Dear, and I am to feel a de Pulse of de Pation.
DORC.   Yes, but I am no Patient, Sir, nor want no Physicion, good Dr. *Ragou*.
        [...]
GREG.   Dis is not a proper Place, dis is too publick, for sud anyone pass bye while I taka dis Physick, it vil preventa de operation.
DORC.   What Physic, Doctor?
GREG.   In your Ear, dat.   [*Whispers.*
DORC.   And in your Ear, dat Sirrah. [*Hitting him a Box.*] Do you dare affront my Virtue, you Villain! (pp. 24–25)

This type of mock French accent and language is found in numerous translations of Molière's plays; its inclusion is designed to gesture to the French origins of the play, and to exploit the comic effect of making fun of old rival neighbours. Gregory's suggestion that he take Dorcas's pulse is inspired by the fake medical practice that Sganarelle conducts in the French source-text. Sganarelle encourages

Léandre (disguised as an apothecary) to 'tend' to Lucinde the patient: 'Allez-vous-en, Monsieur l'Apothicaire, tâter un peu son pouls, afin que je raisonne tantôt, avec vous, de sa maladie' (III.6; *OC*, I, 761). This suggestion has sexual undertones which are exaggerated in Fielding's English translation: the repetition of the reference to Dorcas's 'Pulse', for example, is a deliberate emphasis on the designs that the mock-physician has on her 'Virtue'. Apart from the closely translated plays in the first collected works in English, all the initial translations of Molière's medical satires include the sexual imagery and punning found in the original plays, but use the wider English medical vocabulary to offer the audience a dose of bawdy comedy.

English translators chose between the terms 'doctor' and 'physician' depending on the comic effect they were aiming to transplant from the French context to the English. The title 'doctor' could either be adopted or jettisoned with ease, and its use in English as a common designation meant it could be attached to colourful adjectives to deride the mock doctor figures. The term 'physician' played into the hands of those English translators who sought to intensify the sexual connotations in the French plays and to perpetuate a dramatic tradition presenting doctors as sexually predatory.

Quack

This chapter began with the observation that a fake doctor would not style himself a 'quack', so the term had to be used sparingly in order for it to have maximum comic impact in the English translations. The term 'quack' comes from 'quacksalver', a borrowing from Dutch meaning 'a person who heals using homemade salves'. Its etymology has been linked to the early modern Dutch *quacken* (*kwaken*), 'to boast, quack', thus suggesting that quacksalvers were voluble in advertising their wares. 'Quacksalver' in early modern English was a derogatory term: Thomas Blount's *Glossographia* defines 'Qwacksalver (Belg.)' as 'a peddling Chyrurgeon; a Simpler, that cures with Simples; a Simple Physician, a Mountebank'.[24] 'Mountebank' was a borrowing from the Italian *montambanco*, a contraction of *monta in banco* meaning literally 'mount on bench' and relating to the selling technique. Blount describes a 'mountebank' as 'a base deceitful Merchant (especially of Apothecaries Drugs) that, with impudent lying, does, for the most part sell counterfeit stuff to the common people'. So a 'mountebank' was more akin to a dubious apothecary than a dubious doctor, though the term is often used synonymously with 'quack'. The nearest equivalent in French was *charlatan*, though this term also related more closely to drug-selling than to medical examination. Blount's dictionary demonstrates the hazy distinctions between the terms. 'Charlatan (Fr.)' is defined as 'a Mountebank, a cousening Drug-seller, a pratling Quacksalver'.[25] How, then, were such terms used in translations from French?

Aphra Behn's adaptation of parts of *Le Malade imaginaire* and *L'Amour médecin* in *Sir Patient Fancy* was so loose that reference to quackery could be included in it easily. When Sir Patient is about to consult with his band of physicians (an episode inspired by Act II of *L'Amour médecin*), Leander suggests that Sir Patient should get rid of all his 'couzening Quacks' (p. 75) and instead uncover his wife's lack of devotion (he then proceeds to execute the plan that Toinette devises in *Le Malade imaginaire*). The quacks to which Leander refers end up arguing amongst themselves, and the foppish Sir Credulous, disguised as one of the physicians, attacks the 'Fat Doctor' thus: 'pray how long is't since you left Toping and Naping, for Quacking?' (p. 82). 'Toping and naping' means 'cheating at dice', so by association 'quacking' is understood to be a dishonourable practice.

The association of quackery and gambling is also present in Owen McSwiny's translation of *L'Amour médecin*. At the end of Act II of Molière's play Sganarelle is suddenly inspired to buy 'l'orviétan', a supposed miracle remedy that the Italian charlatan Jeronimo Ferranti claimed to have brought from Orvieto to seventeenth-century Paris. In McSwiny's *The Quacks*, however, this scene is changed so that Sir Patient Carefull's niece Lysette offers an alternative to the unimpressive group of physicians:

> If you would have my Cousin cur'd, there is a Mountebank in Town, that do's wonders; has a particular Method without Druggs or nasty Physick. [...]

These Fellows [the doctors] are all Cheats and Ignorant Quacks, their Consultation was only which Horse ran best at *Newmarket*, and how they might at the same time, Preserve a patient from Dying, and growing well. (p. 23)

So quackery was associated with gaming, and was suggestive of gambling with lives. Lysette's implication, however, demonstrates the range of medical or pseudo-medical figures whose advice could be and was sought in early modern England and mirrors the medical options presented in the French source-text. Just as Molière's Sganarelle is lured by the thought of the miracle remedy 'l'orviétan', McSwiny's Sir Patient Carefull is persuaded by Lysette that the 'mountebank' might be able to cure his daughter (this turns out to be true because the mountebank is her beloved in disguise). Lysette promotes the mountebank as 'a Seventh Son of a seventh Son' who 'laughs at all your College Doctors' (p. 25). It was a commonplace myth that seventh sons had a talent for medicine, though the term was applied to alternative practitioners rather than degree-holders. Such folklore is employed by Lysette to convince Carefull and to invite the audience to laugh at his gullibility.

The multiple English terms available to describe dubious medical practice invited translators to vary them to explore the attitudes of the dupes as well as to satirize medical figures themselves. The actress-dramatist Susanna Centlivre adds the character of Belliza into *Love's Contrivance; or, Le Médecin malgré lui* in order to give range to the plot. Belliza helps her cousin Lucinda to contravene her father's wishes and so win her beloved. While Molière's Géronte is earnest in his belief that his daughter is ill, Centlivre's equivalent character Selfwill needs more persuading. When he is told that his daughter cannot stomach the marriage match he has in mind for her he responds that he will force her to comply. Belliza tries to reason with him:

> BELL.   Ay, but Uncle that seldom digests well, and what don't digest well throws the Body into a Feaver.
> SELF.   Does it so, Mrs. Quack, — Do ye hear, I suspect a Trick. (p. 33)

Given that medicine was a masculine domain it is unusual in drama of the time for the term 'quack' to be applied to a female character. Yet throughout *Love's Contrivance* Susanna Centlivre expands the female roles through her translation choices to reinforce her stance on the value of promoting women's interests. Belliza is shown to be sharp-witted when she replies to her suitor's declaration that she is 'the only Physician can save [his] life' with the remark: 'You had best not trust to my Skill, for I am but a Quack, as my Uncle says' (p. 34). Selfwill rightly suspects Belliza's tricks and therefore justifies his use of the name 'Mrs Quack', but this quackery-trickery is a crucial and comical dramatic device that works towards the resolution of the plot.

A Mountebank Stage

In all of Molière's medical satires the doctor role is presented as a theatrical performance. In the first translations this is conveyed not only through the visual and physical potential of drama, but also through reference to specific vocabulary choices. At the beginning of McSwiny's *The Quacks; or, Love's the Physician*, the game is given away to the audience when Lucinda reveals to her cousin that her suitor will 'make his Man Personate a Mountebank' (p. 6). It transpires that her suitor himself also disguises himself and the scene is set at the start of Act III. The stage directions read '*A Mountebank Stage &c. Enter* Clitander *and* Harry *drest like Mountebanks*'. The very etymology of 'mountebanks' refers to the staging of performance, albeit one intended to sell medical wares or services. Reference to the practice allows McSwiny to include a play-within-a-play that self-referentially points to the illusion of theatre when Clitander explains that he cures by 'Words, Letters, Verses, Charms and Magick Rings' (p. 26), a direct translation from *L'Amour médecin* ('je guéris par des paroles, par des sons, par des lettres, par des talismans, et par des anneaux constellés', III.5; *OC*, I, 628).

In Henry Fielding's *The Mock Doctor*, a hint of the eponymous character's qualification to perform the role of physician is suggested at the beginning of the play. In Molière's French, the seed of Martine's idea to take revenge on Sganarelle comes from her husband's boastful comment: 'trouve-moi un faiseur de fagots, qui sache, comme moi, raisonner des choses, qui ait servi six ans, un fameux médecin, et qui ait su dans son jeune âge, son rudiment par cœur' (1.1; *OC*, I, 731). This is embellished slightly in Fielding's version:

> Find me out a Maker of Fagots that's able, like my Self, to reason upon Things, or that can boast such an Education as mine. [...] a regular Education; first at the Charity-School, where I learnt to read; then I waited on a Gentleman at *Oxford*, where I learnt very near as much as my Master; from whence I attended a travelling Physician six Years, under the facetious Denomination of a *Merry Andrew*, where I learnt Physick. (p. 1)

A 'Merry-Andrew' was a term meaning a joker or buffoon, or a mountebank's assistant. The name was associated with performer-merchants at Bartholomew Fair from the 1660s onwards. In McSwiny's translation of *L'Amour médecin*, *The Quacks*,

Clitander as Mountebank claims that his 'patient' is struggling to recognize people and so will pretend that his 'Merry-Andrew' is a notary so that she thinks her desire to marry has been fulfilled (p. 32). The trick is that a real notary is in fact brought in and the lovers united. So mountebanking, and its close counterpart, quackery, are types of performance; allusions to such activity correspond with the dramatic devices and tricks of Molière's medical comedies.

The links between quackery and theatrical performance are emphasized in the very form of Fielding's *The Mock Doctor*. Like Molière in his *comédies-ballets L'Amour médecin* and *Le Malade imaginaire*, Fielding includes musical interludes in his translation of *Le Médecin malgré lui*. In the English version, Gregory's wife has just been promoting her husband as an eminent doctor, though one of the servants in search of the physician is unsure that her man will fit the bill. The servant's doubting comment in the French source-text is: 'Mais est-il bien vrai, qu'il soit si habile, que vous le dites?' (1.4; *OC*, I, 737). Fielding renders it slightly differently so that it leads into a satirical song:

> JAMES   Sure this Quack understands as much as the whole College of Physicians?
> DORC.   College of Physicians!
>
> AIR V. Set by Mr. SEEDO
>
> *In formal dull Schools,*
> *By Forefathers Rules*
> *The Doctor's equipt out for Slaughter;*
> *If according to Art,*
> *The Patient depart,*
> *He never is blam'd for it after.*
>
> *The Quack still succeeds*
> *Or falls by his Deeds,*
> *If he kills you he gets not a Shilling;*
> *But who denies Fees*
> *To the Quack whose Degrees*
> *Once give him a Licence for killing?* (p. 10)

The first verse of the song responds to the French by satirizing the fusty school of learned doctors. The servant's comment and the second verse of the song show the flexibility with which terminology relating to medical figures could be used. The servant's use of the term 'quack' emphasizes the scepticism of the original French, and helps to identify the quack as a figure considered separate from the College of Physicians. The second verse seems at first to support the servant's distinction between the quack and the learned doctor, though it suggests that the quack may be more honourable than the doctor because he does not receive payment if he kills you. The final turn of the song, however, comes in the penultimate line when the learned doctor is renamed 'Quack', thereby suggesting that the whole medical sphere is a mere act.

The individual cases of doctor-impersonating in Molière's medical comedies satirize the Parisian medical community by suggesting that their practice could be smoke and mirrors, but the various ways of labelling the impersonators in English translation ('doctor', 'physician', 'quack', 'mountebank') offer additional satirical elements based on the connotations of vocabulary.

Milady Malady: Gender and Translation

One might ask whether it was mere coincidence that two female dramatists, Behn and Centlivre, contributed to the early transposition of Molière's medical satires into English theatre. Having shown that the comedy of 'physick' often centred on the innuendo that arises from a doctor's, or a fake doctor's, access to the bodies of his patients, did the female dramatists make modifying translation choices to give their female characters more agency and control over their bodies and the social transactions that they represent?

Recent studies have addressed the intersection of translation studies and gender studies, noting their shared characteristics of a political focus, the challenges of defining their subjects, and 'the 'struggle over meaning that marks both fields'.[26] Aphra Behn's preface to *Sir Patient Fancy* also evokes the overlap between writing, gender, and translation by answering charges levelled against her in such a way as to show that the motivations behind her detractors are interlinked:

> I Printed this Play with all the impatient haste one ought to do, who would be vindicated from the most unjust and silly aspersion, Woman could invent to cast on Woman; and which only my being a Woman has procured me; *That it was Bawdy,* the least and most Excusable fault in the Men writers, to whose Plays they all crowd, as if they came to no other end than to hear what they condemn in this; *but from a Woman it was unnaturall:* but how so Cruell an unkindness came into their imaginations I can by no means guess [...]. But if such as these durst profane their Chast ears with hearing it over again, or taking it into their serious Consideration in their Cabinets; they would find nothing that the most innocent Virgins can have cause to blush at: but confess with me that no Play either Ancient or Modern has less of that Bug-bear Bawdry in it. Others to show their breeding (as *Bays* sayes,)[27] cryed it was made out of at least four *French* Plays, when I had but a very bare hint from one, the *Malad Imagenere,* which was given me translated by a Gentleman infinitely to advantage: but how much of the *French* is in this, I leave to those who indeed understand it and have seen it at the Court. The Play had no other Misfortune but that of coming out for a Womans: had it been owned by a Man, though the most Dull Unthinking Rascally Scribler in Town, it had been a most admirable Play. Nor does its loss of Fame with the Ladies do it much hurt, though they ought to have had good Nature and justice enough to have attributed all its faults to the Authours unhappiness, who is forced to write for Bread and not ashamed to owne it, and consequently ought to write to please (if she can) an Age which has given severall proofs it was by this way of writing to be obliged, though it is a way too cheap for men of wit to pursue, who write for Glory, and a way which even I despise as much below me. (A1)

While it is true that only some parts of *Sir Patient Fancy* are taken from *Le Malade imaginaire*, and even they were mediated through the translation 'by a Gentleman', the model is clearly Molière's play. As explored in Chapter 2, Susanna Centlivre presents herself as a translator in the preface to *Love's Contrivance*, yet Behn, having borrowed sections of a translation, does not present herself as a translator of any kind but as an author who needs to write to earn her keep and to satisfy the expectation that sex sells. She therefore avoids laying the charges of bawdy at Molière's door; such a move would in any case contradict her implicit argument that bawdy comedy written by a woman should be no more censured than that written by men. Her initial denial that there is anything bawdy in the play is disingenuous: in its transformation from *Le Malade imaginaire* to *Sir Patient Fancy*, certain episodes do become more sexually charged, even where they were suggestive in the French source.

At first glance, it may seem that the issues of the gender of the author and the degree to which she offered an unacknowledged though indirect translation of a French play are separate. But there is a pointedness with which Behn comments that she was given the *Malade imaginaire* 'translated by a Gentleman', particularly when the sentence in which the comment features is immediately followed by the defensive assertion that the 'Play had no other Misfortune but that of coming out for a Womans'. Is there, then, an implicit suggestion that a woman's translation of a play written by a man, however indirect, is expected to reframe the content to suit the theoretical sensibilities of the author's gender? And does Behn's adaptation of the 'Gentleman''s translation deliberately diverge from social expectations to emphasize women's agency over their bodies and fortunes in a play in which the male protagonist presents himself at the mercy of his supposedly ailing body?

The pronouns in Behn's comment 'how much of the *French* is in this, I leave to those who indeed understand it and have seen it at the Court' are confusing. By 'the *French*' and 'it' Behn means the play *Le Malade imaginaire*, and she may be referring to a recent production at Whitehall in the winter of 1677–78. Henri Pitel (known as 'Sieur de Longchamp'), his wife Charlotte née Legrand, their daughter Anne and her husband Michel du Rieu, and their other daughter Françoise (who later became the famous Mademoiselle Raisin) were bound for Nijmegen when adverse weather conditions forced them to redirect to London. They arrived in late November or early December 1677 and their first performance was probably on 5 December at the Hall Theatre in Whitehall.[28] This demonstrates that the public theatres were confronted with competition from the French comedians at court at the time *Sir Patient Fancy* was first performed and that French drama was at the forefront of court spectators' minds, thereby perhaps explaining the readiness with which detractors accused Behn of having plagiarized French plays. The fact that Pitel's troupe was in London that winter also colours Behn's comment about *Le Malade imaginaire*. Although surviving records do not indicate which plays the French comedians performed, Behn's remark suggests that *Le Malade imaginaire* may have been amongst them. Janet Todd, writing about editing the works of Behn, argues that the dramatist:

> Would have felt irritation, even anger at that aspect of editing that demands mention of allusions, borrowings and echoes. [...] it was not a 'bare hint' that she had taken from *Le Malade Imaginaire*. But happily for her no one seems to

have pursued the point in the 1670s or taken her to task in print [...]. She would not have expected a scholar with more time than sense and no connection whatsoever with a court to place the play beside Molière's and note the similarities.[29]

Yet it can be argued that by taking inspiration from *Le Malade imaginaire* at a time when French plays were being performed at court would inevitably invite comparison, and Behn herself refers to having perused a translation of the play, so her comments do not stand up to scrutiny, not least because the very title of her play evokes that of Molière's work.

An unpublished but surviving translation of *Le Malade imaginaire* by James Wright, a Middle Temple lawyer, bears so much linguistic resemblance to parts of *Sir Patient Fancy* that it is highly likely that this is the translation 'by a Gentleman' to which Behn refers.[30] An inspection of the manuscript provides insight into the intersection of translation and gender relations in the cross-channel migration of the comedy because it allows us to see which sections of his translation Aphra Behn cherry-picked and which sections she innovated upon along gendered lines.[31] In fact James Wright did not translate *Le Malade imaginaire* quite as it was written by Molière. Owing to the French playwright's sudden death in February 1673, *Le Malade imaginaire* had not been prepared for print publication by the author and several unauthorized versions appeared. The first of these was a 1674 text entitled *Le Malade imaginaire, comédie en trois actes mêlés de danses et de musique* published in Amsterdam by Daniel Elzevir, whose name and address were also attached to further unauthorized editions printed in Paris and Lyon.[32] This text was pieced together from a spectator's recollections of the 1673 performances and almost all of the characters' names were altered, probably to cover the counterfeiters' tracks. Some of these names are anglicized by James Wright in his manuscript translation, and some are adopted by Behn in *Sir Patient Fancy*.

Although Behn's female characters in *Sir Patient Fancy* are generally more forthright in their pursuit of their desires than they are in Molière's source, Derek Hughes points out some limitations to the apparent liberation of these characters by focusing on their use of language to exert control over others:

> The gathering of doctors in the consultation scene is a display of the traditions of formalized gibberish which are the public pretexts and instruments of male authority. [...] In satirizing man's linguistic supremacy, however, it also raises problems about women's attempts to wrest it from them. There is no sense that beyond the rival jargons lies a unified, dominant language of authority whose acquisition can give power to a woman. Power in *Sir Patient Fancy* lies in controlling the distance between the signifying word and the signified body.[33]

Beyond the plot events within the play, it is important to ask to what extent women's ventriloquization of the language of men is enacted by Behn's use of the translation by a 'Gentleman' in her construction of *Sir Patient Fancy*.

In regard to the exact language taken from James Wright's translation of the unauthorized edition of *Le Malade imaginaire*, Behn is justified in writing that she had a 'bare hint', even though in terms of plot events she took more inspiration from the French source. But what she does with the sections she takes from Wright's translation are telling. The first full scene to be transposed into *Sir Patient Fancy* is Act I, scene 7 (Act II, scene 14, in the unauthorized French edition), in which the invalid reveals to his wife that with a view to his supposedly impending death he has laid aside some money for her. In the authorized edition of the French play a notary is on hand to organize proceedings, but in the rudimentary unauthorized edition husband and wife discuss the affairs alone. In the illicit, 'oral' edition published by Elzevir, Argan's name is changed to 'Orgon' (not to be confused with the dupe in *Le Tartuffe*) and Béline's name is change to 'Mariane' (not to be confused with the daughter in *Le Tartuffe*):

MARIANE	Mon Dieu! Pourquoy prens-tu plaisir à m'affliger de la sorte? me parler de ta mort, c'est me parler de la mienne. Que je serois malheureuse! Ils sont, dis-tu, dans ton cabinet derriere le lambris en entrant à gauche? [...]
ORGON	Ma chere ame, je vois que tu m'aimes trop, et je ne pourray jamais assez reconnoître ton affection. Nous vivrons l'un et l'autre autant qu'il plaira au Ciel. Mets-toy en repos [...] et avant toutes choses, viens reconnoistre dans mon cabinet l'endroit que je t'ay marqué, et qui n'est sceu au monde que de nous deux.
MARIANE	Allons, puisque tu le veux de la sorte.[34]

James Wright translated this in a literal manner:

MA.	Good God! Why should you take a pleasure to afflict me thus? In speaking of your Death you speak of mine. Unhappy woman that I am! — In your Closet say you? Behind the Wainscot, on the left hand coming in? [...]
ORG.	My dear Love, I see thou hast too great a Love for me, and I can never sufficiently reward thy Affection. We will both live so long as heaven pleases. Comfort thyself. [...] But in the first place come along with me to my Closet and I will show thee the place, which no one in the World knows of but we two.
MA.	Well, since it is your pleasure, I'le attend you. *Exeunt.*[35]

But Behn reconfigures this section so that Lady Fancy is the one to encourage her husband to lead her to the sequestered money, ironically enough by feigning physical weakness:

LA. FA.	Good Heavens! Why shou'd you take such pleasure in afflicting me. [*Weeps.*] — Behind the Wainscot say you? [...] Oh my Spirits fail me, — lead me, or I shall faint, — lead me to the Study and shew me where 'tis. (p. 57)

This is a simple enough adaptation, but it is one that emphasizes the wife's agency, albeit an act of deceit. Her feigning of weakness also foreshadows the husband's trick at the end of the play where he pretends to be dead in order to learn whether his wife truly loves him, thereby highlighting the lack of authentic communication between the pair.

Behn also makes use of Wright's translation as a means of flying in the face of audiences' expectations of female writers by intensifying the bawdiness of the scene in which the protagonist questions his younger daughter on the amorous exploits of the elder (Act II, scene 8, in the authorized edition of the play, Act II, scene 6, in the unauthorized edition). Louison's name is changed to 'Fanchon' in the early edition, hence the anglicization to the name 'Fanny' in Wright's translation and Behn's *Sir Patient Fancy*:

ORGON	N'entendîtes-vous pas ce qu'ils disoient?
FANCHON	L'homme parloit à ma sœur et luy disoit.... tout-cy, tout-ça, en luy jettant les fleurs de jasmin. [...]
FANCHON	Elle luy disoit: Mon Dieu, je vous prie, allez-vous en, j'ay peur que l'on ne vous voye icy, et aprés le luy avoir dit deux ou trois fois, il luy baisa la main, et s'en alla par la porte de derriere dont ma sœur avait la clef. (p. 42)

Wright translates this closely but expands the last lines to provide a response from the suitor:

FA.	She said, let me see — I, she said, Lord! My dear we forget ourselves, prithee be gone now, I tremble for fear you shall be seen, and this he said two or three times: I kiss your sweet hands, dearest mistress, Oh! I could live here for ever! And so went out at the back door, of which my sister has a key. (fol. 10^r)

Behn extends this section to make Fanchon ventriloquize the words of her sister's suitor, which become somewhat more detailed and fulsome than in the French:

FA.	The Man talked to my sister a great deal, and told her — this and that, I don't know what, and all the while he spoke he threw Jasmin flowers into her Bosom.
SIR PAT.	And thou didst not hear a word they said all the while?
FA.	Yes I did Sir, and the man talked a great deal of this, and of that, and of t'other, and all the while threw Jesimine in her bosome [...]
SIR PAT.	Ah, very fine, — then what said he?
FA.	Then he said, Well if I must be gone, let me leave thee with this hearty curse, A Pox take thee all over for making me love thee so confoundedly. [...] — Oh I cou'd live here for ever, — that was when he kist her — her hand only, are you not a Damn'd woman for making so fond a Puppy of me? [...]
SIR PAT.	[...] Oh I am heart-sick. (p. 63)

Whereas Fanny is supposedly merely parroting the words of her elder sister's suitor, her comment that he kissed her 'hand only' hints at her precociousness and plants a further seed of doubt in Sir Patient's mind. The father is thus laid low by his daughter's words; his self-diagnosis of heart-sickness is an ironic nod to the way in which his imagination can make him ill, but we sense in Behn that this imagination is being manipulated by a young daughter who is rendered less innocent in translation.

In contrast to Behn, Susanna Centlivre translated directly from Molière, although she only incorporated select scenes from *Le Médecin malgré lui* in *Love's Contrivance; or, Le Médecin malgré lui*. Not only is the inclusion of the French title as a subtitle indicative of the wish to draw attention to the Frenchness of the source-text, but the move away from Lacy's earlier title *The Dumb Lady* is telling, especially given that it was restored in Fielding's 1732 English adaptation, *The Mock Doctor*. In fact, although Centlivre's heroine initially feigns dumbness to avoid an unwanted marriage, this approach is quickly dispensed with in favour of more direct action.

Even before Lucinda is examined by the *médecin malgré lui*, the idea that Centlivre is challenging any notion that women should be seen and not heard is evoked in the early exchanges between the mock doctor and his wife. The very name of Centlivre's faggot-maker turned doctor seems to be inspired by the name of the protagonist's wife in *Le Médecin malgré lui*: Molière's 'Sganarelle' becomes Centlivre's 'Martin' whereas Molière's 'Martine' simply becomes 'Martin's wife'. In the English translation these two characters were played by the acting couple Mr Henry Norris and Mrs Sarah Norris, a casting choice which was perhaps intended to add metatheatrical irony. While the title 'Martin's wife' might seem to label the female character as a mere appendage to the husband, this idea is challenged through some slight amendments to the characters' dialogue in translation. When the audience first meets Sganarelle and his wife in Molière's play they are arguing about the roles of husbands and wives:

> SGANARELLE Non, je te dis que je n'en veux rien faire: et que c'est à moi de parler et d'être le Maître.
> MARTINE Et je te dis, moi, que je veux que tu vives à ma fantaisie: et que je ne me suis point mariée avec toi pour souffrir tes fredaines. (1.1; OC, I, 731)

This is expanded slightly in Centlivre's translation to read as follows:

> MAR. I say I won't work to Day; and if I say I won't, I won't; and so you had as good hold your Tongue.
> WIFE 'Tis very fine indeed, a Woman must not speak.
> MAR. I say 'tis my Business to speak, and to act too; pray who am I, am not I your Lord and Master?
> WIFE And who am I, if you go to that? Am not I the Wife of your Bosom? What did I marry you for? to bear with all your mad Freaks? No, no, I'd have you know, I shall make you turn over a new Leaf. (p. 10)

There is a frequent and pointed use of the term 'a Woman' in Centlivre's text as she capitalizes on the double meaning of *femme* as wife and as woman to identify Martin's wife not only as a put-upon spouse but also as a woman in society. The emphasis on speech, and in particular women's speech, establishes language as a means to gain power over the body and is thus a common theme in the medical satires and their translations.

As the argument between the married couple escalates and they are observed, Molière's Monsieur Robert exclaims 'Quelle infamie, peste soit le Coquin, de battre ainsi sa Femme' (1.2; *OC*, I, 733), whereas Centlivre's Octavio cries 'What insolence is this? Are you not ashamed to beat a Woman!' (p. 12), thereby once again broadening the female character's identity from wife to woman in society. It turns out that the wife rejects the offer of support and responds to the abuse from her husband by seeking revenge on him. Molière's Martine hints at the potential to cuckold Sganarelle, but decides that she wants her vengeance to be less subtle and less personally compromising: 'Je sais bien qu'une femme a toujours dans les mains, de quoi se venger d'un Mari: mais c'est une punition trop délicate pour mon Pendard' (1.3; *OC*, I, 735) Hence she comes up with the rather unconventional trick of pretending he is an accomplished doctor who can only be persuaded to treat patients if he is beaten soundly; she achieves this end through manipulating language. In Centlivre's translation, this scheme is preceded by the comment: 'And am I always to be used thus? — well, if I am not reveng'd, I am no Woman' (p. 15), thereby suggesting her action is a form of female power and self-defence rather than simply a response to a personal marital tiff.

Centlivre was selective in the scenes that she translated from *Le Médecin malgré lui*, interweaving them with sections of her own invention, but she does include the 'consultation scene' (Act II, scene 4) in which Lucinde/Lucinda is assessed by the 'doctor' at home. Whereas John Lacy expanded the prefatory advances of the mock doctor towards the household's nurse in order to develop bawdy wordplay surrounding clysters, Centlivre dispenses with this exchange. She focuses instead on the mute 'patient' whom she does not allow to remain dumb for long. Whereas Molière has Lucinde blurt out her rejection of her father's choice of husband for her only after she has remained remote and silent for several scenes, Centlivre tweaks the plot so that the fake doctor encourages her to take instant action by writing to her preferred suitor, Mr Bellmie, to declare: 'I am not dumb, only as the last Remedy to prevent my barbarous Father's Designs, who was resolutely bent to marry me that Moment' (p. 44). This letter, however, is immediately discovered by her father, who reads it out and echoes her words: 'Huzzy, I'll marry you to my Scullion, I will, huzzy, if I please; counterfeited with a Pox, I'll counterfeit you, I'll yerk the sullen Devil out of you I will so' (p. 45). Whereas Derek Hughes notes that in Behn's *Sir Patient Fancy* an act of writing can often 'help to control the male body', in *Love's Contrivance* it betrays its authoress.[36] But this failed communication increases the dramatic tension and forces Lucinda to try a different linguistic tack; she speaks at length to Sir Toby Doubtful, her unsatisfactory intended, in order to conjure up a manipulated image of the life she envisions with him: 'I assure you when I marry I hope to be my own Mistress, and follow my own Inclination, which will carry me to the utmost Pinnacle of the Fashion' (p. 47). An ironic nod to the source text of the play is then made when Lucinda continues her theme of fashion to ask for a French chariot, to which Sir Toby reacts with horror at the thought of being mistaken for a Jacobite (p. 48). The result of Lucinda's carefully calculated verbal onslaught is an attack of the 'Vapors' for Sir Toby, for which he receives mock sympathy from Lucinda: ''tis a Disease that afflicts abundance of People — but our Marriage, I hope, will dissipate that' (p. 49). The language of illness and remedy is therefore shifted from the central focus of the farce in Molière to the linguistic trickery of the female character who gains power over a male body through language.

One final significant adaptation in translation occurs in the resolution of the plot. In Molière, Lucinde's beloved discovers by a chance and opportune letter that he has inherited his uncle's fortune and now has the confidence to seek permission to marry her. In Centlivre, however, the couple marry in secret and Lucinda's father reacts angrily: 'Why then take her, but not a Groat of mine along with her [...] there's five hundred a Year her Grandmother left her, which I can't hinder her of, I wish I cou'd, you should starve together' (p. 65). It is noteworthy that in translation the bride receives an inheritance, however modest, from a grandmother, rather than the groom's inheriting a fortune from a male relation. Centlivre's addition of the character Belliza, Lucinda's cousin, means that Selfwill must part with another female relative when she decides to marry Bellmie's friend Octavio: 'I wish you much Joy, if there can come any such thing from the Sex, for I'm in doubt if there can or no; she has a good Fortune, as long as that lasts you may live well enough' (p. 65). There seems, therefore, to be a sustained effort on Centlivre's part to show female characters capable of solving their own predicaments.

These observations of the ways in which female translators dealt with the source texts do not necessarily demonstrate an organized feminizing approach to translation, but they do indicate some effort to present an alternative view of gender relations through subtle changes in translation. It is important to note that the printer of Centlivre's *Love's Contrivance* deliberately included incorrect initials in the dedication to hide the fact that it had been the work of a woman. This move clearly angered Centlivre; she published an advertisement in the *Daily Courant* to emphasize that the initials were false, and in her dedication to her later play *The Platonick Lady* (also published anonymously) she wrote that this injustice meant that 'passing for a Man's' *Love's Contrivance* 'has been play'd at least a hundred times'.[37] It could be argued that the concealment of the author allowed her forthright female characters in the play to reach a wider audience, especially if readers were as prejudiced as she claimed:

> Some have arm'd themselves with resolution not to like the Play [...] and [...] if in spite of Spleen they have been pleas'd against their Will, have maliciously reported it was none of mine, but given me by some Gentleman: Nay, even my own Sex, which shou'd assert our Prerogative against such Detractors, are often backward to encourage a female Pen.[38]

It is significant that Centlivre should hint at the pathology of prejudice against female writers by using the expression 'in spite of Spleen' in reference to a medical satire. Centlivre's assertion echoes Behn's preface to *Sir Patient Fancy*, though Behn acknowledges that she had been given *Le Malade imaginaire* 'translated by a

Gentleman'. Despite her discussion of her having 'touched the colours' of Molière's text 'with an English pencil' in the preface to *Love's Contrivance* (a2^v), Centlivre does not address the grey area of translation and authorship, which in the case of *Love's Contrivance* involves both a male 'source' pen and a female translating pen. A close inspection of the translation shows that the female pen relies on the male, but enhances the language of the female characters so that they can exert more direct control over their own fates to remedy gendered power imbalance.

The public backlash against female dramatists perhaps explains why Behn and Centlivre chose to put Molière's medical satires on the stage rather than plays that focus on women in society at large such as *Les Précieuses ridicules* or *Les Femmes savantes*, though Lady Knowell in *Sir Patient Fancy* bears some comparison with Molière's learned ladies Bélise and Philamante. Of course, it could be argued that Behn and Centlivre might not seek to transpose satirical portraits of educated women, but on the other hand the potential for a recalibration of their portrayal in translation could have provided an opportunity for the female writers to promote the status of women. Yet given the unjust obstacles that Centlivre outlines to the 'Generous Encouragers of Female Ingenuity' in her dedication to *The Platonick Lady*, female writers were forced to present their ideas covertly. The medical satires provided opportunities to present familiar episodes of farce surrounded by translations or re-translations of plot elements that demonstrate greater agency on the part of female characters, thereby addressing the social malady of imbalanced gender power relations within the limits prescribed by early modern audiences.

La Faculté

Molière's medical comedies not only ridicule individual patients and doctors but also address the medical *faculté* as a whole, as well as the tensions between individual doctors within a professional group. In *Le Malade imaginaire* Molière includes a self-referential pun in which Argan condemns Molière himself for ridiculing learned doctors, claiming that he would confront the dramatist with the instruction: 'crève, crève, cela t'apprendra une autre fois à te jouer à la Faculté' (III.3; *OC*, II, 727). But 'la Faculté', at least in the comic world, is not really a united group, as Molière demonstrates in Act II of *L'Amour médecin*. When the physicians Messieurs Tomès, des Fonandrès, Macroton, and Bahys are called in to diagnose the depressed daughter, they find they cannot come to a consensus. The doctors' names are all based on well-known physicians practising in Paris and at court in the seventeenth century. The first English translators of these scenes therefore took the opportunity to relocate the doctors by alluding to the London medical scene.

Aphra Behn produced the first imitation of the extended consultation scenes in *L'Amour médecin*. In Behn's *Sir Patient Fancy* a motley mix of doctors attends a consultation requested by Sir Patient. Monsieur Turboon, Sir Patient's usual doctor, hails from France and is inspired by James Wright's translation of the early unauthorized edition of *Le Malade imaginaire* in which a 'Monsieur Turbon' rather than the authorized edition's Monsieur Purgon appears. Behn's Turboon is bribed to allow the presence of other doctors so that they can distract Sir Patient Fancy while the young Lodwick Knowell slips away to marry Isabella Fancy. Turboon is accompanied by 'An Amsterdam Doctor', 'A Leyden Doctor', 'A Fat Doctor' referred to as 'Mr Hedlberg', 'Brunswick' (a mock 'high Dutch'/German doctor), and a comic knight Sir Credulous Easy playing the role of a doctor from Cologne. When Sir Patient first sets eyes on them he asks 'Are they *English* pray?' (p. 77); the various nationalities of the doctors are emphasized to reflect the cosmopolitan nature of the London medical scene in the late seventeenth century. The medical faculties of Amsterdam and Leiden were famous and several Dutch and German physicians settled in London.[39] Monsieur Turboon introduces Sir Credulous as a 'Collender', thereby inviting the fool's exclamation: 'What a pox does the Fellow call me a Cullender?' (p. 77); and there follows an explanation from Lodwick that 'he means a *high-Dutch* man of the Town called *Collen*'. When Lodwick exits to marry Isabella he is replaced by his friend 'Brunswick', who also plays the role of a German doctor. Sir Credulous is unusually sharp in recognizing the trick, 'The Rascall's drest like *Vanderbergen* in the *Strand*' (p. 84), but he plays along by introducing Brunswick as a fellow 'high *Dutch* Doctor' (p. 79). The localized reference to a resident doctor in London would have encouraged the first audiences of the play to consider how the onstage action might reflect the medical practices in the environs of the Duke's Theatre, where the play was being performed.

A similar adaptation technique is undertaken in Owen McSwiny's early eighteenth-century translation of *L'Amour médecin*, *The Quacks*. McSwiny extends Sganarelle's request 'qu'on m'aille quérir des Médecins, et en quantité' (II.6; *OC*, I, 616) to provide portraits of the various doctors to be found in London. He calls for Dr Medly, 'the Hard favour'd Fellow, that took his Degree at *Glasgow*' and who lays 'Wagers upon the Scotch Gelding' (p. 9), Doctor Tickle-Purse, who often accompanies 'a young Lord, a Jacobite Polititian' and pores over a valuable Roman coin 'a Medal of *Otho's*' (p. 9), Doctor Trinket who 'has a farm in *Essex*, and takes all his Rent out in Shells and Butter-flies', Doctor Caudle whose Coach drives round the [Covent] Garden very slow' (p. 10), and finally Doctor *Pauvre Hugonot De Refugee*, 'the French Gascon Physician in *Sohoo*' (p. 10). All of the references point to the money-grasping tendencies of these characters, and some recall the links between gambling and quackery outlined in several of the first translations of Molière's medical satires. The reference to the Huguenot doctor at the end of this scene may gesture, in tongue-in-cheek fashion, to the importation of Molière's comedy into English. But McSwiny's Sir Patient Carefull, unlike Molière's Sganarelle, seems to realize that a collective of doctors may prove just as useless as an individual: 'What an Inundation of Doctors have I sent for! but 'tis the Fashion, no body Dyes without 'em' (p. 10). *L'Amour médecin* in translation is fashioned so that the play represents the diverse medical world just beyond the London theatre and thus satirizes it as sharply as Molière mocked the Parisian *faculté*.[40]

Although some words in French and English relating to medical practice shared etymological links, a broader range of common words were available in English to describe the impersonators or incompetent doctors satirized in Molière's plays. The translators sought to make Molière's texts fit into an existing tradition of English anti-quack satire. In order to do so they employ the terms 'quack' and 'mountebank' within the remarks of the more sceptical characters. Such references prime audiences to anticipate the theatrical elements that had long been associated with quacks and mountebank stages. Spectators are invited to enjoy the impersonation scenes as recognizable scenarios and to laugh at the dupes who are easily drawn in by the illusions. The translators aim to make the scenes resonate with city audiences by including specific references relating to the time and place in which the translations were performed.

In order for there to be doctors present in Molière's comedies there must be patients. Molière exploits the sexual innuendo that arises from the doctor's ability to gain access to a patient at close quarters, but the common trait in the English translations is for the innuendo to be exaggerated, particularly through using the connotations of a female patient as the recipient of 'physic'. While in Molière's plays the mock female patients are 'cured' by being united with their preferred suitors, the English translators make use of bawdy wordplay to invite audiences to consider the physical remedial advantages of the marriages. In these cases the first English translations of Molière's medical comedies could be understood as titillating translations. Yet in the translations of Behn and Centlivre there is a certain resistance to the idea that male doctors, whether real or fake, exercise control over female bodies and the marriage market in which they circulate.

It is likely that English doctors witnessed performances of the translations of Molière's satires, just as Parisian doctors likely saw the original plays. The translator of *Le Médecin malgré lui* in the *Select Comedies* seems to make a bold step in dedicating the parallel French-English text to a London physician called Dr Mead. He makes sure to explain, however, that 'As 'twas perverted Medicine alone, and its quack Professors that were the Subject of his [Molière's] Ridicule' Dr Mead could not 'be displeas'd with a Satire he could not fear' (II, A3^v). The dedicator goes on to explain that the following text and its translation can only be understood as a time-locked satire of late seventeenth-century Parisian medicine. This chapter has shown, however, that previous and contemporaneous translations of Molière dispensed plenty of bitter pills to English physicians as well as to the French. In taking care to translate the medical satires appropriately, the translators sought to broadcast Molière's suggestion that laughter provoked by comedy can have widespread curative effects.

Notes to Chapter 6

1. *The Hypocondriack*, trans. by anon., *The Monthly Amusement*, 4 (July 1709).
2. Molière, *The Works*, trans. by Ozell and others, VI. In the dedication to volume I Ozell explains that *The Hypocondriack* and *The Misantrope*, both of which appeared in 1709 in *The Monthly Amusement*, were translations by 'other Persons' (A9^r). An advertisement in issue 4 of the periodical states that the two Molière translations were by different people, but they are not identified. The personal correspondence of John Hughes indicates that he translated *Le Misanthrope*. All further references to *The Hypocondriack* are taken from the 1714 *Works* and are given after quotations in the text.

3. Roy Porter, *Health for Sale: Quackery in England, 1660–1850* (Manchester: Manchester University Press, 1989), p. 1.
4. Richelet, 'Patient', in *Dictionnaire françois*, II, 135.
5. John Lacy (*c*.1615–81) was a Yorkshire-born actor-dramatist in the King's Company, known for his dialect performance. He used French-style farce in his own works and played the part of Drench in *The Dumb Lady*.
6. John Lacy, *The Dumb Lady; or, The Farriar Made Physician* (London: printed for Thomas Dring, 1672), p. 20. Further references are given after quotations in the text.
7. Williams, 'Glister Syringe', in *A Dictionary of Sexual Language and Imagery in Shakespearean and Stuart Literature*, II, 601–02. See also Shakespeare's *Othello*, II.1.167–77, when Iago plots to use Cassio's chivalrous behaviour towards Desdemona to fabricate a fiction of adultery: 'Very good, well kissed, and excellent courtesy: 'tis so indeed! Yet again, your fingers to your lips? Would they were clyster-pipes for your sake!'. Ben Saunders interprets the image as part of a purgative metaphor representative of Iago's civilizing process by which he seeks to 'expunge Venetian society of everything he associates with lower-body functions: women, people of color, sexual desire' ('Iago's Clyster: Purgation, Anality, and the Civilizing Process', *Shakespeare Quarterly*, 55.2 (2004), 148–76). In contrast Drench's 'gentile glister' evokes sexual desire, though there may be an ironic echo of the civilizing drive in the different meanings of 'gentile' as relating to gentility, the state of being gentile, or a type of worm.
8. Phillips, 'Gentil', in *The New World of English Words*; Elisha Coles, 'Gentil', in *An English Dictionary* (London: printed for Samuel Crouch, 1676).
9. See Williams, 'Physic', in *A Dictionary of Sexual Language and Imagery in Shakespearean and Stuart Literature*, II.
10. Aphra Behn (*c*.1640–89) was a dramatist, poet, and fiction-writer. Her early life is mysterious but by 1670 she began to establish herself as a playwright for the Duke's Company and had at least nineteen plays performed, several of which mocked the Whigs. The epilogue to *Sir Patient Fancy* supports the role of women in theatre. Aphra Behn, *Sir Patient Fancy* (London: printed by E. Flesher for Richard Tonson and Jacob Tonson, 1678), A^v. Further references are given after quotations in the text.
11. See n. 1 above.
12. Thomas Willis, 'Hypochondriac', in 'The Table of Hard Names' appended to *Dr Willis's Practice of Physick* (London: printed for T. Dring, C. Harper, and J. Leigh, 1681).
13. 'Hypochondre', in *Dictionnaire de l'Académie françoise*, I, 577.
14. Le Boulanger de Chalussay, *Élomire hypocondre, ou Les Médecins vengés* (Paris: printed by Charles de Sercy, 1670).
15. Patrick Dandrey, 'Molière auto-portraitiste: du masque au visage', in *Le Statut littéraire de l'écrivain*, ed. by Lise Sabourin, Travaux de Littérature, XX (Geneva: Droz, 2007), pp. 107–19 (p. 110).
16. For a detailed analysis of Argan's supposed problem in *Le Malade imaginaire* see Patrick Dandrey, *La Médecine et la maladie dans le théâtre de Molière*, 2 vols (Paris: Klincksieck, 1998), II.
17. The 'College', or medical faculty, is of course composed of male doctors, so Lady Knowell's comment could be seen as a challenge to the patriarchal medical world. On the other hand, Behn's presentation of the learned lady, though less ridiculous than Molière's Bélise in *Les Femmes savantes* (1672), is not entirely positive. Derek Hughes points out that Lady Knowell 'gullibly seeks proficiency in the fraudulent jargon of medicine. Her learning bestows no authority; it merely adds another dialect to Babel [...] she never writes, even though the play is full of acts of writing — often ones which help to control the male body' (Derek Hughes, *The Theatre of Aphra Behn* (Basingstoke & New York: Palgrave Macmillan, 2001), p. 104).
18. Samuel Johnson, 'Hypochondriack', in *A Dictionary of the English Language*, 2 vols (London: printed by W. Strahan, 1755), I.
19. 'Docteur', in *Dictionnaire de l'Académie françoise*, I, 339.
20. Wilkins, 'Farrier', in the dictionary table appended to *Essay Towards a Real Character, and Philosophical Language*; Kersey, 'Farrier', in *A New English Dictionary*.
21. Robert Campbell, *The London Tradesman: A Compendious View of All the Trades Now Practised in London and Westminster* (London: printed by T. Gardner, 1747), p. 37.

22. See Williams, 'Physician', in *A Dictionary of Sexual Language and Imagery in Shakespearean and Stuart Literature*, II, 1019–20.
23. Williams, 'Seamstress', in ibid., III, 1216.
24. Blount, 'Qwacksalver', in *Glossographia* (1656). Medicinal simples are medical preparations that require only one active ingredient.
25. Blount, 'Mountebank', in *Glossographia* (1656).
26. Luise von Flotow and Joan W. Scott, 'Gender Studies and Translation Studies: "Entre braguettes" — Connecting the Disciplines', in *Border Crossings: Translation Studies and Other Disciplines*, ed. by Yves Gambier and Luc van Doorslaer (Amsterdam & Philadelphia: John Benjamins Publishing Company, 2016), pp. 349–73 (p. 366).
27. Bays is a character in Buckingham's *The Rehearsal*: 'Mark that: I Makes 'em both speak *French* to shew their breeding'. George Villiers, Duke of Buckingham, *The Rehearsal* (London: printed for Thomas Dring, 1672, first performed 1671), p. 14 (II.2).
28. The Lord Chamberlain's records include an order dated 4 December 1677 to alter the stage for the French comedians. Contemporary letters also indicate that they performed at court on 18 January 1677/8. See *The London Stage, 1660–1800*, ed. by Van Lennep, Avery, and Scouten, pp. 261, 266–67. See also W. J. Lawrence 'Early French Players in England', *Anglia*, 32 (1909), 61–89 (pp. 83–84). The *Calendar of Treasury Books* shows that a warrant was issued on 12 April 1678 to examine their goods before they were exported to Dieppe, suggesting the actors left London that month. See Nicol, *A History of Restoration Drama, 1660–1700*, p. 253.
29. Janet Todd, '"Pursue that Way of Fooling, and be Damned": Editing Aphra Behn', *Studies in the Novel*, 27.3 (Fall 1995), 304–19 (p. 306).
30. James Wright was an antiquarian and author from Oxfordshire. He was a student at New Inn in London before moving to the Middle Temple in 1670. As a man of letters he had a wide range of interests and became a historian of Jacobean and Caroline theatre. He published several anonymous translations and original works.
31. Wright's manuscript is held in the Folger Shakespeare Library, Washington, DC (MS V.b.220). A hand other than Wright's has curiously recorded the title as 'La Mallad', though the content of the direct translation suggests this is a grammatical error rather than a deliberate ironic adaptation of the title.
32. The edition published by Daniel Elzevir in Amsterdam appeared without a printer's address, but with the Elzevirs' sphere device, as *Le Malade imaginaire, comédie en trois actes meslés de danses et de musique, suivant la Copie imprimée à Paris* ([Amsterdam: Daniel Elzevir], 1674). Unauthorized French editions of the same text falsely used Elzevir's address and included the prologue and *intermèdes* as appendices: *Le Malade imaginaire, comédie en trois actes mélez de danses et de musique* (Amsterdam: Daniel Elzevir [but France], 1674).
33. Hughes, *The Theatre of Aphra Behn*, pp. 106–07.
34. Molière, *Le Malade imaginaire, comédie en trois actes mélez de danses et de musique* (Amsterdam: Daniel Elzevir [but France], 1674), pp. 68–69. Further references are given after quotations in the text.
35. 'La Mallad [Le Malade imaginaire] Translated by Mr Wright', [*c.* 1678?], Washington, DC, Folger Shakespeare Library, MS V.b.220, fol. 15^v. Further references are given after quotations in the text.
36. Hughes, *The Theatre of Aphra Behn*, p. 104.
37. *Daily Courant*, 16 June 1703.
38. Susanna Centlivre, *The Platonick Lady* (London: printed for James Knapton, and Egbert Sanger, 1707), a2^v.
39. See Silke Meyer, 'The Germans as the Alter-Ego of the English?: The German Doctor in Eighteenth-century Debate', *Ethnologia Europaea*, 36.1 (2006), 58–69.
40. This chapter has centred on the way that Molière and his translators lampoon medical figures but the French playwright also satirizes the practice of medicine itself. In *Dom Juan* the titular character draws a parallel between religious belief and faith in medicine in which he suggests that both are futile, leading his servant to ask 'vous êtes aussi impie en Médecine?' (III.1; *OC*, II, 874).

CHAPTER 7

Bourgeoisie and Urbanity

The term *mamamouchi* exists in both French and English and can be used to refer to a mock honour or title, a person who assumes such a title, or someone who misguidedly seeks social elevation. It was a name invented by Molière in *Le Bourgeois gentilhomme* (1670), in which Monsieur Jourdain is fooled into believing that a Grand Turk is conferring an honorary title on him and is made to believe that his daughter's suitor is the Sultan. The name 'Mamamouchi' first appeared in English in Edward Ravenscroft's *The Citizen Turn'd Gentleman* (1672), renamed *Mamamouchi; or, The Citizen turned Gentleman* for the 1674 edition. This play combines two of Molière's *comedies-ballets* in translation, *Monsieur de Pourceaugnac* (1669) and *Le Bourgeois gentilhomme*.[1] It is not surprising that Ravenscroft should choose to combine these plays, because themes of social status and the relative importance of titles and names are common to both.

This chapter will explore the ways in which Ravenscroft and other translators transposed the theme of social relations in the *comédies-ballets* into works that reflected English society of the late seventeenth and early eighteenth century. Ravenscroft's hybrid *The Citizen Turn'd Gentleman* will be considered in relation to John Ozell's *Monsieur de Pourceaugnac; or, Squire Trelooby* (1704), *The Gentleman Cit* (1714), and the 1732 *Select Comedies* translations of the respective Molière plays. The chapter will demonstrate that the main characters' preoccupation with social origin required translators to recontextualize the theme with reference to English geography and locales; in order to do this, however, knowledge of the French cultural allusions in Molière's original plays was of utmost importance.

Bourgeoisie and urbanity are helpful terms of reference in this exploration because they represent the complexities of social status in their very meanings. *Bourgeoisie* is a term that comes from the Old French *borgesie* referring to the citizenry of a town or borough. In seventeenth-century French it came to refer to the professional urban members of the Third Estate and the values supposedly typical of these groups, but when it was first carried over into English in the late sixteenth century the term generally referred to the citizenry of French or continental towns, rather than being fully recontextualized to relate to English townships. The English term 'urbanity' was originally borrowed from the Middle French *urbanité* and the Latin *urbanitas,* the former of which originally referred to the interactions of people in an urban setting and the latter to the courtesy and social refinement supposedly typical of city-dwellers. Both senses lingered in the English uses of the word 'urbanity', along with the occasional sense of the general character of a town.² The nuances of terms relating to social groupings are explored in both *Monsieur de Pourceaugnac* and *Le Bourgeois gentilhomme*, and adapted for specific satirical effects in their first English translations.

What's in a Name?

The importance that socially pretentious characters place on names and titles is ridiculed in the very titles of Molière's plays, which offer an immediate ironic angle. In the play-title *Monsieur de Pourceaugnac*, for example, Molière takes the French word for 'swine' (*pourceau*) and adds a Gascon-Occitan provincial surname-ending (*-gnac*) and a prepositional particle (*de*) that indicates nobility, making the name is a mixture of comically disparate elements. Indeed, the Limousin region from which Pourceaugnac hails was and is well-known for its pig-farming, but this defining feature does not complement the dignified title of *Monsieur*. Even before audiences meet the eponymous character, they are invited to laugh at his name. Nérine, servant to Monsieur de Pourceaugnac's intended bride, expresses disgust for the name in the first scene of the play: 'Le seul nom de Monsieur de Pourceaugnac m'a mis dans une colère effroyable. J'enrage de Monsieur de Pourceaugnac. Quand il n'y aurait que ce nom-là, Monsieur de Pourceaugnac, j'y brûlerai mes Livres' (1.1; OC, II, 204). Nérine feels a strong aversion to Pourceaugnac because her mistress is unwilling to marry him and instead loves Éraste. Her venom also stems from her disdain for his provincial origins as a Limousin; she wonders why he comes to Paris to find a bride rather than simply marrying someone from his own region. Furthermore, her reaction conveys an instinctual disgust for the porcine nature of the name. Names and titles provoke strong reactions in plays that mock the pretensions of individuals who are excessively concerned with status.

In many respects, Monsieur de Pourceaugnac is a prototype of Monsieur Jourdain in *Le Bourgeois gentilhomme*; only a year separates the plays' first performances. The key difference, however, is that Pourceaugnac is a provincial visitor to Paris, whereas Jourdain is a social parvenu within Paris. The name Jourdain, which includes the word *jour*, is suggestive of the everyday and therefore undermines the character's aspirations to be *mondain*, a socialite. The links between names and places are fundamental to the representations of the socially ambitious figures within the plays; the first translators of these works needed to be attuned to this and to adapt both social titles and place-names accordingly. Although social standing and geography are interlinked, this chapter begins by addressing the various ways in which English translators conveyed social status before going on to consider the effects of geographical recontextualization of the plays for new urban environments. These changes in translation were designed to make audiences or readers 'see themselves' in the works, thereby making the translated plays work in self-reflexive ways.

Despite the influx of French terms and vocabulary into English in the late seventeenth century, marks of social status were so deep-rooted in the histories of France and England respectively, that they posed particular problems in translation.

It is worth beginning the exploration of the concept of 'bourgeoisie' by considering the difficulty of translating the title *Le Bourgeois gentilhomme* into English. Olive Classe notes that:

> *Le Bourgeois Gentilhomme* is an oxymoronic title that has caused no end of trouble, since a literal translation into English could not carry the same precise connotations as the French original and might nowadays seem offensive to liberal ears. Whether Ravenscroft's *The Citizen Turn'd Gentleman* quite caught the tone in 1672 is doubtful, though the 1675 variant *Mamamouchi: or the Citizen Turn'd Gentleman*, has a more humorous irony to commend it.[3]

The 'same precise connotations' of the title will be analysed in the following sections. Why the lengthier title should be more ironic is unclear, other than emphasizing the easy and futile assumption of dubious social titles within the action of the play. The nineteenth-century translator and teacher Henri Van Laun, writing in his *Works of Molière* (1875–76), offers some views on the early eighteenth-century translations of the play-title *Le Bourgeois gentilhomme*:

> It is difficult to give the correct meaning of the French title, *Le Bourgeois Gentilhomme*. Mr. Ozell translates it, *The Gentleman Cit*, which to my mind gives the idea of a gentleman who was also a citizen. In the translation of the select Comedies, published in 1732, [...] this play is called *The Cit turned Gentleman*, which is not correct, for Monsieur Jourdain never became a gentleman. Besides, in Molière's time the word *Gentilhomme* indicated a certain noble descent or rank, and was also bestowed upon the holders of some offices [...]. M. Jourdain was not a noble by manners or birth, but does his best to imitate one.[4]

Van Laun is wrong in his definition of *gentilhomme* because it was a title conferred only by birth. He also reads the verb 'turned' too rigidly; it is possible to argue that the 'citizen' might have turned gentleman temporarily, and in an imaginary rather than a literal sense. The word 'turned' could be read as suggestive of the character's theatrical gentility. Van Laun attempts to spell this out by opting for *The Citizen Who Apes the Nobleman*. It is curious that Van Laun, translating in the late nineteenth century, should retain the term 'citizen' rather than attempting to incorporate the English term 'bourgeois'. By the nineteenth century the word 'bourgeois' had come to be used generally in English to describe the middle classes, sometimes with disparaging connotations intensified by use of the term by Karl Marx; perhaps the word's increasingly politicized connotations dissuaded Van Laun. The term 'bourgeois', however, could mean different things to different people in seventeenth-century France, depending on the particular value they placed on social labels; this complexity contributes to the comedy and satire in Molière's comedies about socially pretentious characters.

C'est un bon Bourgeois

In contrast to the French terms that have been described in previous chapters, *bourgeois* was not carried into common English in the years immediately following the Restoration. It was, in English, used to refer specifically to citizens of a French town; only in the late eighteenth century did it start to be associated with the middle class of any country and with shop-keeping or mercantile groups. In late seventeenth-century French, *bourgeois* referred to town-dwellers, though it was used to distinguish them from the peasant classes below and the noble classes above. Antoine Furetière's 1690 *Dictionnaire universel* illustrates the various meanings of the noun and adjective, with reference to Molière's use of it:

> Nom collectif. L'assemblage du peuple qui habite dans une ville. [...]
> BOURGEOIS, se dit aussi de chaque particulier habitant de la ville. Ce Marchand, cet Advocat est un bon *bourgeois*.
> BOURGEOIS, se dit aussi pour marquer les gens du tiers Estat, à la distinction des Gentilshommes et des Ecclesiastiques, qui joüissent de plusieurs privileges dont le peuple ne joüit pas. Les charges de l'Estat sont portées par le *bourgeois*. On dit en ce sens, Un tel est Gentilhomme, et un tel n'est que *bourgeois*.
> BOURGEOIS, se dit quelquefois en mauvaise part par opposition à un homme de la Cour, pour signifier un homme peu galant, peu spirituel, qui vit et raisonne à la maniere du bas peuple. C'est un franc *bourgeois*. Molière a dit plaisamment dans les Femmes sçavantes, Un corps composé d'atomes plus *bourgeois*. Le Gentilhomme *bourgeois*.[5]

The blurred distinction between collectivity and individuality in these dictionary entries is of interest in the exploration of social terms in comedy. While Molière's socially ambitious characters seek to mark themselves out as important individuals, they attempt to do so by shunning one group and joining another, supposedly more select group. They therefore have to be judged according to the standards of the new group, and the ensuing mockery is at the core of the comedy.

In *Le Bourgeois gentilhomme* Madame Jourdain tries to curb her husband's pretentions by pointing out that both his father and her father were tradesmen, *marchands*. Unsurprisingly, she is unsuccessful in her attempt:

> MADAME JOURDAIN Descendons-nous tous deux que de bonne Bourgeoisie?
> MONSIEUR JOURDAIN Voilà pas le coup de langue.
> MADAME JOURDAIN Et votre Père, n'était-il pas Marchand aussi bien que le mien?
> MONSIEUR JOURDAIN Peste soit de la Femme. Elle n'y a jamais manqué. Si votre Père a été Marchand, tant pis pour lui; mais pour le mien, ce sont des malavisés qui disent cela. Tout ce que j'ai à vous dire, moi, c'est que je veux avoir un Gendre Gentilhomme. (III.12; *OC*, II, 309)

Madame Jourdain's reference to their families' social status as 'bonne Bourgeoisie' demonstrates pride in her background, though her use of the term can cause confusion. Seventeenth-century dictionary definitions do not provide clear explanations of what her wording might mean. Some clues are offered in a 1791 article by an anonymous revolutionary journalist which claims that before the revolution there existed several types of bourgeoisie in Paris: *la petite*, *la haute*, and *la bonne*. The latter two, the author explains, were often confused. While the *haute bourgeoisie* was aristocratic in manner, it was not as energetically loyal to the monarchy as the nobility. People such as magistrates and other officials were amongst this group. The *bonne bourgeoisie*, however, was a more open, self-assured group that included businesses that took pride in fulfilling transactions, as well as committed lawyers, some men of letters, artists, and some doctors. The *petite bourgeoisie* was a larger group that included merchants, artisans, clerks, and some writers.[6] The term *petit bourgeois* was not especially derogatory until the emergence of Marxist theory, but Richelet's 1680 dictionary notes that it could be used to describe an unremarkable bourgeois 'qui ne fait pas figure'.[7] So the Jourdain family's mercantile heritage is viewed by Madame Jourdain as *bonne bourgeoisie* and by Monsieur Jourdain as *petite bourgeoisie*, though he rejects the term *bourgeoisie* in relation to himself and instead tries to deflect attention towards his aspirations for his 'noble' future.

The eighteenth-century account provided above of the different types of bourgeoisie is of course coloured by the revolutionary stance of its author, but reveals the difficulty of describing the early modern bourgeoisie in Paris. Charles Mazouer summarizes the seventeenth-century types of bourgeoisie that have been identified by historians:

> *Haute bourgeoisie* — celle qui s'occupe de la finance, du négoce, du grand commerce ou est en charge des emplois les plus importants du service royal — une *moyenne bourgeoisie* — titulaires des offices, rentiers, membres des professions libérales, marchands aisés — et une *petite bourgeoisie* — celle de la boutique ou petite négoce. L'existence des bourgeois, qui sont gens des villes, est fondée sur le travail réellement exercé, et leur travail les enrichit; il enrichit aussi le pays.[8]

Similarities between the categories drawn up by the eighteenth-century journalist and those outlined by Mazouer are evident. The *moyenne bourgeoisie* equates to the *bonne bourgeoisie* in terms of the social roles of its members. The term *bonne bourgeoisie* as used by Madame Jourdain also implies stability, reliability, and lack of pretention. In Furetière's 1690 dictionary, for example, the term *bon bourgeois* is included in various entries that suggest it is a metaphor for being on middle or solid ground: 'Cet homme est un bon bourgeois qui ne fait ni bien, ni *mal* à personne', 'C'est un bon bourgeois qui a un esprit paisible, qui vit bien avec tout le monde', 'C'est un bon bourgeois qui vit de ses rentes'.[9] In contrast to the positive connotations of the *bonne bourgeoisie*, however, the qualifier *bon* can also be used alongside *bourgeois* to mean 'a plain old bourgeois', as when the upper-class trickster Dorante describes Monsieur Jourdain as a 'bon bourgeois assez ridicule [...] dans toutes ses manières' (3.16). It is precisely the unremarkable, middling status of the *bon bourgeois* that Monsieur Jourdain disdains, and so this would be a cutting insult to him. Little wonder, then, that the comment is muttered as an aside. Given the complexity of the term *bourgeois* and its connotations in seventeenth-century France, specifically English terms had to be employed for the translations of the social groupings described in Molière's plays.

'Poor old silly Citt'

The first translators of *Le Bourgeois gentilhomme* chose the term 'citizen' to denote the bourgeois origins of Monsieur Jourdain. The closeness in meaning of the terms 'bourgeois' and 'citizen' is suggested in Guy Miège's entry for 'city' in his 1677 French-English dictionary: 'Ville, Cité. [...] Citizen, bourgeois, citoyen. Citizen-like, en bourgeois'.[10] The term 'bourgeois', when used in seventeenth- and early eighteenth-century English, referred to the inhabitants of French and occasionally other continental towns. The first translation of *Le Bourgeois gentilhomme*, however, appeared in Ravenscroft's *The Citizen Turn'd Gentleman*, in which the scene is changed from Paris to London. Ravenscroft therefore needed to choose a term that conveyed the particular bourgeois social type in a London setting. 'Citizen' could be used both to describe an ordinary town-dweller and to distinguish him from a landed nobleman or a labourer; the term could also be shortened to 'cit', or 'citt', which was used to refer derogatively to a tradesman. The abbreviated form is adopted in Ravenscroft's *The Citizen Turn'd Gentleman*, in which Madame Jourdain's confrontation with her husband is adapted into an exchange between 'Mr Jorden' and his daughter.[11] Lucia argues that her grandfather brought up Mr Jorden according to his means and station. Mr Jorden responds scathingly:

> Your Grand-father! alas poor old silly Citt, I cannot but laugh to think what an Asse he was to imagine that I would stand sneaking in my Shop all my life with my Cap in my hand, crying, What do you lack, Gentlemen, choice of good Silkes: I'd have you to know *Lucia,* I have no such Mechanick Spirit in me. (p. 8)

'Citizen', then, and 'cit' or 'citt' especially, connotes a trader and a shopkeeper. Ironically, Mr Jorden is so pompous that he likens shop-keeping to 'mechanic' work, which is etymologically linked to 'machinery', and is suggestive of manual labour rather than to a bourgeois occupation. The main appeal of the term 'silly Citt' is probably its alliteration, though the term 'silly' could be used to refer to lowly status and simple-mindedness as a well as general foolishness, so might be applied readily to citizen-tradesmen by those of higher social standing or those who sought higher social status.[12]

The expression 'silly Citt' has a similar impact to 'bon bourgeois' when the latter is uttered in a condescending tone. The irony is that while Jourdain brands other people a 'bourgeois', or, in English translation, a 'cit', other characters label *him* the same way. Dorante's description of Jourdain as 'un bon Bourgeois assez ridicule [...] dans toutes ses manières' (III.16; *OC*, II, 313) is translated in similar ways in all three of the first translations of *Le Bourgeois gentilhomme*. In *The Citizen Turn'd Gentleman* Ravenscroft translates it literally when 'Trickmore' mutters that Mr Jorden is 'as good a ridiculous Cit as e'er was seen' (p. 48). Ravenscroft appears not to detect that 'bon bourgeois' is used in an ironic and condescending sense in the original French and therefore translates 'bon' as an intensifier rather than as a component of the social label. In Ozell's *The Gentleman Cit* in *The Works of Monsieur de Molière*, however, the abbreviated term 'cit' is understood to be derogatory enough; the phrase 'bon bourgeois assez ridicule' simply becomes 'a ridiculous Cit' (IV, 266). The translators of *The Cit Turn'd Gentleman* in the 1732 *Select Comedies* rely on a literal translation style in rendering the description: 'a downright Cit, ridiculous enough [...] in his whole Behaviour' (II, 155). The term 'cit' as opposed to 'citizen' is used much more frequently in the early eighteenth-century translations of *Le Bourgeois gentilhomme* compared to the sections translated for *The Citizen Turn'd Gentleman*. This is partly because the translation of *Le Bourgeois gentilhomme* is not complete in Ravenscroft's version because he mixes it in with sections translated from *Monsieur de Pourceaugnac*. Furthermore, the titles of the latter both include the term 'cit' rather than the more neutral 'citizen'. The term 'cit' is absent from many late seventeenth-century English dictionaries, though it does appear in the first English dictionary of slang in 1699.[13] By the mid-eighteenth century, however, it seems to have been established as a term of derision: Samuel Johnson's 1755 dictionary defines 'cit' as 'an inhabitant of a city, in an ill sense. A pert low Townsman; a pragmatical Tradesman'.[14] The use of the term as a label for the English reincarnations of Monsieur Jourdain is suitably ironic given the character's distaste for the meaning it conveys.

Certain characters, however, do not view their bourgeois status in such negative terms. As explored, Madame Jourdain has a healthier view of her origins in the 'bonne bourgeoisie'; she is absent from Ravenscroft's *The Citizen Turn'd Gentleman*, though her viewpoint is offered through that of her daughter, Lucia. In early eighteenth-century versions of *Le Bourgeois gentilhomme* the term *cit* is played off against the term *citizen*. When Molière's Monsieur Jourdain confronts his wife, he claims that his frequenting of noble circles is 'plus beau que de hanter votre Bourgeoisie' (III.3; *OC*, II, 293). This is rendered in Ozell's *Works* as "tis better than conversing with the Cits' (p. 248) and in the *Select Comedies* as 'that's much better than herding with your Cit' (p. 89). *Cit* could be used to describe a body of citizens rather than just individuals and was often used in opposition to the court body. When Madame Jourdain points out that both she and her husband descend from the 'bonne bourgeoisie', the early eighteenth-century translations include the term *citizen* rather than *cit*. Thus, in Ozell's version Mrs Jordan describes their ancestors as 'good Citizens' (p. 262) and in the *Select Comedies* she describes them as 'plain citizens' (p. 141), both of which point to the idea of reliability and solidity that the term 'bonne bourgeoisie' can evoke. The apparent plainness of the citizen, however, is the cause of Jordan's aversion to the role; his interest lies elsewhere.

Bourgeois: gentilhomme?

A *bourgeois* is identified not only by what he is but also by what he is not. In an early modern social context, *bourgeois* is not a *gentilhomme*, which is why the title *Le Bourgeois gentilhomme* is comically oxymoronic. A *gentilhomme* is a *noble de race*. As Furetière's 1690 dictionary states, a *gentilhomme* is an 'homme noble d'extraction, qui ne doit point sa Noblesse ni à sa charge, ni aux Lettres du Prince'.[15] The close equivalent in English is 'gentleman'. Blount's *Glossographia* records that 'gentleman' 'seems to be confounded of two words, the one French (gentile, id est honestus, vel honesto loco natus;) the other Saxon (mon) as if you would say, a man well born'.[16] Blount based his entry on the definition provided in John Cowell's *The Interpreter; or, Book Containing the Signification of Words* (1607). Cowell's definition is more detailed and includes the insight that:

> The Frenchmen call him also gentil houme, so that gentlemen bee those, whom their blood and race doth make noble and knowne. [...] But by the course and custome of England, Nobilitie is either major or minor; the greater

contained all titles and degrees from Knights upward: the lesser all from Barons downward.[17]

Cowell goes on to point out that some individuals can lose the inherited title of 'gentleman' if they fall into poverty, or can regain the title by dint of virtue and fortune. Furthermore, a herald can sometimes allow a prosperous man to start carrying the title of 'gentleman'. So although the etymology of the title 'gentleman' refers to noble birth, it could in English be applied more generally to individuals of social distinction. The English reincarnations of Monsieur Jourdain are more realistic in their ambitions than their French model. The translators, however, used various terms to indicate that the anglicized Jourdain is out of his social depth.

Monsieur Jourdain refers to his noble acquaintances (and exploiters) as 'Gens de Qualité' or 'personnes de qualité'. He aims to become a *personne de qualité* himself, and his first step towards doing so is to dress like one. In all but one instance the complete English translations from the early eighteenth century render the term *gens de qualité* as 'people of Quality', meaning people of high birth or rank. On occasion it is translated simply as 'Quality' to denote the collective. Given the general sense of 'gentleman' in seventeenth- and eighteenth-century English compared to the French related term *gentilhomme*, the inclusion of the term 'people of Quality' in translations of *Le Bourgeois gentilhomme* helps to emphasize the character's misguided ambition in seeking to join a specific social group which *he* defines and labels as 'high quality'. Audiences are invited to consider that the character's quality of judgement is poor.

In Ravenscroft's hybrid play *The Citizen Turn'd Gentleman*, Mr Jorden is apparently au fait with the technicalities of genealogy in relation to gentility. This is not least because his plan is to marry off his daughter Lucia to one 'Sir Simon Softhead', an adaptation of the character Monsieur de Pourceaugnac. Ravenscroft's hybridizing process is facilitated by his addition of the character of 'Young Jorden', Lucia's half-brother, whose status is explained to her in detail by Mr Jorden:

> Your Brother — puh — he can ne'r be a Gentleman. I was born a Citizen my self, and his Mother was a Citizen born, he was not allyed to gentility on either side, [...] but for you daughter, because you are a gentlewoman by your Mothers side, I have provided better; you shall be married to the *Suffolk* Knight that will be here anon. [...] if he comes time enough. (p. 9)

This passage links the plot of *Monsieur de Pourceaugnac* with the plot of *Le Bourgeois gentilhomme*. It has to be placed early in the play, so Mr Jorden has not yet heard a false report from 'Trickmore' that Mr Jorden *père* was a gentleman. Although the English term 'gentleman' was more flexible than the term *gentilhomme*, gentle birth was still considered the most highly valued qualification for the title, hence Mr Jorden's reasoning. He goes on to explain that he longs 'to have a Gentleman, and a Knight, for a Son-in-law' thereby expanding upon the original French 'je veux avoir un Gendre Gentilhomme' (III.12; *OC*, II, 309). Ravenscroft therefore introduces yet another title into the social mix of the play. This is in order to distinguish between the urban social scene of which the Jordens are a part, and the country environment from which the 'Suffolk Knight' has hailed.

The Gentleman is a Knight

In many respects *Monsieur de Pourceaugnac* is a forerunner to *Le Bourgeois gentilhomme*. The main difference is that Pourceaugnac is an outsider in Parisian society; he is a provincial, supposedly a 'Gentilhomme Limosin'. Pourceaugnac makes a point of emphasizing his status as a *gentilhomme* when he first arrives in the bustling city. Sbrigani, employed to prevent the proposed marriage between Pourceaugnac and the young Julie, is there to greet him and ready to trick him through flattery. Sbrigani arranges for a group of town-dwellers to mock the provincial so that he can pretend to come forward in Pourceaugnac's defence:

SBRIGANI	Qu'est-ce que c'est, Messieurs? que veut dire cela? à qui en avez-vous? faut-il se moquer ainsi des honnêtes Étrangers qui arrivent ici?
M. DE POURCEAUGNAC	Voilà un Homme raisonnable celui-là.
	[...]
SBRIGANI	Apprenez à connaître les Gens.
M. DE POURCEAUGNAC	C'est bien dit.
SBRIGANI	Monsieur est d'une mine à respecter.
M. DE POURCEAUGNAC	Cela est vrai.
SBRIGANI	Personne de condition.
M. DE POURCEAUGNAC	Oui, Gentilhomme Limosin.
SBRIGANI	Homme d'esprit.
M. DE POURCEAUGNAC	Qui a étudié en Droit.
SBRIGANI	Il vous fait trop d'honneur, de venir dans votre ville.

(1.3; *OC*, II, 206–07)

This exchange introduces the 'Étranger' and also demonstrates how Sbrigani is trying to win Pourceaugnac's trust. It also makes Pourceaugnac declare his origins and the way he defines himself in society. Sbrigani's observation that he is a 'personne de condition' is probing. Labelling someone *personne de condition* was akin to labelling him *personne de qualité*, but was often used with a qualifying adjective, as in the term *personne de condition servile*. 'Personne de condition' therefore includes an element of ambiguity that Pourceaugnac is quick to remove by stating that he is a 'Gentilhomme Limosin', a native gentleman of the Limousin region. In Richelet's 1680 dictionary the entry for *condition* states that it means 'Qualité' and that 'le mot de condition, en ce sens, n'a point de pluriel et est moins usité que celui de *qualité*. [C'est un homme de condition. C'est un fat de condition, on dit plutôt *c'est un fat de qualité*]'.[18] Pourceaugnac's 'condition', however, is called into question throughout the play.

The terms *gentilhomme* and *personne de qualité* and their cognates are not used as frequently in *Monsieur de Pourceaugnac* as in *Le Bourgeois gentilhomme*. The references, however, are charged with significance because it is suggested that Monsieur de Pourceaugnac is feigning his status as *gentilhomme*. When Sbrigani plans for two women to accuse Pourceaugnac of bigamy, the provincial *gentilhomme* responds with a detailed legal defence. This prompts Sbrigani to respond that he must be a practising lawyer, to which Pourceaugnac responds with 'je suis gentilhomme', claiming he simply recalls what he has read in books (Act II, scene 10), despite having already mentioned in Act I, scene 3, that he studied law. He also reveals that the threat of being hanged concerns him because were that to happen to him he would lose his reputation as a *gentilhomme*, not because he would perish (Act III, scene 2). The comic climax of Pourceaugnac's ordeal occurs when Sbrigani encourages him to dress as a woman in order to evade the officials. Sbrigani cheekily throws back at Pourceaugnac the latter's own term when he says that in disguise he looks like a 'Femme de condition' (III.2; *OC,* II, 241). Pourceaugnac seems to betray his status when he claims that he is confident he can ape the language and manners of a 'Personne de qualité' because he has seen 'les Personnes du bel air' (III.2; *OC,* II, 242), people who carry themselves well and in accordance with their high status. The distanced perspective from which Pourceaugnac makes this comment suggests that he does not really count himself amongst their number.

How, then, were the first English translators to carry across all the subtleties of meaning contained in these social labels? As explained, the term 'gentleman' could be used more flexibly in English than in French, though given a clear context it could be understood as referring to native nobility. The first translation of *Monsieur de Pourceaugnac* appeared in hybrid form with *Le Bourgeois gentilhomme*, so the designations of both socially pretentious characters could become confusing. Ravenscroft lighted on the term 'Knight' to describe his version of Monsieur de Pourceaugnac, who 'Mr Jorden' believes is a true knight called 'Sir Simon Softhead'. Ravenscroft was perhaps inspired by Sbrigani's tongue-in-cheek reference to the possibility that Pourceaugnac's title of *écuyer* could be removed were he tried for bigamy. According to Thomas Corneille's 1694 dictionary, an *écuyer* was a 'Titre qui marque la qualité de Gentilhomme. C'estoit autrefois une dignité fort considerable, et qui venant immediatement aprés celle de Chevalier, estoit un degré pour y parvenir. Cela estoit cause que les Chevaliers faisoient ordinairement leurs fils Ecuyers'.[19] So Ravenscroft 'promotes' his version of Pourceaugnac to a *chevalier*/Knight rather than an *écuyer*/Squire, but this is in order to keep Mr Jorden's ambition outrageous in wishing to marry Lucia to Sir Simon. Furthermore, the feudal origins of the title 'Knight' meant that it could be associated with specifically country gentlemen. A 'Knight of the Shire' was a gentleman who represented a country or shire in Parliament. Within the social world of the play, Sir Simon is meant to be a stereotypical representative of the county of Suffolk, thereby corresponding with the Limousin origin of Pourceaugnac.

In Ravenscroft's *The Citizen Turn'd Gentleman* the first exchange between Sbrigani and Pourceaugnac is adapted to focus on the concept of Sir Simon as a knight:

> TRICK. Go, go home, and learn better breeding.
> SIR SIM. That's good counsel, and take it y'ad best.
> TRICK. The Gentleman is a Knight.
> SIR SIM. Aye.
> TRICK. The heir of an honourable Family.
> SIR SIM. Aye.
> TRICK. His Ancesters deserv'd well of his Country.
> SIR SIM. Aye. (p. 21)

Pourceaugnac's recasting as a knight reinforces the divide between town and country. It also allows for some extra ridiculing of Softhead, whom Trickmore encourages to act as a 'Knight errant' in order to trick him into marrying the 'damsel in distress', 'Betty Trickmore' (a character added to ease the hybridization of the two Molière plays). In the parallel plot-thread Mr Jorden is also given the false promise of a knighthood. So Sir Simon's obsession with his supposed status as a knight and Mr Jorden's hopes to become a knight help to intensify the references to being a *gentilhomme* in the source text and to emphasize the characters' ineffectual attempts at social climbing.

Your Squireship

In *Le Bourgeois gentilhomme* the servant Nicole supports Madame Jourdain's assertion that it is better to marry a well-turned-out rich man than a poor, unimpressive *gentilhomme* by drawing on her own observation: 'Cela est vrai. Nous avons le Fils du Gentilhomme de notre Village, qui est le plus grand Malitorne et le plus sot Dadais que j'aie jamais vu' (III.12 ; *OC*, II, 309). In the *Select Comedies* of 1732 this is translated with more licence than these translators generally allow themselves: 'That's very true. We have a young 'Squire in our Town, who is the most awkward Looby, the veriest Driv'ler that I ever set eyes on' (p. 143). 'Squire', a shortened form of 'esquire', was originally a title to designate a young nobleman who attended on a knight. In later usage it came to be used as a title for a country gentleman or a principal landowner in a village or district. Additionally, it could refer to a man who waited upon ladies as a gallant or lover. In the context of Nicola's comment about the unsuitability of her village's high-born gentleman as a potential husband, the term 'squire' can be interpreted with some irony. So it seems appropriate that 'le fils d'un gentilhomme' should be translated as 'squire' in this section of *Le Bourgeois gentilhomme*. The translators of *The Cit Turn'd Gentleman* in the *Select Comedies* may also have been inspired to translate this section with reference to *Squire Lubberly*, the title of their translation of *Monsieur de Pourceaugnac*. The term 'squire' also features in the first complete translation of *Monsieur de Pourceaugnac*, the title of which was translated as *Squire Trelooby* in the version by Congreve, Vanbrugh, and Walsh performed in 1704, and in the printed edition believed to be translated by John Ozell. Whereas the acted version does not survive in print, the latter version appeared as a single text in 1704 and was reprinted in Ozell's *The Works of Monsieur de Molière* in 1714. It is likely that Ozell adopted the character-names used in the acted version in order to exploit its success on the London stage. But the names also demonstrate the way in which the social titles in Molière's play were carried into an English context.

Molière's Monsieur de Pourceaugnac is tricked to such a degree that he falls out with his intended bride's father, the merchant Oronte. In *Squire Trelooby* Oronte is renamed 'Tradewell' in order to emphasize the supposed difference in their social status. The designation 'squire', however, could be used comically or ironically in some circumstances and this is put to use in translation. When Tradewell and Trelooby have both been given false information and are arguing over their status, the merchant sarcastically refers to his opponent as 'your Squireship' (p. 35), thereby calling into doubt his title. Trelooby responds with a great deal of personal pride by pompously referring to himself as '*Leonard Trelooby* Esq.' (p. 37). These variations are all inspired by Sbrigani's reference to Pourceaugnac's 'Titre d'Écuyer' in Molière's play (III.2; *OC*, II, 242). Pourceaugnac himself acknowledges that 'Ce n'est pas tant la peur de la mort qui me fait fuir, que de ce qu'il est fâcheux à un Gentilhomme d'être pendu, et qu'une preuve comme celle-là ferait tort à nos Titres de Noblesse' (III.2; *OC*, II, 242). This section is translated with an additional pun in *Squire Trelooby* when the eponymous character envisages this loss as a 'Blot in one's Scutcheon' (p. 47), a stain on one's coat of arms, one's family name, and heraldry, and thus a figurative term used to describe a besmirched reputation. Pourceaugnac's concern about the possible transience of his title belies his confidence in his social status but confirms his status as a figure of ridicule in the dramatic context.

Town and Country

Monsieur de Pourceaugnac and *Le Bourgeois gentilhomme* are both set in Paris and this urban society has an impact on the way that individuals react to each other. Although Monsieur de Pourceaugnac presents himself as a gentleman, he is still treated as an outsider and complains constantly of the busy urban scene in Paris. Monsieur Jourdain belongs in urban Paris but is anxious to climb up to a new social sphere within it. The concept of urbanity is helpful in exploring the comic techniques employed to represent these tensions because it can refer both to urban life and the manner of behaviour deemed most worthy in a town setting. The social relations of city-dwellers are the basis of the satire of both plays. In order for them to be carried into English with the same satirical effect, the urbanity of the settings and character behaviour had to be adapted in translation.

In *Monsieur de Pourceaugnac* there is a clear divide between Paris and the provinces. From the first scene Pourceaugnac is presented as an interloper who is to be driven away. He has arrived by a slow and inexpensive coach, a mode of transport that calls into question his supposed status as a *gentilhomme*. Pourceaugnac himself no sooner arrives than he wishes to be rid of the city again, describing it as 'la sotte Ville' (I.3; *OC*, II, 206). His provincial origin in Limoges is highlighted at frequent intervals. At first the 'small talk' regarding his background is a means for his rival to win his trust:

ÉRASTE	Comment est-ce que vous nommez à Limoges ce lieu où l'on se promène?
M. DE POURCEAUGNAC	Le cimetière des Arènes?
ÉRASTE	Justement; c'est où je passais de si douces heures à jouir de votre agréable conversation. Vous ne vous remettez pas tout cela?
M. DE POURCEAUGNAC	Excusez-moi, je me le remets. (*À Sbrigani.*) Diable emporte, si je m'en souviens.
SBRIGANI	Il y a cent choses comme cela qui passent de la tête.
ÉRASTE	Embrassez-moi donc, je vous prie, et resserrons les nœuds de notre ancienne amitié. (I.4; *OC*, II, 210)

The comedy lies in the audience's awareness that Éraste, with Sbrigani's assistance, is fishing for information about specific locales of Limoges in order to give the impression that he is an old acquaintance. This also weakens Pourceaugnac's faith in himself as he understandably fails to remember this 'acquaintance'. 'Le cimetière des Arènes' was a cemetery on the site of the old Roman amphitheatre and was a popular place for walking in Limoges, hence Pourceaugnac's quick response. This exchange represents the beginning of Pourceaugnac's 'public trial' performed in the name of entertainment for the tricksters and the audience of the play. Much of the comedy lies in the characters' exploitation of the specific 'background' information that they gain about the outsider. The audience is in on the trick. This is why *Monsieur de Pourceaugnac* is recontextualized to a significant degree in its first translations into English; it plays on the pleasure of local familiarity and the displeasure of unfamiliarity.

In Ravenscroft's *The Citizen Turn'd Gentleman* Pourceaugnac is transformed into Sir Simon Softhead, a 'Suffolk Knight' visiting London in search of a wife. The exact place from which he hails is not revealed until the scene in which Cleverwit ('Éraste' in the original) tries to persuade Softhead that he is an old friend. After enquiring about the people at the local hostelry in 'Berry' (Bury St Edmunds), Cleverwit asks where they used to walk. Softhead replies with the comically predictable 'the *Green*' as if this is a remarkable revelation. The comedy lies in the gradual pinpointing of a familiar locale and the way that shared mundane experience can engender trust (however misplaced it may be in this situation). There is perhaps an extra significance in choosing Bury St Edmunds as Softhead's place of origin: not only was it a major town in largely rural Suffolk, but it had also been the site of several witch trials and hangings. Softhead's fear of hanging (because it would be 'below the dignity of Knighthood', p. 77) is all the more comical, and possibly resonant, given the knowledge that he comes from Bury. Unlike the French original, Softhead is not accused of bigamy, but of trying to evade hanging after a quarrel with Mr Jorden and 'Young Jorden'. Softhead is persuaded that he has killed 'Young Jorden' in a quarrel he has had with Mr Jorden over his supposed debts to some 'Norwich merchants'. This episode is inspired by the quarrel between Oronte and Monsieur de Pourceaugnac, in which the latter is accused of owing money to some Flemish merchants. Ravenscroft localizes his translation by making reference to the interactions of characters from a specifically East Anglian context (Norwich held a major market for the whole area from the eleventh century on). While the recontextualization is a way for Ravenscroft to put his own stamp on the work, it also contributes to the firm and comic divide drawn between the urban life of London and the supposedly mundane concerns of nearby rural areas.

A recontextualizing process occurs to an even greater degree in the next translation of *Monsieur de Pourceaugnac*, *Squire Trelooby*. Squire Trelooby's name is inspired by the Cornish mining term 'treloobing', the act of stirring the earth of tin in a slime-pit so that the ore can settle to the bottom. In the English translation, then, the French swine-based name of the protagonist becomes slime-based. Trelooby's origins are made explicitly clear in Nerina's tirade against him in the first scene. She exclaims that her mistress Julia is not 'made for a Cornish Hug' (p. 2). This is a comic 'elaboration in translation' of Nérine's observation that Julie is not 'faite pour un Limosin' (1.1; *OC*, II, 204). A 'Cornish Hug' is a squeezing grip in wrestling, a particular 'lock' used by Cornish wrestlers. The image is intended to bring to mind a provincial brute. The English Nerina's enhanced colourful language is also evident in the translation when the comment 'nous renverrons à Limoges Monsieur de Pourceaugnac' (1.1; *OC*, II, 204) is rendered 'I'll send him to the Land's end again, — or the Devil's Arse i'th'Peak — Squire *Trelooby*!' (p. 3). The pun on 'Land's end' works in both a metaphorical and a literal sense, given the squire's origins. The latter location is an impetuous bawdy addition from Nerina, who refers to the colloquial name of a famous cavern in the Peak District. From the outset, the aim of the urban characters is to send the country outsider packing.

In translating *Monsieur de Pourceaugnac* Ozell is at pains to identify geography in order to present Squire Trelooby as a native of an isolated corner of the country that in itself is a source of mockery. In Molière's play, when Éraste begins to trick Pourceaugnac, he claims that 'Il n'y a pas un Pourceaugnac à Limoges que je ne connaisse depuis le plus grand jusques au plus petit' (1.4; *OC*, II, 209). In *Squire Trelooby*, 'Lovewell' comments that 'There is n't a *Trelooby* at Penzance in the Hundred of *Penwith* in the County of *Cornwall*, but I know 'em from the first to the last' (p. 8). In Molière's original, Éraste aims to flatter Pourceaugnac's ego by suggesting that his family is very influential in Limoges. The same effect is present in Lovewell's observation, but the added hyperbole lays extra emphasis on the idea that Trelooby has come from a faraway place by giving him a suggestion of parochial pride. The imagined scene is narrowed even further in the exchange about the popular walking place, here a 'fine long Walk in *Penzance*' which Trelooby reliably informs is called '*Church-lane*' (p. 9). All of these exchanges are intended to entertain a London audience or reader delighting in the references to localized detail.

Regional Accents and Local Colour

In Molière's *Monsieur de Pourceaugnac* there are numerous characters who represent regional stereotypes, though they are part of Sbrigani's mockery of Pourceaugnac. These stereotypes are changed in *Squire Trelooby* to be comical to English audiences. Thus, the Flemish merchant of the original is changed to a French merchant in *Squire Trelooby*, thereby allowing for the type of French-accented English that recurs frequently in English translations of Molière.[20] Lucette, the 'feinte Gasconne' who falsely claims she is married to Pourceaugnac, becomes 'A *Woman with 2 children*' who claims Trelooby is her husband (p. 38). Nérine, disguised as a *Picarde* (II.8; *OC*, II, 235), becomes '*A North-Country-Woman*' who is concerned about her 'poor bairn' (p. 38). When Trelooby denies the marriages, the northern woman claims that 'Aw the Noorth roong of it Neeght and Deay' and the other woman claims that 'All the South assisted at my Wedding' (p. 40). The trickster-women in both the original and the translation aim to suggest that the provincial had 'sown his wild oats' far and wide.

Beyond the joke being played on Pourceaugnac/Trelooby, the various cod accents employed are intended to provoke laughter through mimicking identifiable regional accents. Philip S. Wadsworth notes that Molière's use of foreign accents and regional dialects derives from Italian comedy and that *Monsieur de Pourceaugnac* is full of sound effects:

> Strange-sounding French is particularly plentiful in the mystifications throughout the last two acts [...]. The intruder from Limousin, who may himself have a rustic accent, is hounded by all sorts of people who speak in exaggerated dialects [...] the two shrill women [Lucette and Nérine], each one claiming Pourceaugnac as her husband, have a barbarous pronunciation.[21]

Pourceaugnac's speech, however, is written in standard French throughout, allowing for the interpretation that that he is suppressing his provincial accent. Recent scholarship has argued that Molière's use of dialect is a celebration of the plurality of ways of speaking that responds to seventeenth-century debates about standardizing pronunciation; the dialects are not considered comically barbarous in themselves but rather contrast with Pourceaugnac's slavish following of convention.[22] In *Squire Trelooby* the translation of the women's false claims in Act II, scene 8, works slightly differently. Neither woman speaks in a Cornish dialect nor in the Cornish language to emphasize Trelooby's pretension. Instead, one woman is given a 'North-Country' English accent, apparently with a north-eastern twang; the dialect words are shared by several northern regions so cannot be ascribed to a particular area:[23]

> I WOMAN   We ha been teed together these tweavle Month
> II WOMAN And I have been his Wife these Seven Years —
> I WOMAN   Aw the Toon kens it well.
> II WOMAN And all my Country knows it — . (p. 40)

The similar content of their expressions means that 'Woman II' almost provides a translation of 'Woman I''s northern dialect, thereby heightening the pantomimic effect. The dramatic irony, by which the audience understands that the women are play-acting within a play, is also highlighted by the contrast in accents.

The translators of the *Select Comedies* of 1732 pride themselves in staying as close to the original French as possible. They keep the setting of *Monsieur de Pourceaugnac/ Squire Lubberly* as Paris and do not change the identities of the townspeople in disguise. Yet a few localized references are absorbed into the translation. When 'Squire Lubberly' first appears on stage he exclaims 'Eh, ye Cocknies, mind your own Business' (p. 13). This is perhaps inspired by Ozell's Squire Trelooby who frequently refers to the nuisance of 'Cocknies'. Later in *Squire Lubberly* the two Swiss guards who have heard news that Squire Lubberly will be hanged hurry to the place of execution. In the French original one guard says to the other: 'Allons, dépêchons, Camerade, li faut allair tous deux nous à la Crève' (III.3; *OC*, II, 243). By 'la Crève' the guard means the Place de Grève where public executions in Paris used to take place. This is translated in English with a Romansh dialectical twang as: 'Come aloong, Broder, make hasht; ush both musht away to *Teyburn*' (p. 119). Despite the scene's purportedly being Paris, even in translation the London execution site is named. The potential pleasure of witnessing the public execution is highlighted by the guards' enthusiasm and is exploited for comic effect when they meet Lubberly in disguise and encourage him to accompany them to Tyburn. This scene is recontextualized in order to allow readers of the translation to appreciate the full comic irony of the suggestion and to reflect on the behaviour of groups in an urban environment.

Just as groups may gather at the place of a public execution, they also gather in theatres to watch plays that tell them about the society in which they live. The satire on group behaviour in the dramatic content of the play is to some extent played out by the gathering of different individuals in the theatre. This is why the presentation of urbanity is localized to a significant degree in the first translations of *Monsieur de Pourceaugnac*. It is difficult to know what a Cornish gentleman may have made of *Squire Trelooby*. According to Ozell, the acted version enjoyed so much success on the London stage that 'the whole Town' was asking for it to be printed because they believed it was in part a satire against 'West-Country Gentlemen' (π4ʳ). Ozell also explains that the acted version included a topical reference to a local scandal; when Julia feigns interest in Trelooby, her father wonders if she has been whipped into submission, thereby alluding to 'a certain whipping Story now in every Body's Mouth' (π4ʳ). This comment probably relates to the story of 'Whipping Tom', a sexual attacker who spanked his victims in London alleys in 1681 and who reportedly acted with such speed that he was thought to have supernatural powers. The story took hold of the city's imagination to such a degree that the nickname 'Whipping Tom' became a term for a flagellator. A translation of a Molière play, then, could be used as a way of both presenting a new urban setting and of engaging audiences in discussion of character-types, events, and even gossip within the urban environment surrounding the theatre. By comparing urban life with the country life of outsiders the identity of the town is reinforced.

If the satire of *Monsieur de Pourceaugnac* defines the city by what it is not (the country), *Le Bourgeois gentilhomme* explores what it is to be an urbane member of a city. In the latter play Jourdain wrongly believes that the quality of urbanity can be adopted through social climbing by dressing like a nobleman and hiring a dancing master, a music teacher, a fencing master, and a philosophy teacher. Yet despite his best efforts, Jourdain's mundane concerns contrast easily with his trickster's natural and easy urbanity of manners. Most of the exchanges between Jourdain and his teachers are translated closely in the English versions of the text. English standards of urbanity are largely similar to the French, particularly given the prevalence of French fashions and modes of behaviour in late seventeenth- and early eighteenth-century England. One significant difference in the first translation of *Le Bourgeois gentilhomme* in Ravenscroft's *The Citizen Turn'd Gentleman* is that 'Mr Jorden' does not study the 'Nature of Letters' as he does in subsequent translations, but he studies 'French'.[24] A certain 'Jacques' inspired by the character 'Maître Jacques' in Molière's *L'Avare* teaches Mr Jorden some French vocabulary, noting that 'all travellers give te ver many littil graces to their discourse vith te tange of te French' (p. 5). This observation is supported by the inclusion of numerous French terms in the various English translations of Molière that preceded Ravenscroft's attempt. But this chapter has demonstrated that the concepts of bourgeoisie and urbanity had to be rendered in English by terms specific to the social structure of the 'target country' and even to specific locales within that country.

There are many thematic similarities between *Monsieur de Pourceaugnac* and *Le Bourgeois gentilhomme*, but it should also be noted that they were both *comédies-ballets*. The influence of dance, ceremony, and song, performed in turn by individual actors and groups of actors, complements the theme of social relations in the dramatic plots and mirrors the tension between individual ambition and the behaviour of the collective. This chapter has focused on the linguistic transfer of social labels in order to represent urban social exchange in translation, but the impact of spectacle should not be underestimated. Although the eighteenth-century translations of *Monsieur de Pourceaugnac* and *Le Bourgeois gentilhomme* that survive were intended for readers rather than spectators, they still include the songs that contribute to the public mockery of the main characters. This is because these two plays by Molière demonstrate that urban social interactions are themselves forms of theatre and performance.

Notes to Chapter 7

1. A few elements, such as the presence of one Maître Jacques, are inspired by Molière's *L'Avare* (1668).
2. Phillips, 'Urbanity', in *The New World of English Words*: '(lat.) the fashion of the City, civility, courtesie, gentlenesse in speech, or behaviour'.
3. *The Encyclopedia of Literary Translation into English*, ed. by Classe, II, 1397.
4. Molière, *The Dramatic Works of Molière*, trans. by Henri Van Laun, 6 vols (Edinburgh: William Paterson, 1875–76), III, 255, n. 1.
5. Furetière, 'Bourgeois', in *Dictionnaire universel*, I, 311–12.
6. *Révolutions de Paris*, 12 March 1791.
7. Richelet, 'Bourgeois', in *Dictionnaire françois*, I, 88–89.
8. Charles Mazouer, *Trois comédies de Molière: étude sur Le Misanthrope, George Dandin, Le Bourgeois gentilhomme* (Pessac: Presses universitaires de Bordeaux, 2007), p. 48.
9. Furetière, 'Insulte', 'Mal', 'Paisible', and 'Rente', in *Dictionnaire universel*, II, 361, 528; III [no page numbers].
10. Miège, 'City', in *A New Dictionary, French and English, with Another English and French*.
11. While there is a pun on the concept of the everyday in the French name 'Jourdain', the English equivalent 'Jorden' has different and earthier connotations, its slang meaning being 'chamber pot'. The seventeenth-century English translators of Molière tend to intensify puns in order to satisfy audience expectation for bawdiness in comedy. In the case of the name/term 'Jorden' no work is required.
12. See, for example, this comment in Aphra Behn's *The False Count* (1681): Is it think you for a little silly Cit, to complain when a Don does him the Honour to visit his Lady?' (Act II, scene 2) (Aphra Behn, *Five Plays*, ed. by Margaret Duffy (London: Methuen Drama, 1990), p. 337).
13. B. E., 'Cit', in *New Dictionary of the Terms Ancient and Modern of the Canting Crew*.
14. Johnson, 'Cit', in *A Dictionary of the English Language*.
15. Furetière, 'Gentilhomme', in *Dictionnaire universel*, II, 164.
16. Blount, 'Gentleman', in *Glossographia* (1656).
17. John Cowell, 'Gentleman', in *The Interpreter; or, Book Containing the Signification of Words* (Cambridge: Legate, 1607).
18. Richelet, 'Condition', in *Dictionnaire françois*, I, 162.
19. Thomas Corneille, 'Écuyer', in *Le Dictionnaire des arts et des science*, I, 351–52.
20. The first translation of a Molière play appears in William D'Avenant's *A Playhouse to be Let*

(1663), which includes *Le Cocu imaginaire* in French-accented English.
21. Philip S. Wadsworth, *Molière and the Italian Tradition* (Birmingham, AL: Summa Publications, 1987), p. 120.
22. Claude Bourqui, '*Monsieur de Pourceaugnac* et les enjeux de la prononciation du français', *Littératures Classiques*, 87.2 (2015), 163–73.
23. See, for example, 'Ken' in Joseph Wright, *The English Dialect Dictionary*, 6 vols (London: Henry Frowde, 1898–1905), III, 418.
24. There has been recent scholarly interest in language learning in early modern English society, and its representations on stage. See John Gallagher, *Learning Languages in Early Modern England* (Oxford: Oxford University Press, 2019).

CONCLUSION

The translators of the 1732 *Select Comedies of Mr de Moliere* sought to present their work as a fresh departure from the range of translations that had preceded it. An advertisement published in several newspapers from May 1732 emphasizes that 'the Translation is entirely New' and that:

> Particular Care has been had to keep as close as possible to the Original, and to observe the very Words of the Author as well as his Sense, so far as was consistent with giving it a spirited and easy Comick Stile, in order to make it the more serviceable to those of our own nation who are Learners of the French Language; as likewise to Foreigners who desire to be acquainted with ours.[1]

The idea that Molière's texts represented 'originals' and that the translators were distinct from the 'author' had not been articulated so explicitly in earlier English versions of Molière's plays, and the stress on the closeness of the translation suggests it is a novel technique that had not hitherto been observed. The parallel format of the text complements the two-way pedagogical aims of the work, which eschew mere assimilation of Molière's texts into English in favour of a comparative assessment of the sources and their translations. But was the contribution and legacy of Molière in translation before 1732 so far removed from Baker, Miller, and Clare's approach? *The Select Comedies* attest to the fact that Molière had reached a prominent position in the dramatic literary landscape of the 1730s, and this elevation is due in large part to the translating experimentation of the previous seventy years.

The translations of Molière that emerged in the 1660s brought the French dramatist's work into English through hybridized plays such as D'Avenant's *The Playhouse to be Let* (1663) and Flecknoe's *The Damoiselles à la mode* (1667). The composite nature of these plays reflects the early tentative search for direction in Restoration drama as well as the haste with which dramatists sought to find new material for the newly reopened theatres. Derek Hughes observes a particularly intense period of Molière anglicizations from 1668 to 1672.[2] During this phase the first translation of a single play by Molière emerged in the form of Medbourne's *Tartuffe; or, The French Puritan* (1670). This translation of a work by a contemporary French dramatist was actually a vehicle for looking back to the anti-Puritan tradition of early seventeenth-century English theatre and its revival in the years following the Restoration when the fall of the Puritan Commonwealth was still fresh in the minds of audiences. While several other translations of the 1670s focused on single plays, the hybridized forms still persisted in versions such as Ravenscroft's *The Citizen Turn'd Gentleman* (1672).

There was a short hiatus in Molière translations in the mid-1670s, when sex comedy based on contemporary English life was dominant, but Molière did not remain far from view and the influence of his plotting and characters was combined with the themes of the evolving sex comedy in Wycherley's *The Country Wife* (1674/5). Towards the end of the 1670s Aphra Behn turned to Molière by adapting James Wright's manuscript translation of *Le Malade imaginaire* into *Sir Patient Fancy* (1677/8), which also drew on the sex comedy genre to present women attempting to gain agency over their bodies within the limits of their social environment. This idea was echoed over twenty years later in the subtle reconfigurations of dialogue in Susanna Centlivre's translation of *Le Médecin malgré lui* in *Love's Contrivance* (1703). Yet translations did not merely represent interactions between near-contemporaneous works; in Dryden's successful *Amphitryon* (1690), for example, both Molière's and Plautus's works were carried into a new context. Above all, it is important to recall that patterns of translation over the period were not linear; furthermore, audience tastes constantly fluctuated and while translators sought novel approaches to their work, they also responded to previous translations in their reworkings.

The most noticeable shift in the first decades of the eighteenth century was towards close translations of single Molière plays for reading audiences, with clear acknowledgement of the author of the source text. The year 1709 saw the publication of translations of *Le Misanthrope* and *Le Malade imaginaire* in *The Monthly Amusement*, and newspaper advertisements of the translations indicate a growing interest in Molière amongst the reading public. At this time John Ozell was the most prolific, if not always the most proficient, translator of Molière for print, and the first to present a collected works translation (including translations 'collected' from other translators). New translations of Molière for the stage dropped significantly in number in the 1720s and it was not until 1732 that interest was re-energized with the appearance of Fielding's *The Mock Doctor* for the stage and the *Select Comedies* for print. This revitalization, however, could not have occurred without the recollection of the diverse translations of the Restoration, and the promise of new interactions with Molière's texts in the future. In his *Lettres philosophiques* or *Lettres sur les Anglais* (1734) Voltaire famously assessed the influence of Molière on English Restoration theatre after his voluntary exile in England. But he also enacted a 'return trip' for Molière's play *Le Misanthrope* in the sense that it was the model for William Wycherly's *The Plain Dealer* (1676), which in turn was adapted into Voltaire's *La Prude* (1739).[3] Voltaire was at pains to point out that *La Prude* was 'bien moins une traduction qu'une esquisse légère de la fameuse comédie de Wicherley', but the connection between the plays of Molière, Wycherley, and Voltaire had been fostered by the interest sustained in Molière through the various translations that surrounded them.[4] The dual pedagogical aims of the translators of the *Select Comedies* is paralleled in the two-way theatrical exchanges that translations of Molière inspired.

By approaching the study of Molière in early modern England from the perspective of translation, the various English versions of the French plays have been explored as individual literary transformations, and assessed in relation to each other in order to show the evolving nature of theatre that travels across nations.

John Wilcox's strong reaction to the view that Restoration dramatists saw Molière as their main inspiration led him to disregard their interest in translation, arguing instead that pre-Civil War English theatrical forms remained dominant. Wilcox writes:

> There was little need to experiment with importations of the strange form and the stranger spirit of foreigners, even of the successful contemporary Molière. To benefit by his superior skill and experience in things theatrical, they waylaid him, and turned out his pockets to steal all his rare tricks of the stage; but they ignored his ideas and spirit as coin not readily current in the land of Charles and Nell.[5]

There is clearly evidence that challenges this assessment in the many translations that appeared from 1663 onwards. Contrary to Wilcox's view, I argue that English dramatists repeatedly found the need to experiment with French dramatic imports because the texts were both foreign and yet familiar in a country that looked across the Channel in order to assess itself. Far from ignoring Molière's 'ideas and spirit', they engaged with them by considering their impact in France and conceiving of ways to present them with the same sense of immediacy to English audiences.

While previous studies of Molière in England have made some reference to historical context and theatre conditions, they have neglected to address the ways in which the first translations reacted to and fed into a broader discourse on the role and functions of theatre. In order to fill this gap I have read the plays and their translations alongside a broad range of theoretical writings in French and English, against paratextual material such as prefaces, prologues, and epilogues, and against dictionary definitions of key terms. Beyond these texts, the impact of Molière's plays in early modern England is also evident in journalistic writing of the period. Issue 34 of the early eighteenth-century journal *Visions of Sir Heister Ryley* includes the following comments, supposedly conceived by the fictitious editor of the newspaper after he had perused some books in the library of Sion College, London:

> I find that a certain Gentleman has disobliged many People by contradicting those who say, that no Modern Author can be compared with *Homer* and *Virgil*, *Demosthenes* and *Cicero*, *Aristophanes* and *Terence*, *Sophocles* and *Euripides*. [...] I think I may say, that among the Productions of the Pen, there are few things wherein so many people have acknowledged the Superiority of our Age, as in the Comical Pieces. Perhaps the Reason of it is, that the Beauties and Niceties of *Aristophanes* are not known to all those who are sensible of M. *de Molière's* Wit and Charms. [...] There are some Beauties of Wit in Fashion at all Times. One would think that Molière is more copious in that respect than the Ancient Comick Poets. He has some Beauties that would vanish away in a Translation or in a Country of a different Taste from that of *France*; but he has many others that would be preserved in all sorts of Translations, and approved, whatever the Taste of the Readers might be, provided they understood the Essence of a good Thought.[6]

It is odd that 'Sir Heister Ryley', writing from a college in London, should choose Molière over an English dramatist as an example of a modern author to compare and contrast with the ancients. The reason why this is the case is that this extract is in fact lifted from a 1710 translation into English of Pierre Bayle's *Dictionnaire historique et critique* (1697).[7] The anonymous newspaper editor adapts the beginning of the extract so that the name of the *moderne*, Charles Perrault, is replaced with the vague designation 'a certain Gentleman' and suggests that the comments are relevant to an English audience. This was a public that had come into contact with many versions of Molière's plays from the 1660s onwards, and which would therefore be receptive to Bayle's comments about Molière several years after they were first published in French.

In placing the comments in a new journalistic context the 'editor' in a sense enacts the ideas put forward in the article. The appearance of the extract in an English journal suggests that English audiences appreciated the comic appeal of Molière as readily as French audiences, while also drawing attention to the numerous translation options to which his plays are suited. It is worth tracing these comments about Molière back to Pierre Bayle's original dictionary entry in French:

> [Molière] a des beautés qui disparaîtraient dans les versions, et à l'égard des pays où le goût n'est pas semblable à celui de France; mais il en a un grand nombre d'autres qui passerait dans toutes sortes de traductions, et de quelque goût que les lecteurs fussent, pourvu qu'ils entendissent l'essence des bonnes pensées.[8]

Bayle allows for the possibility that countries which have a similar taste to France may preserve the 'beauties' or insights of Molière's plays, and states that even where the taste will diverge from the French there are elements that will nonetheless carry across successfully.

Voltaire, however, writing a few decades later in a 1748 revised edition of his *Lettres philosophiques*, claims that some elements of Molière's works were wholly unfamiliar to English audiences. He argues that *Le Tartuffe*, for example, had not been successful on the English stage because, he declares, there are neither 'vrais dévots' nor 'faux dévots' in England and that 'on ne se plaît guère aux portraits des gens qu'on ne connaît pas'.[9] So both Bayle and Voltaire acknowledge that audiences of comedy are required to experience a sense of familiarity, and so the practical construction and content of translated plays must fit with this theory. Voltaire criticized the translation of Molière into English, stating that the English 'ont déguisé, ont gâté la plupart des pièces de Molière'.[10] Critics have used this remark to explore the ways in which English dramatists who adapted Molière did or did not acknowledge him in their prefaces, but it is worth pondering the significance of the idea that the plays had been 'disguised'.

While a disguise is meant to alter appearance to conceal an established identity, the pleasure of a disguise sometimes derives from the awareness of the true identity of whatever lies beneath it. Most of the first English translators were conscious of the comic pleasure of disguise and so drew attention to the French origins of their source texts while on the surface they 'dressed them up' as English plays. This dual approach is manifested in analysis of the translators' treatment of plot, translation practice, prosody, and vocabulary.

As Part I on the theory and form of the first English translations of Molière demonstrates, the translators embedded his plots within frame texts, mixed two or more plots together, or added extra characters. These modifications were a response to the theory that comedy should be familiar to spectators, and in the case of English theatre should satisfy the audiences' expectations of multiple plot events and interactions. But the mixing of plots and the addition of characters was possible because the concentrated form of French comedies had been shaped by the development of the theory of the unities of time, place, and action based on interpretations of Aristotle's *Poetics*. The multiplicity of Molière's stories in hybridized plots contributes to Bayle's suggestion that comic insights can be repeatedly presented in 'toutes sortes de traductions'. Yet some translations also demonstrate an awareness of common themes amongst Molière's corpus. Flecknoe mixed *L'École des maris* and *Les Précieuses ridicules* together because they share themes of gender politics and marital satire; Ravenscroft combined *Monsieur de Pourceaugnac* and *Le Bourgeois gentilhomme* because they both ridicule middle-class pretension. In the case of mixed plots audiences are invited to draw parallels between Molière's plays and to observe how the French dramatist repeated and reworked ideas in different works. This in turn allows the translators to demonstrate that they too have revised the themes and invented new ways to present them to their audiences. There is theatrical appeal in the awareness that the stories of Molière's characters are being retold in new forms.

A seemingly paradoxical approach is at play in which translators sought to anglicize the French source-texts but at the same time relished engagement with the foreign elements of the plays, be they the dramatic form, the metrical composition, or the vocabulary. This is why the choice between domesticating and foreignizing approaches to translation is pertinent to the first translations of Molière. Despite the fact that the concepts of 'domestication' and 'foreignization' have been defined in twentieth-century translation theory, it is helpful to consider them as two poles between which the first translators of Molière navigated their route through the adaptation process.

As Part II ('Lexical Choices and Recontextualizations') has shown, the linguistic boundaries between the domestic and the foreign were distorted during a period in which some elements of the vocabulary of the source text were being absorbed into the target language. This is particularly true of the vocabulary surrounding the codes and connotations of gallantry. Some terms in the target language, such as 'zeal', though etymologically linked to French and close in essential meaning, carried particularly potent satirical charge within the theatrical tradition, so its usage in translation contributed to a cultural recontextualization. Certain terms in the target language, such as the title 'quack', could label the figures of Molière's satire appropriately but with a cynical edge that could not reflect the naivety of Molière's dupes. Some terms that are now familiar in English as well as in French, such as 'bourgeois', had not yet been transferred in the late seventeenth and early eighteenth century and therefore had to be replaced with terms that had equivalent satirical connotations within a localized frame of reference. So a negotiation between a domesticating and a foreignizing translation style was required so that audiences could recognize familiar character behaviour while also acknowledging its initial resonance in its French context. Audiences could take pleasure in the thought that a play that had a satirical impact in France was adapted so that it had a satirical impact in England.

Molière's plays did not undergo a complete decontextualization in order for them to be recontextualized for the English stage or page. Instead, a certain awareness of the origins of the translated play was often maintained through the retention of French characters or through reference to French fashions or modes of behaviour. Even a play such as *Squire Trelooby*, in which the localized French references of *Monsieur de Pourceaugnac* were swapped for localized English references, was known as a play by Molière. Susan Cannon Harris explains a curious theatrical reference to *Squire Trelooby* which demonstrates a conflation of source-text and translation in a 1740s play by Thomas Sheridan, first performed in Dublin:

> *The Brave Irishman* was never an original text. In [...] manuscript versions, the intriguer Schemewell admits to having stolen his best ideas about how to bedevil an Irishman from a French playwright: 'Molière's Squire Trelooby has furnished me with something I believe I have improved'. A half-century of cross-cultural plagiarism nests inside that sentence. Molière never named anything or anyone 'Squire Trelooby'. He did write a farce called *Monsieur de Pourceaugnac* (1669) in which the daughter of a rich Parisian merchant conspired with her urbane lover and an army of intriguing accomplices to prevent her father from forcing her to marry a dim-witted provincial bourgeois.[11]

Cannon Harris reads the comment relating to Molière in the manuscript version as an insight into Shadwell's approach to the 'theft' of the French playwright's piece. Given that it is a line attributed to a scheming character within the play, however, it is more convincing to read it as a metatheatrical reference that works as a comically ironic allusion to the absorption of Molière into English from the early 1660s onwards. Molière did not name anyone 'Squire Trelooby', but Squire Trelooby was, in a sense, 'Molière's' because the character emerged from a translation of the French playwright's work. The very concept of the local and the foreign is repeatedly explored in the various early English translations of Molière, both in terms of the theory and practice of translation and within the plays' satirical themes. The late seventeenth- and early eighteenth-century period was rich in cross-cultural translation rather than cross-cultural plagiarism.

Recent theatre scholarship has come to acknowledge the insights to be gained from rejecting the view that a playtext is a fixed object in favour of a more flexible concept of drama that gives due weight to the collaborative, sometimes improvisatory nature of creating and putting on plays. This assessment of the first translations of Molière complements this theoretical current and suggests that dramatic translation be treated in a similarly elastic way to show that dramatic texts, from their inception, are repeatedly remodelled not only through directors' or stage managers' choices, but through translators' changes of form, composition, vocabulary, and satirical focus, all of which are informed by an interpretation of the initial context of the play, whether or not this has been filtered through previous translations.

Molière's plays were imported from France into England and their Gallic origins mattered to the dramatists who translated them. This is evident in the analysis of the translators' negotiation with plot formation, with theoretical concepts of translation, and with prosody, as well as in the exploration of their treatment of the key cultural models of marital politics, religion, healthcare, and social status. The very act of anglicization required an acknowledgement of both the differences and the similarities between French and English dramatic theory, society, and language, a process that precluded the dismissal of textual origins and encouraged the promotion of the source.

The first English translations of Molière represent repeated reworkings of the French plays, and their recontextualization is characterized by a continuous accumulative translating approach that helped to establish new audiences for the French plays. The recurring remodelling set in motion the continued translation of Molière, from the close translations of the nineteenth century, and the various innovative translations of the twentieth century.[12] Late twentieth- and early twenty-first-century translations of Molière have largely returned to the localizing approaches of the pioneering translators of the early modern period, proving Bayle correct in the view that Molière's ideas could be preserved in 'toutes sortes de traductions' and by extension in 'toutes sortes d'époques'.

Notes to the Conclusion

1. *Daily Journal*, 10 May 1732.
2. Hughes, *English Drama 1660–1700*, pp. 117–60.
3. See Russell Goulbourne, *Voltaire Comic Dramatist* (Oxford: Voltaire Foundation, 2006), pp. 102–17.
4. Voltaire, *Complete Works of Voltaire / Œuvres complètes de Voltaire*, 20C: *'Micromégas' and Other Texts (1738–1742)*, ed. by Nicholas Cronk, Thomas Wynn, and others (Oxford: Voltaire Foundation, 2017), p. 159.
5. Wilcox, *The Relation of Molière to Restoration Comedy*, p. 201.
6. [Anon.], 'From Sion College, November 4', *Visions of Sir Heister Ryley*, 6 November 1710, in *The Visions of Sir Heister Ryley: With Other Entertainments*, ed. anon. [Charles Povey? or Daniel Defoe?] (London: printed for the author and sold by Mrs Sympson and others, 1711), pp. 135–36.
7. Pierre Bayle, 'Poquelin', in *An Historical and Critical Dictionary*, trans. anon., 4 vols (London: printed for C. Harper and others, 1710), IV, 2672–76 (p. 2673).
8. Pierre Bayle, 'Poquelin', in *Dictionnaire historique et critique*, 2 vols (Rotterdam: chez Reinier Leers, 1697), II, 869–72 (p. 871).
9. Voltaire, 'Lettre XIX', in *Lettres philosophiques, ou Lettres anglaises*, ed. by Raymond Naves (Paris: Garnier Frères, 1964), p. 246.
10. Ibid.
11. Susan Cannon Harris, 'Mixed Marriage: Sheridan, Macklin, and the Hybrid Audience', in *Players, Playwrights, Playhouse: Investigating Performance, 1660–1800*, ed. by Michael Cordner and Peter Holland (New York: Palgrave Macmillan, 2007), pp. 189–212 (pp. 191–92).
12. See, for example, Molière, *The Dramatic Works*, and Noël Peacock, *Molière in Scotland* (Glasgow: University of Glasgow French and German Publications, 1993).

APPENDIX

Table of English Translations and Adaptations of Molière, 1663–1732

Included in the following table are all plays that were modelled on Molière plots, regardless of whether or not they contain lexical translations. This is in order to demonstrate the variety of ways in which the French playwright's works were absorbed into English theatre in the period.

Where plays are recorded as having the same production year I have ordered the works according to their dates of first performance. In working out this ordering I am indebted to *The London Stage, 1660–1800: A Calendar of Plays, Entertainments and Afterpieces. Part 1: 1660–1700*, ed. by William Van Lennep, Emmet L. Avery, and Arthur H. Scouten (Carbondale: Southern Illinois University Press, 1965) and *The London Stage', 1660–1800: A Calendar of Plays, Entertainments and Afterpieces. Part 2: 1700–1729*, ed. by Emmet L. Avery (Carbondale: Southern Illinois University Press, 1960). Translations cited in the text are also listed in the bibliography.

Some explanation of reasons why certain plays were repeatedly translated in the period is offered in the Introduction. Readers may be surprised to see that plays that are now considered minor farces, such as *Le Cocu imaginaire*, were given a lot of attention. This is partly owing to the relative ease with which the one-act play could be hybridized with other plays. It is also worth bearing in mind that *comédies-ballets* that were originally performed with elaborate scenery before the court and are now considered major works were either neglected by early modern translators or remodelled to lay the focus on character interaction, thereby suiting the rapid production of London public theatre.

First appearance (on stage or in print)	Title	Molière Source	Translator / Adaptor	First print edition
1663 Duke's Theatre, Lincoln's Inn Fields	*The Playhouse to be Let*	Act 2 is a condensed translation of *Sganarelle ou le Cocu imaginaire* (1660)	William D'Avenant	Published in *The Works of Sir William D'Avenant*, printed in London by T. N. for Henry Herringman, 1673

1667	*The Damoiselles à la mode*	Translation and hybridization of *Les Précieuses ridicules* (1659), *L'École des maris* (1661). Character elements from *L'École des femmes* (1662)	Richard Flecknoe	Printed in London for the author, 1667. 'Licensed 15th May 1667 by Roger L'Estrange', but not acted
1667 Duke's Theatre, Lincoln's Inn Fields	*Sir Martin Mar-all; or, The Feign'd Innocence*	Adapted translation of *L'Étourdi* (1658) by the Duke of Newcastle, with added sub-plot from Quinault's *L'Amant indiscret* (1656)	John Dryden	Printed in London for H. Herringman, 1668; reissued in 1691 with Dryden named author
1668 Duke's Theatre, Lincoln's Inn Fields	*The Sullen Lovers; or, The Impertinents*	Modelled on *Les Fâcheux* (1661). Elements from *Le Misanthrope* (1666)	Thomas Shadwell	Printed in the Savoy for Henry Herringman, 1668
1668 Theatre Royal, Bridges Street	*The Mulberry-garden*	Modelled on *L'École des maris* (1661)	Charles Sedley	Printed in London for H. Herringman, 1668
1668 Theatre Royal, Bridges Street	*An Evening's Love; or, The Mock Astrologer*	Scenes translated from *Le Dépit amoureux* (1656), but mostly an adaptation of Thomas Corneille's *Le Feint Astrologue* (1648)	John Dryden	Printed in London by T. N. for Henry Herringman, 1671
1669 Theatre Royal, Bridges Street	*The Dumb Lady; or, The Farriar Made Physician*	Hybridized translations of *L'Amour médecin* (1665) and *Le Médecin malgré lui* (1666)	John Lacy	Printed in London for Thomas Dring, 1672
1670 Theatre Royal, Bridges Street	*Tartuffe; or, The French Puritan*	Translation of *Le Tartuffe* (1664, 1669) with some additional scenes and adaptations.	Matthew Medbourne	Printed in London by H. L. and R. B. for James Magnus, 1670
1670 Duke's Theatre, Lincoln's Inn Fields	*Sir Salomon; or, The Cautious Coxcomb*	Modelled on *L'École des femmes* (1662). Parts translated closely from French, e.g. Act II, scene 5.	John Caryl	Printed in London for H. Herringman, 1671

1670? Duke's Theatre, Lincoln's Inn Fields	*The Amorous Widow; or, The Wanton Wife*	Translation of *George Dandin, ou Le Mari confondu* (1668), combined with a prose translation of Thomas Corneille's *Le Baron d'Albikrac* (1667)	Thomas Betterton	Printed in London for W. Turner, 1706
1671/2 Duke's Theatre, Lincoln's Inn Fields	*The Gentleman Dancing-Master*	Borrowings from *L'École des maris* (1661)	William Wycherley	Printed in London for Herringman and Dring, 1673
1672 Theatre Royal, Bridges Street	*A Comedy Called The Miser*	Adaptation of *L'Avare* (1668)	Thomas Shadwell	Printed in London for Thomas Collins and John Ford
1672 Duke's Theatre, Lincoln's Inn Fields	*The Citizen Turn'd Gentleman*	Hybridized translations of *Monsieur de Pourceaugnac* (1669) and *Le Bourgeois gentilhomme* (1670)	Edward Ravenscroft	Printed in London for Thomas Dring, 1672
1673 Duke's Theatre, Lincoln's Inn Fields	*The Careless Lovers*	Borrowings from Act II, scene 8, of *Monsieur de Pourceaugnac* (1669) and Act III, scene 9, of *Le Bourgeois gentilhomme* (1670)	Edward Ravenscroft	Printed in London, William Cademan, 1673
1674/5 Theatre Royal, Drury Lane	*The Country-wife*	Borrowings from *L'École des maris* (1661)	William Wycherley	Printed in London for Thomas Dring, 1675
1674/5 Duke's Theatre, Dorset Garden	*Psyche*	Part-translation, part-adaptation of *Psyché* by Molière, Pierre Corneille, and Quinault (1671)	Thomas Shadwell	Printed in London by T. N. for Henry Herringman, 1675
1675/6 Duke's Theatre, Dorset Garden	*The Countrey Wit*	Modelled on *Le Sicilien, ou L'Amour peintre* (1667)	John Crowne	Printed in London for J. Draby, A. Bettesworth, and F. Clay, 1675

1676 Theatre Royal, Drury Lane	*The Libertine*	Adaptation of *Le Festin de Pierre/Dom Juan* (1665). Shadwell also draws on the versions by Dorimon, Villiers, and Rosimond.	Thomas Shadwell	Printed in London by T. N. for Henry Herringman, 1676
1676 Duke's Theatre, Dorset Garden	*The Wrangling Lovers; or, The Invisible Mistress*	Modelled on *Le Dépit amoureux* (1656)	Edward Ravenscroft	Printed in London for William Crook, 1677
1676/7 Duke's Theatre, Dorset Garden	*The Cheats of Scapin* (at the end of a translation of Racine: *Titus and Berenice*)	Translation of *Les Fourberies de Scapin* (1662)	Thomas Otway	Printed in London for R. Tonson, 1677
1676/7 Theatre Royal, Drury Lane	*The Plain Dealer*	Modelled on *Le Misanthrope* (1666)	William Wycherley	Printed in London by T. N. for James Magnes and Rich Bentley, 1677
1677 Duke's Theatre, Dorset Garden	*Tom Essence; or, The Modish Wife*	*Sganarelle, ou Le Cocu imaginaire* (1660), several scenes translated closely	Thomas Rawlins	Printed in London by T. M. for W. Cademan, 1677
1677 Theatre Royal, Drury Lane	*Scaramouch a Philosopher, Harlequin a School-Boy, Merchand and Magician*	Modelled on *Les Fourberies de Scapin* (1662), *Le Mariage forcé* (1664), borrowings from Act II, scenes 2–3, of *Le Bourgeois gentilhomme* (1670)	Edward Ravenscroft	Printed in London for Robert Sollers, 1677
1677/8 Duke's Theatre, Dorset Garden	*Sir Patient Fancy*	Plot from *Le Malade imaginaire* (1673), and scenes from a translation by James Wright. Plot elements from *L'Amour médecin* (1665), character inspiration from *Les Femmes savantes* (1672)	Aphra Behn	Printed in London, E. Flesher for R. Tonson, 1678

c. 1678/8	*Le Malade imaginaire* [ms title: 'La Mallad']	Manuscript translation of an early unauthorized edition of *Le Malade imaginaire* (1673) [*Le Malade imaginaire, comédie en trois actes meslés de danses et de musique*, 1674]	James Wright	Not printed. Washington, DC, Folger Shakespeare Library, MS V.b.220
1680 Duke's Theatre, Dorset Garden	*The Souldier's Fortune*	Modelled on *Sganarelle ou le Cocu imaginaire* (1660) and *L'École des maris* (1661)	Thomas Otway	Printed in London for R. Bentley and J. Magnes, 1681
1681 Duke's Theatre, Dorset Garden	*The False Count; or, A New Way to Play an Old Game*	Modelled on *Les Précieuses ridicules* (1659)	Aphra Behn	Printed in London by M Flesher for Jacob Tonson, 1682
1681 Duke's Theatre, Dorset Garden	*The London Cuckolds*	Modelled on *L'École des femmes* (1662)	Edward Ravenscroft	Printed in London for Jos. Hindmarsh, 1682
1685 Theatre Royal, Drury Lane	*Sir Courtly Nice; or, It Cannot Be*	Modelled on *Les Précieuses ridicules* (1659)	John Crowne	Printed in London by H. H. Jun. for R. Bently, 1685
1689 Theatre Royal, Drury Lane	*Bury-fair*	Modelled on *Les Précieuses ridicules* (1659)	Thomas Shadwell	Printed in London for James Knapton, 1689
1689 Theatre Royal, Drury Lane	*The English Frier; or, The Town Sparks*	Modelled on *Le Tartuffe* (1664, 1669)	John Crowne	Printed in London for James Knapton, 1689, 'As it is Acted by Their Majesty's Servants'
1704/5 Theatre Royal, Drury Lane	*The Quacks; or, Love's the Physician*	Adaptation of *L'Amour médecin* (1665)	Owen McSwiny	Printed in London for Benjamin Bragg, 1705
1705 Theatre Royal, Drury Lane	*The Tender Husband; or, The Accomplish'd Fools*	Modelled on *Le Sicilien, ou L'Amour peintre* (1667)	Richard Steele	Printed in London for Jacob Tonson, 1705

1705 Queen's Theatre, Haymarket	The Mistake	Translation of Le Dépit amoureux (1656)	John Vanbrugh	Printed in London for Jacob Tonson, 1706
1707	The Cuckold in Conceit (lost)	Translation (?) of Sganarelle, ou Le Cocu imaginaire	John Vanbrugh	Not printed
1709	The Misantrope; or, Man-Hater	Translation of Le Misanthrope (1666)	John Hughes	Printed in London by D. Midwinter and B. Lintott, The Monthly Amusement, 2, May 1709; reprinted in Ozell's Works (1714)
1709	The Hypocondriack	Translation of Le Malade imaginaire (1673)	(?)	Printed in London by D. Midwinter and B. Lintott, The Monthly Amusement, 4, London, July 1709; reprinted in Ozell's Works (1714)
1714	The Works of Monsieur de Molière	Translation of prefatory material and plays from the first major collected works in French, Œuvres de Monsieur de Molière (1682)	John Ozell	Printed in London for Bernard Lintott, 1714. Not acted
1714/5 New Lincoln's Inn Fields Theatre	The Perplex'd Couple; or, Mistake Upon Mistake	Borrowings from Sganarelle ou le Cocu imaginaire (1660)	Charles Molloy	Printed in London for W. Meares, and J. Brown, 1715
1717 Theatre Royal, Drury Lane	Three Hours After Marriage	Borrowings from Sganarelle ou le Cocu imaginaire (1660)	John Arbuthnot, John Gay, and Alexander Pope	Printed in London for Bernard Lintott, 1717
1718	The Non-juror	Adaptation of Le Tartuffe (1664, 1669)	Colley Cibber	Printed in London for J. L, 1718

1721 Theatre Royal, Drury Lane	*The Refusal; or, The Ladies Philosophy*	Adaptation of *Les Femmes savantes* (1672)	Colley Cibber	Printed in London for B. Lintot and W. Chetwood
1732	*The Comical Revenge; or, The Doctor in Spite of His Teeth* (lost)	Translation (?) of *Le Médecin malgré lui* (1666). Advertised as 'taken from Molière', see *Daily Post*, 2, 11 May 1732	(?)	Not printed
1732 Theatre Royal, Drury Lane	*The Mock Doctor; or, The Dumb Lady Cur'd*	Part adaptation, part contracted translation of *Le Médecin malgré lui* (1666)	Henry Fielding	Printed in London for J. Watts, 1732
1732	*Select Comedies of Mr. de Molière, in French and English*	Translation of plays and prefatory material from the first major French edition of Molière, *Œuvres de Monsieur de Molière* (1682)	Henry Baker, James Miller, and Martin Clare	Printed in London for J. Watts, 1732

BIBLIOGRAPHY

Editions of Molière's Works Discussed in the Text

MOLIÈRE, *Œuvres complètes*, 2 vols, ed. by Georges Forestier and Claude Bourqui (Paris: Gallimard, 2010)
—— *Les Œuvres de Monsieur de Molière*, 8 vols (Paris: printed by Denys Thierry, Claude Barbin, and Pierre Trabouillet, 1682)
—— *Le Malade imaginaire, comédie en trois actes meslés de danses et de musique, suivant la Copie imprimée a Paris* ([Amsterdam: Daniel Elzevir], 1674)
—— *Le Malade imaginaire, comédie en trois actes mélez de danses et de musique* (Amsterdam: Daniel Elzevir [but France], 1674)

Translations of Molière Discussed in the Text

BEHN, APHRA, *Sir Patient Fancy* (London: printed by E. Flesher for Richard Tonson and Jacob Tonson, 1678)
BETTERTON, THOMAS, *The Amorous Widow; or, The Wanton Wife* (London: printed for W. Turner, 1706)
CENTLIVRE, SUSANNA, *Love's Contrivance; or, Le Médecin malgré lui* (London: printed for Bernard Lintott, 1703)
—— *The Platonick Lady* (London: printed for James Knapton, and Egbert Sanger, 1707)
CIBBER, COLLEY, *The Non-juror, a Comedy* (London: printed for T. J., 1718)
D'AVENANT, WILLIAM, *The Works* (London: printed by T. N. For Henry Herringman, 1673)
DRYDEN, JOHN, *Amphitryon; or, The Two Socia's [sic]* (London: printed for J. Tonson, 1690)
—— *Amphitryon; or, The Two Sosias*, in *Four Restoration Marriage Plays*, ed. Michael Cordner and Ronald Clayton (Oxford: Oxford University Press, 1995)
—— *Plays: Albion and Albanius, Don Sebastian, Amphitryon*, ed. by Earl Miner, George R. Guffey and Franklin B. Zimmerman, The Works of John Dryden, 15 (Berkeley, Los Angeles, & London: University of California Press, 1976)
FIELDING, HENRY, *The Mock Doctor; or, The Dumb Lady Cur'd. A Comedy. As it is Acted at the Theatre-Royal in Drury Lane, by His Majesty's Servants. With the Musick prefix'd to each Song* (London: printed for J. Watts, 1732)
FLECKNOE, RICHARD, *The Damoiselles à la mode* (London: printed for the author, 1667)
LACY, JOHN, *The Dumb Lady; or, The Farriar Made Physician* (London: printed for Thomas Dring, 1672)
MCSWINY, OWEN, *The Quacks; or, Love's the Physician* (London: printed for Benjamin Bragg, 1705)
MEDBOURNE, MATTHEW, *Tartuffe; or, The French Puritan* (London: printed by H. L and R. B. for James Magnus, 1670)
MOLIÈRE, *The Dramatic Works of Molière*, trans. by Henri Van Laun, 6 vols (Edinburgh: William Paterson, 1875–76)
—— *The Hypochondriack*, trans. anon. [John Hughes?], *The Monthly Amusement*, 4 (July 1709)

—— 'La Mallad [sic] Translated by Mr Wright', [c. 1678?], Washington, DC, Folger Shakespeare Library, MS V.b.220

—— *Monsieur de Pourceaugnac; or, Squire Trelooby*, trans. anon. [John Ozell?] (London: printed for Bernard Lintott, 1704)

—— *Select Comedies of Mr. de Molière, in French and English*, trans. by Henry Baker, James Miller, and Martin Clare, 8 vols (London: printed for J. Watts, 1732)

—— *The Works of Monsieur de Molière*, trans. by John Ozell and others), 6 vols (London: printed for Bernard Lintott, 1714)

—— *The Works of Mr. de Molière, French and English*, trans. by Henry Baker, James Miller, and Martin Clare, 10 vols (London: printed for J. Watts, 1739)

RAVENSCROFT, EDWARD, *The Citizen Turn'd Gentleman* (London: printed for Thomas Dring, 1672)

RAWLINS, THOMAS, *Tom Essence; or, The Modish Wife* (London: printed by T. M. for W. Cademan, 1677)

French Dictionaries

BAYLE, PIERRE, *Dictionnaire historique et critique*, 2 vols (Rotterdam: chez Reinier Leers, 1697)

—— *An Historical and Critical Dictionary*, trans. anon., 4 vols (London: printed for C. Harper and others, 1710)

CORNEILLE, THOMAS, *Le Dictionnaire des arts et des sciences*, 2 vols (Paris: Jean Baptiste Coignard, 1694)

Le Dictionnaire de l'Académie françoise dedié au Roy, 2 vols (Paris: printed for Coignard, Veuve Jean-Baptiste, 1694)

FURETIÈRE, ANTOINE, *Dictionnaire universel*, 3 vols (The Hague & Rotterdam: Arnout and Reinier Leers, 1690)

GODEFROY, Frédéric, *Dictionnaire de l'ancienne langue française*, 8 vols (Paris: F. Vieweg, Émile Bouillon, 1881–1902)

RICHELET, PIERRE, *Dictionnaire françois*, 2 vols (Geneva: Jean Herman Widerhold, 1680)

English Dictionaries

B. E., *The New Dictionary of the Terms Ancient and Modern of the Canting Crew* (London: printed for W. Hawes, 1699)

BLOUNT, THOMAS, *Glossographia* (London: printed by Tho. Newcomb, 1656)

—— *Glossographia*, 3rd edn (London: printed by Thomas Newcomb, 1670)

COLES, ELISHA, *An English Dictionary* (London: printed for Samuel Crouch 1676)

COWELL, JOHN, *The Interpreter; or, Book Containing the Signification of Words* (Cambridge: Legate, 1607)

JOHNSON, SAMUEL, *A Dictionary of the English Language* (London: printed by W. Strahan, 1755)

KERSEY, JOHN, *A New English Dictionary* (London: printed for Henry Bonwicke and Robert Knaplock, 1702)

NORTON DEFOE, BENJAMIN *A New English Dictionary* (Westminster: printed for John Brindley, Olive Payne, John Jolliffe, Alexander Lyon, Charles Corbett, and Richard Wellington, 1735)

PHILLIPS, EDWARD, *The New World of English Words* (London: printed by E. Tyler for Nath. Brooke, 1658)

PRESTON, HENRY, *Brief Directions for True-spelling: 1674* (Menston: Scolar Press, 1968)

SIMPSON, JACQUELINE, and STEVE ROUND, *A Dictionary of English Folklore* (Oxford: Oxford University Press, 2000)

VIENNE-GEURRIN, NATHALIE, *Shakespeare's Insults: A Pragmatic Dictionary* (London: Bloomsbury, 2016)
WILKINS, JOHN, *Essay Towards a Real Character, and Philosophical Language* (London: printed for Sa: Gellibrand and John Martyn, 1668)
WILLIAMS, GORDON, *A Dictionary of Sexual Language and Imagery in Shakespearean and Stuart Literature*, 3 vols (London: Athlone Press, 1994)
WRIGHT, JOSEPH, *The English Dialect Dictionary*, 6 vols (London: Henry Frowde, 1898–1905)

Bilingual Dictionaries

COTGRAVE, RANDLE, *A Dictionarie of the French and English Tongues* (London: printed by Adam Islip, 1611)
ESTIENNE, Robert *Dictionaire françois-latin, augmenté* (Paris, 1539)
FLORIO, JOHN, *Queen Anna's New World of Words; or, Dictionarie of Italian and English Tongues* (London: printed by Melchisedec Bradwood, 1611)
MIÈGE, GUY, *A New Dictionary, French and English, with Another English and French* (London: printed by Thomas Dawks, 1677)
RIDER, JOHN, *Bibliotheca scholastica* (Oxford: printed by Joseph Barnes, 1589)
THOMAS, WILLIAM, *Principal Rules of the Italian Grammar* (London: printed by Thomas Berthelet, 1550)

Other Works

ARISTOTLE, *Poetics*, trans. by Stephen Halliwell in *Aristotle, 'Poetics', Longinus, 'On the Sublime', Demetrius, 'On Style'*, Loeb Classical Library, 199 (Cambridge, MA: Harvard University Press, 1995)
ABLANCOURT, NICOLAS PERROT D', *Lucien, de la traduction de N. Perrot, sr. d'Ablancourt*, 2 vols (Paris: Augustin Courbé, 1654)
—— *Les Œuvres de Tacite de la traduction de N. Perrot sieur d'Ablancourt*, 2 vols (Paris: Augustin Courbé, 1658)
[ANON.], 'From Sion College, November 4', *Visions of Sir Heister Ryley*, 6 November 1710, in *The Visions of Sir Heister Ryley: With Other Entertainments*, ed. anon. [Charles Povey? or Daniel Defoe?] (London: printed for the author and sold by Mrs Sympson and others, 1711), pp. 135–36
—— *Hell Upon Earth; or, The Town in an Uproar* (London: printed for J. Roberts and A. Dodd, 1729)
AUBIGNAC, FRANÇOIS HÉDELIN, ABBÉ D', *La Pratique du théâtre*, ed. by Hélène Baby (Paris: Champion, 2001)
—— *The Whole Art of the Stage, Made English*, trans. anon. (London: printed for the author, 1684)
AVERY, EMMET L., ed., *The London Stage, 1660–1800: A Calendar of Plays, Entertainments and Afterpieces. Part 2: 1700–1729* (Carbondale: Southern Illinois University Press, 1960)
BAKER, MONA, ed., *Routledge Encyclopedia of Translation Studies* (London & New York: Routledge, 2019)
BARBEAU GARDINER, ANNE, 'Medbourne's *Tartuffe* (1670): A Satire on Land-Acquisition during the Interregnum', *Restoration and Eighteenth-century Theatre Research*, 9.1 (1994) 1–16
BARBER, CHARLES LAURENCE, *Early Modern English*, 2nd edn (Edinburgh: Edinburgh University Press, 1997)
BASSNETT, SUSAN, and ANDRÉ LEFEVERE, *Constructing Cultures: Essays on Literary Translation* (Clevedon: Cromwell Press, 1998)

BAXTER, RICHARD, *Church-history of the Government of Bishops and their Councils Abbreviated* (London: printed for Thomas Simmons, 1680)

BEHN, Aphra, *Five Plays*, ed. by Margaret Duffy (London: Methuen Drama, 1990)

BESING, MAX, *Molières Einfluss auf das englische Lustspiel bis 1700* (Borna-Lepizig: Buchdruckerei Robert Noske, 1913)

BEVINGTON, DAVID, *Shakespeare: The Seven Ages of Human Experience*, 2nd edn (Malden, MA: Wiley-Blackwell, 2005)

BEVIS, RICHARD W., *English Drama: Restoration and Eighteenth Century 1660–1789* (London: Longman, 1988)

BOURQUI, CLAUDE, 'Monsieur de Pourceaugnac et les enjeux de la prononciation *du français*', *Littératures Classiques*, 87.2 (2015), 163–73

BOURQUI, CLAUDE, and CLAUDIO VINTI, *Molière à l'école italienne: le 'lazzo' dans la création moliéresque* (Turin, Paris: L'Harmattan Italia, 2003)

BRAGA RIERA, JORGE, *Classical Spanish Drama in Restoration England (1660–1700)* (Madrid: Complutense University of Madrid, 2009)

BRÉMOND, GABRIEL DE, *The Fair One of Tunis; or, The Generous Mistres [sic]: A New Piece of Gallantry*, trans. by Charles Cotton (London: printed for Henry Brome, 1674)

BRÉMOND, SÉBASTIEN, *The Pilgrim: A Pleasant Piece of Gallantry*, trans. by Peter Belon (London: printed for R. Bentley and M. Magnes, 1680)

BRUHN, JØRGEN, ANNE GJELSVIK, and EIRIK FRISVOLD HANSSEN, eds, *Adaptation Studies: New Challenges, New Directions* (London: Bloomsbury, 2013)

BIAGIO, GIAN, *Latin Literature: A History*, trans. by Joseph Solodow (Baltimore, MD, & London: John Hopkins University Press, 1994)

CAMERON, DERRICK, 'Tradaptation: Cultural Exchange and Black British Theatre', in *Moving Target: Theatre Translation and Cultural Relocation*, ed. by Carole-Anne Upton (London & New York: Routledge, 2000), pp. 17–24

CAMPBELL, ROBERT, *The London Tradesman: A Compendious View of All the Trades Now Practised in London and Westminster* (London: printed by T. Gardner, 1747)

CANFIELD, J. DOUGLAS, *Tricksters and Estates: On the Ideology of Restoration Comedy* (Lexington: University Press of Kentucky, 1997)

CANNON HARRIS, SUSAN, 'Mixed Marriage: Sheridan, Macklin, and the Hybrid Audience', in *Players, Playwrights, Playhouse: Investigating Performance, 1660–1800*, ed. by Michael Cordner and Peter Holland (New York: Palgrave Macmillan, 2007), pp. 189–212

CANOVA-GREEN, MARIE-CLAUDE, 'Molière, ou comment ne pas reconnaître sa dette: le théâtre de la Restauration en Angleterre', in *La France et l'Europe du Nord au XVIIe siècle: de l'Irlande à la Russie*, ed. by Richard Maber, Biblio 17 (Tübingen: Narr Francke Attempto, 2017), pp. 109–20

CAVAILLÉ, FABIEN, and BÉNÉDICTE LOUVAT-MOLOZAY, 'Les Compétences linguistiques des comédiens professionnels au XVIIe siècle', *Littératures Classiques*, 87.2 (2015), 317–32

CHARLANNE, LOUIS, *L'Influence française en Angleterre au XVIIe siècle* (Paris: Société Française d'Imprimerie et de Librairie, 1906)

CLASSE, OLIVE, ed., *The Encyclopedia of Literary Translation into English*, 2 vols (London, Chicago: Fitzroy Dearborn, 2000)

COFFEY, JOHN, and PAUL C. H. LIM, eds, *The Cambridge Companion to Puritanism* (Cambridge: Cambridge University Press, 2008)

CORNEILLE, PIERRE, *Œuvres complètes*, ed. by Georges Couton, 3 vols (Paris: Gallimard, 1987)

COWLEY, ABRAHAM, *Poems: i. Miscellanies. ii. The Mistress. iii. Pindarique Odes. iv. Davideis.* (London, 1656)

Daily Courant (London), Wednesday, June 16, 1703

———, Wednesday, May 10, 1732

DANDREY, PATRICK, *La Médecine et la maladie dans le théâtre de Molière*, 2 vols (Paris: Klincksieck, 1998)
—— 'Molière auto-portraitiste: du masque au visage', in *Le Statut littéraire de l'écrivain*, ed. by Lise Sabourin, Travaux de Littérature, XX (Geneva: Droz, 2007), pp. 107–19
DEMETRIOU, TANIA, and ROWAN TOMLINSON, eds, *The Culture of Translation in Early Modern England and France, 1500–1660* (New York: Palgrave Macmillan, 2015)
DENHAM, JOHN, *The Destruction of Troy: An Essay upon the Second Book of Virgils Æneis, Written in the Year, 1636* (London: printed for Humphrey Moseley, 1656)
DENIS, DELPHINE, *Le Parnasse galant: institution d'une catégorie littéraire au XVIIe siècle* (Paris: Champion, 2001)
DILLON, WENTWORTH, EARL OF ROSCOMMON, *Essay on Translated Verse* (London: printed for J. Tonson, 1685)
DOBSON, MICHAEL, 'Adaptations and Revivals', in *The Cambridge Companion to English Restoration Theatre*, ed. by Deborah Payne Fisk (Cambridge: Cambridge University Press, 2000), pp. 40–51
DRYDEN, JOHN, *Plays: The Indian Emperour, Secret Love, Sir Martin Mar-all*, ed. by John Loftis and Vinton A. Dearing, The Works of John Dryden, 9 (Berkeley, Los Angeles, & London: University of California Press, 1966)
—— *Plays: The Tempest, Tyrannick Love, An Evening's Love*, ed. by Maximillian E. Novak and George R. Guffey, The Works of John Dryden, 10 (Berkeley, Los Angeles, & London: University of California Press, 1970)
—— *Poems, 1649–1680*, ed. by Edward Niles Hooker and H. T. Swedenberg, Jr., The Works of John Dryden, 1 (Berkeley, Los Angeles, & London: University of California Press, 1956)
—— *The Poems of John Dryden: Volume 1, 1649–1681*, ed. by Paul Hammond (London: Longman, 1995)
—— *Prose 1668–1691: An Essay of Dramatick Poesie and Shorter Works*, ed. by Samuel Holt Monk and A. E. Wallace Maurer, The Works of John Dryden, 17 (Berkeley, Los Angeles, & London: University of California Press, 1971)
—— *Prose: The History of the League, 1684*, ed. by Alan Roper and Vinton A. Dearing, The Works of John Dryden, 18 (London: University of California Press, 1974)
ETHEREGE, GEORGE, *The Comical Revenge; or, Love in a Tub* (London: printed for Henry Herringman, 1664)
FLOTOW, LUISE VON, and JOAN W. SCOTT, 'Gender Studies and Translation Studies: "Entre braguettes" — Connecting the Disciplines', in *Border Crossings: Translation Studies and Other Disciplines*, ed. by Yves Gambier and Luc van Doorslaer (Amsterdam & Philadelphia: John Benjamins Publishing Company, 2016), pp. 349–73
FRANCE, PETER, *The Oxford Guide to Literature in English Translation* (Oxford: Oxford University Press, 2001)
GALLAGHER, JOHN, *Learning Languages in Early Modern England* (Oxford: Oxford University Press, 2019)
GOULBOURNE, RUSSELL, *Voltaire Comic Dramatist* (Oxford: Voltaire Foundation, 2006)
HAWCROFT, MICHAEL, *Molière: Reasoning with Fools* (Oxford: Oxford University Press, 2007)
HODGES, JOHN C., 'The Authorship of *Squire Trelooby*', *The Review of English Studies*, 4.16 (1928), 404–13
HOLDEN, WILLIAM P., *Anti-Puritan Satire 1572–1642* (New Haven, CT: Yale University Press, 1954)
HOLLAND, ANNA, and RICHARD SCHOLAR, eds, *Pre-histories and Afterlives: Studies in Critical Method for Terence Cave* (London: Legenda, 2009)
HOLLAND, PETER, *The Ornament of Action: Text and Performance in Restoration Comedy* (Cambridge: Cambridge University Press, 1979)

HOPKINS, DAVID, and STUART GILLESPIE, eds, *The Oxford History of Literary Translation in English: Volume 3, 1660–1790* (Oxford: Oxford University Press, 2005)

HOWARD, SIR ROBERT, *Four New Plays* (London: printed for Henry Herringman, 1655)

HOWARTH, W. D., *Molière: A Playwright and his Audience* (Cambridge: Cambridge University Press, 1982)

HUME, ROBERT D., *The Development of English Drama in the Late Seventeenth Century* (Oxford: Oxford University Press, 1976)

HUGHES, DEREK, *English Drama 1660–1700* (Oxford: Clarendon Press, 1996)

—— *The Theatre of Aphra Behn* (Basingstoke & New York: Palgrave Macmillan, 2001)

JOHANSSON, BERTIL, *The Adapter Adapted, a Study of Sir John Vanbrugh's Comedy 'The Mistake': Its Predecessors and Successors* (Stockholm: Almqvist & Wiksell International, 1977)

JONES, SUZANNE, 'Printing Stage: Relationships between Performance, Print and Translation in Early English Editions of Molière', *Early Modern French Studies*, 40.2 (2018), 146–65

JONSON, BEN, *Bartholomew Fair*, ed. by Suzanne Gossett (Manchester: Manchester University Press, 2000)

KEARFUL, FRANK J., 'Molière among the English', in *Molière and the Commonwealth of Letters: Patrimony and Posterity*, ed. by Roger Johnson, Guy T. Trail, and Editha Neumann (Jackson: University Press of Mississippi, 1975), pp. 199–217

KERBY, W. MOSELEY, 'Molière and the Restoration Comedy in England' (unpublished doctoral thesis, Université de Rennes, 1907)

KEWES, PAULINA, *Authorship and Appropriation: Writing for the Stage in England, 1660–1710* (Oxford: Clarendon Press, 1998)

KLEIN, H. M. 'Molière in English Critical Thought on Comedy to 1800', in *Molière and the Commonwealth of Letters: Patrimony and Posterity*, ed. by Roger Johnson, Guy T. Trail, and Editha Neumann (Jackson: University Press of Mississippi, 1975), pp. 218–31

KNOWLAND, A.S., ed., *Six Caroline Plays* (Oxford: Oxford University Press, 1962)

KNUTSON, HAROLD C. *The Triumph of Wit: Molière and Restoration Comedy* (Columbus: Ohio State University Press, 1988)

LA MOTTE, ANTOINE HOUDAR DE, *Suite de réflexions sur la tragédie où on répond à Mr. de Voltaire* (Paris: Dupuis, 1730; fac. repr. Millwood, NY: Kraus International, 1983)

LANGBAINE, GERARD, *An Account of the English Dramatick Poets* (Oxford: printed by L.L. for George West and Henry Clements, 1691)

LAWRENCE, W. J., 'Early French Players in England', *Anglia*, 32 (1909), 61–89

LE BOULANGER DE CHALUSSAY, *Élomire hypocondre ou les médecins vengés* (Paris: printed by Charles de Sercy, 1670)

LE PAYS, RENÉ, *The Drudge; or, The Jealous Extravagant: A Piece of Gallantry*, trans. by J. B. (London: printed for Henry Herringman, 1673)

LOUVAT-MOLOZAY, BÉNÉDICTE, 'L'obscénité: du texte à la scène', in *Mettre en scène(s) 'L'École des femmes' selon les sources historiques / Staging 'L'École des femmes' According to Historical Sources*, special issue of *Arrêt sur scène / Scene Focus*, 5 (2016), 101–10, <http://www.ircl.cnrs.fr/productions%20electroniques/arret_scene/arret_scene_focus_5_2016.htm>

LOUVAT-MOLOZAY, BÉNÉDICTE, and FLORENCE MARCH, *Les Théâtres anglais et français (XVIe–XVIIIe siècles): contacts, circulation, influences* (Rennes: Presses universitaires de Rennes, 2016)

MAZOUER, CHARLES, *Trois comédies de Molière: étude sur Le Misanthrope, George Dandin, Le Bourgeois gentilhomme* (Pessac: Presses universitaires de Bordeaux, 2007)

MCBRIDE, ROBERT, *Molière et son premier Tartuffe: genèse et évolution d'une pièce à scandale*, Durham Modern Language Series (Durham: Durham University Press, 2005)

MEYER, SILKE, 'The Germans as the Alter-Ego of the English?: The German Doctor in Eighteenth-century Debate', *Ethnologia Europaea*, 36.1 (2006), 58–69

MILES, DUDLEY H., *The Influence of Molière on Restoration Comedy* (New York: Columbia University Press, 1910)
—— 'The Original of the Non-juror', *Publications of the Modern Languages Association*, 30.2 (1915), 195–214
MILHOUS, JUDITH, and ROBERT D. HUME, 'Dating Play Premieres', *Harvard Library Bulletin*, 22 (1974), 374–405
MONGRÉDIEN, GEORGES, *Recueil des textes et des documents du XVIIe siècle relatifs à Molière*, 2 vols (Paris, 1966)
NEVALAINEN, TERTTU, 'Early Modern English Lexis and Semantics', in *The Cambridge History of the English Language*, ed. by Roger Lass, 6 vols (Cambridge: Cambridge University Press, 2000), III, 332–498
NICOLL, ALLARDYCE, *A History of Restoration Drama, 1660–1700*, 4th edn (Cambridge: Cambridge University Press, 1952)
PARISH, RICHARD, 'How (and Why) not to Take Molière too Seriously', in *The Cambridge Companion to Molière*, ed. by David Bradby and Andrew Calder (Cambridge: Cambridge University Press, 2006), pp. 71–82
PAYNE FISK, DEBORAH, ed., *The Cambridge Companion to English Restoration Theatre* (Cambridge: Cambridge University Press, 2000)
——, ed., *Four Restoration Libertine Plays* (Oxford: Oxford University Press, 2005)
PAULSON, RONALD, *Hogarth's Graphic Works*, 2 vols (New Haven, CT: Yale University Press, 1965)
PEACOCK, NOËL, 'Molière', in *The Encyclopedia of Literary Translation into English*, ed. by Olive Classe, 2 vols (London, Chicago: Fitzroy Dearborn, 2000), II
—— *Molière in Scotland* (Glasgow: University of Glasgow French and German Publications, 1993)
—— 'Molière Nationalised: *Tartuffe* on the British Stage from the Restoration to the Present Day', in *The Cambridge Companion to Molière*, ed. by David Bradby and Andrew Calder (Cambridge: Cambridge University Press, 2006), pp. 177–88
PEPYS, SAMUEL, *The Diary of Samuel Pepys*, ed. by Robert Latham and William Matthews, 11 vols (London: Bell and Hyman, 1970–83)
PHILLIPS, HENRY, 'Authority and Order in Molière Comedy', *Nottingham French Studies*, 33.1 (Spring 1994), 12–19
PLATO, *Selected Dialogues of Plato: The Benjamin Jowett Translation*, rev. and intro. by Hayden Pelliccia (New York: Modern Library, 2001)
PLAYFORD, JOHN, *Choice Songs and Ayres for One Voyce to Sing to a Theorbo-lute or Bass-viol* (London: printed by William Godbid, 1676)
PLOIX, CÉDRIC, *Translating Molière for the English-speaking Stage: The Role of Verse and Rhyme* (New York and Abingdon: Routledge, 2020)
PORTER, ROY, *Health for Sale: Quackery in England, 1660–1850* (Manchester: Manchester University Press, 1989)
POWELL, JOHN S., *Music and Theatre in France, 1600–1680* (Oxford: Oxford University Press, 2000)
PREST, JULIA, *Controversy in French Drama: Tartuffe and the Struggle for Influence* (New York: Palgrave, 2014)
PURE, MICHEL DE, *La Prétieuse, ou le mystère des ruelles*, ed. by Émile Magne, 2 vols (Paris: E. Droz, 1938–39)
QUINAULT, PHILIPPE, *L'Amant Indiscret, ou le maistre estourdi*, ed. by William Brooks (Liverpool: University of Liverpool, Department of French, 2003)
RACINE, JEAN, *Théâtre. Poésie,* ed. by Georges Forestier (Paris: Gallimard, 1999)
Révolutions de Paris, 12 March 1791

RICHARDS, KENNETH, 'The French Actors in London', *Restoration and Eighteenth-century Theatre Research*,14.2 (1 November 1975), 48–52
RICHMOND, HUGH M., *Puritans and Libertines: Anglo-French Relations in the Reformation* (Berkeley, Los Angeles, & London: University of California Press, 1981)
ROBERTS, DAVID, *Restoration Plays and Players: An Introduction* (Cambridge: Cambridge University Press, 2004)
RUNTE, ROSEANN, 'Cross-cultural Influences: Versions of *Tartuffe* in Eighteenth-century France and Restoration England', *Romances Notes*, 36.3 (Spring 1996), 265–76
SACKVILLE, CHARLES, LORD BUCKHURST, SIR CHARLES SEDLEY, and SIR WILLIAM D'AVENANT, eds, *The New Academy of Complements* (London: printed for George Sawbridge, 1671)
SALTER, DENIS, 'Acting Shakespeare in Postcolonial Space', in *Shakespeare: Theory and Performance*, ed. by James C. Bulman (London & New York: Routledge, 1996), pp. 113–32
SAUNDERS, BEN, 'Iago's Clyster: Purgation, Anality, and the Civilizing Process', *Shakespeare Quarterly*, 55.2 (2004), 148–76
SCHERER, JACQUES, *La Dramaturgie classique en France* (Paris: Librairie Nizet, 1986)
SCOTT, CLIVE, *The Riches of Rhyme: Studies in French Verse* (Oxford: Clarendon Press, 1988)
—— *French Verse-art: A Study* (Cambridge: Cambridge University Press, 1980)
SHADWELL, THOMAS, *The Miser, a Comedy* (London: printed for Thomas Collins and John Ford, 1672)
—— *Psyche: A Tragedy* (London: printed by T. N. for Henry Herringman, 1675)
—— *The Sullen Lovers; or, The Impertinents* (London: printed for Henry Herringman, 1668)
SHAPIRO, BARBARA, *Political Communication and Political Culture in England, 1558–1668* (Stanford, CA: Stanford University Press, 2012)
SIMMONS, J. L., 'A Source for Shakespeare's Malvolio: The Elizabethan Controversy with the Puritans', *Huntingdon Library Quarterly*, 36.6 (May 1973), 181–201
SINGH, SARUP, *The Theory of Drama in the Restoration Period* (Bombay: Orient Longmans, 1963)
SMITH, CHRISTOPHER, and ELFRIEDA DUBOIS, eds, *France et Grande-Bretagne de la chute de Charles Ier à celle de Jacques II (1649–1688)*, Actes d'Oxford, Society for Seventeenth-century French Studies (Norwich: University of East Anglia, 1990)
SONDEREGGER, LORI, 'Sources of Translation: A Discussion of Matthew Medbourne's 1670 Translation of Molière's *Tartuffe*', *Papers on Seventeenth-century French Literature*, 27.52 (2000), 553–72
SPURR, JOHN, *English Puritanism 1603–1689* (Basingstoke: Macmillan, 1998)
STEDMAN, GESA, *Cultural Exchange in Seventeenth-century France and England* (Farnham: Ashgate, 2013)
SUCKLING, NORMAN, 'Molière and English Restoration Comedy', in *Restoration Theatre*, ed. by John Russell Brown and Bernard Harris (London: Edward Arnold, 1965)
SWIFT, JONATHAN, *Miscellanies in Prose and Verse* (London: printed for John Morphew, 1711)
THOMAS, DAVID, and ARNOLD HARE, eds, *Restoration and Georgian England, 1660–1788: A Documentary History* (Cambridge: Cambridge University Press, 1989)
TODD, JANET, '"Pursue that Way of Fooling, and be Damned": Editing Aphra Behn', *Studies in the Novel*, 27.3 (Fall 1995), 304–19
TUCKER, JOSEPH E., *Molière in England 1700–1750* (Madison: University of Wisconsin, 1937)
—— 'The Eighteenth-century English Translations of Molière', *Modern Language Quarterly*, 3.1 (March 1942), 83–103
TURNER, DAVID, *Fashioning Adultery, Gender, Sex and Civility in England, 1660–1740* (Cambridge: Cambridge University Press, 2002)
TYTLER, ALEXANDER, *Essay on the Principles of Translation* (London: printed for T. Cadell; and W. Creech, Edinburgh, 1791)

UNGERER, GUSTAVE 'Thomas Shadwell's *The Libertine* (1675): A Forgotten Restoration Don Juan Play', in *SEDERI: Yearbook of the Spanish and Portuguese Society for English Renaissance Studies*, 1 (1990), 222–40
VAN LENNEP, WILLIAM, EMMET L. AVERY, and ARTHUR H. SCOUTEN, eds, *The London Stage, 1660–1800: A Calendar of Plays, Entertainments and Afterpieces. Part I: 1660–1700* (Carbondale: Southern Illinois University Press, 1965)
VENUTI, LAWRENCE, *The Translator's Invisibility* (London & New York: Routledge, 1995)
VIALA, ALAIN, *La France galante* (Paris: Presses universitaires de France, 2008)
—— 'Molière et le langage galant', in *'Car demeure l'amitié': mélanges offerts à Claude Abraham*, ed. by Francis Assaf and Andrew H. Wallis (Paris, Seattle, & Tübingen: Biblio 17, 1997), pp. 99–109
VILLIERS, GEORGE, DUKE OF BUCKINGHAM, *The Rehearsal* (London: printed for Thomas Dring, 1672)
VOLTAIRE, *Complete Works of Voltaire / Œuvres complètes de Voltaire*, 20C: *'Micromégas' and Other Texts (1738–1742)*, ed. by Nicholas Cronk, Thomas Wynn, and others (Oxford: Voltaire Foundation, 2017)
—— *Lettres philosophiques, ou Lettres anglaises*, ed. by Raymond Naves (Paris: Garnier Frères, 1964)
WADSWORTH, PHILIP S., *Molière and the Italian Tradition* (Birmingham, AL: Summa Publications, 1987)
WALLACE, DEWEY D., ed., *The Spirituality of the Later English Puritans: An Anthology* (Macon, GA: Mercer University Press, 1989)
WALSHAM, ALEXANDRA, *Providence in Early Modern England* (Oxford: Oxford University Press, 1999)
Westminster-drollery; or, A Choice Collection of the Newest Songs & Poems both at Court and Theatres, ed. by 'a Person of quality' (London: printed for H. Brome, 1671)
WILCOX, JOHN, *The Relation of Molière to Restoration Comedy* (New York: Benjamin Blom, 1938)
WILLIS, THOMAS, *Dr Willis's Practice of Physick* (London: printed for T. Dring, C. Harper, and J. Leigh, 1681)
WORTH-STYLIANOU, VALERIE, *Practising Translation in Renaissance France: The Example of Étienne Dolet* (Oxford: Clarendon Press, 1988)
—— 'Translatio and Translation in the Renaissance: From Italy to France', in *The Cambridge History of Literary Criticism, III: The Renaissance*, ed. by George Alexander Kennedy and Glyn P. Norton (Cambridge: Cambridge University Press, 1999), pp. 127–35
WYCHERLEY, William, *The Plain Dealer*, in *The Country Wife and Other Plays*, ed. by Peter Dixon (Oxford: Oxford University Press, 2008)
ZUBER, ROGER, *Les Belles Infidèles et la formation du goût classique* (Paris: Colin, 1968; rev. edn Paris: Michel, 1995)

INDEX

Ablancourt, Nicolas Perrot d':
    translating 'fidelity' and 'infidelity' 46–47
Act of Settlement 116
Act of Uniformity 105
Acts of Union 9
Adaptation Studies 44
Anne of Austria 1
Aristotle:
    Poetics 17, 179
Aubignac, François Hédelin, abbé d':
    La Pratique du Théâtre 18, 20, 41

Baker, Henry, James Miller and Martin Clare:
    biographies 57 n. 27
    Select Comedies of Mr. de Molière 6, 35–36, 52–53, 54–55, 99, 175, 176
        The Cit turn'd Gentleman 80, 157, 162, 163, 167; *The Cuckold in Conceit* 87, 88, 90, 91, 95, 96, 97; *A Doctor and no Doctor* 134, 153; *George Dandin; or, The Husband Defeated* 93, 96; *The Hypochondriack* 133; *The Imposter (Tartuffe)* 107, 117, 118–19; *Love the Best Physician* 134; *The School for Wives* 87, 90, 91; *Squire Lubberly* 157, 159, 167, 171–72
    The Works of Mr. de Molière, French and English:
        The School for Wives Criticis'd 100
Barbeau Gardiner, Anne:
    'Medbourne's *Tartuffe* (1670): A Satire on Land-Acquisition' 30
Barber, Charles Laurence:
    Early Modern English 110
Barbieri, Nicolò:
    Il inavvertito 27–28
Baxter, Richard:
    Church-history of the Government of Bishops 119
Bayle, Pierre:
    Dictionnaire historique et critique 178
Behn, Aphra:
    biography 154 n. 10
    gender and translation 11–12
    Sir Patient Fancy 11, 128, 131–32, 134, 139–40, 143–48, 149, 150, 151–52, 153
Betterton, Thomas:
    The Amorous Widow; or, Wanton Wife 5, 92–93, 96–97
    and Lincolns Inn Fields 5
    and the United Company at the Theatre Royal, Drury Lane 5

bourgeoisie 157, 159–61, 173, 179

Cameron, Derrick:
    'Tradaptation: Cultural Exchange and Black British Theatre' 9
Campbell, Robert:
    The London Tradesman 135–36
Cannon Harris, Susan:
    'Mixed Marriage: Sheridan, Macklin, and the Hybrid Audience' 180
Caryl, John:
    Sir Salomon; or, The Cautious Coxcomb 5, 87
Centlivre, Susanna:
    biography 39 n. 36
    gender and translation 11–12
    Love's Contrivance; or, Le Médecin malgré lui 34–35, 50, 128, 140–41, 143–44, 148–51, 153, 176
    The Platonick Lady (preface) 150, 151
Charlanne, Louis:
    L'Influence française en Angleterre au XVIIe siècle 7
Charles II: 3, 44, 105, 106, 108, 177
Charpentier, Antoine 2
Cibber, Colley:
    The Non-juror 116
    and the Theatre Royal, Drury Lane 5
Classe, Olive:
    The Encyclopedia of Literary Translation into English 159
clyster (glister) 130
Cockpit Theatre 1–2, 3
comédie-ballet 2, 3, 76, 78, 142, 157, 173
commedia dell'arte 2, 41, 48, 94
Communauté des librairies 6
Congreve, William, John Vanbrugh and William Walsh:
    translation of *Monsieur de Pourceaugnac* 5, 35, 43, 51, 167
Corneille, Pierre 41, 88
    Discours des trois unités 18–19, 20
    and *liaison des scènes* 19
    Horace 4
    La Mort de Pompée 4
    Nicomède 2
    Psyché 79
Corneille, Thomas 88
    Dictionnaire des arts et des sciences 5
Cowley, Abraham:
    Pindarique Odes (preface) 47–48, 53

Cromwell, Oliver:
   and the Commonwealth period 1, 3, 4, 105, 175
   death 2
Crowne, John:
   The English Frier 116
cuckoldry 85–90, 93–95, 100

Dandrey, Patrick:
   'Molière auto-portraitiste: du masque au visage' 133
D'Avenant, William:
   biography 37 n. 10
   The Cruelty of the Spaniards in Peru 1, 60
   The Duke's Company 5
   The History of Sir Francis Drake 60
   The Playhouse to be Let 3, 21, 44, 60, 65, 86, 88–89, 94–95, 97, 175
Denham, (Sir) John:
   completion of Katherine Philips's *Horace* 4
   The Destruction of Troy (preface) 47
Descartes, René 122, 123
Donneau de Visé, Jean 2
Dryden, John:
   Amphitryon 6, 20, 31–33, 50, 55, 59, 69–76, 79, 176
   Arviragus Reviv'd (preface) 3–4
   biography 37 n. 7
   and the Duke's Company 5
   Essay of Dramatick Poesie 19, 20–21, 23, 25, 26–27, 36, 55
   An Evening's Love 29
   The History of the League (preface) 105–06, 107
   Marriage à la mode 85
   and Nathaniel Lee; *The Duke of Guise* 106
   Ovid's Epistles (preface) 48, 50
   Sir Martin Mar-all; or, The Feign'd Innocence 5, 27–28, 79
   translating tendencies 6

Elzevir, Daniel 145
English Civil War 1, 3, 105, 117
Etherege, George:
   The Comical Revenge 121
   time in France 3
Exclusion Crisis 9

Farmer, Thomas (composer) 78
Fielding, Henry:
   biography 57 n. 28
   The Mock Doctor 52–53, 128, 134, 137, 138, 141–42, 148, 176
Flecknoe, Richard:
   biography 38 n. 13
   The Damoiselles à la mode 21–27, 49, 87, 175
Fronde 1

gallantry 90–100
Garneau, Michel:
   tradaptation 8–9

gender:
   and early modern translation 11–12, 143–51
Glorious Revolution 9, 32

Henrietta of England 3
Hogarth, William 10, 13 n. 24
Holland, Peter:
   The Ornament of Action: Text and Performance in Restoration Comedy 120
Howard, (Sir) Robert:
   Four New Plays (preface) 65, 66
Hughes, Derek:
   The Theatre of Aphra Behn 145, 149
Hughes, John, and John Ozell:
   The Monthly Amusement 127, 176
hypochondria 132–34
hypocrisy 119–21

James I: 110
James II: 32, 116
Jonson, Ben:
   Bartholomew Fair 110, 116

Kearful, Frank K.:
   'Molière among the English' 7–8
Killigrew, Thomas:
   and the King's Company 4–5
   The Parson's Wedding 95
Knutson, Harold C.:
   The Triumph of Wit: Molière and Restoration Comedy 8

Lacy, John:
   The Dumb Lady; or, The Farriar Made Physician 5, 128, 129–31, 134, 135–36, 137
La Mothe le Vayer, François de:
   Du mariage 88
Langbaine, Gerard:
   Account of the English Dramatic Poets 6, 108
Le Boulanger de Chalussay:
   Élomire hypocondre, ou Les Médecins vengés 133–34
libertinism 121–24
Louis XIV 2, 31, 67–68, 105
Lully, Jean-Baptiste 2, 78

McSwiny, Owen:
   biography 57 n. 25
   The Quacks; or, Love's the Physician 51, 127, 128, 132, 138–39, 140, 141–42, 152
Maimbourg, Louis de:
   Histoire de la Ligue 105
malady 128–29
mamamouchi 157
Marais, Théâtre du 2
Mazarin 1
Mazouer, Charles:
   Trois comédies de Molière 161

Medbourne, Matthew:
    biography 38 n. 23
    Tartuffe; or, the French Puritan 5, 20, 29–31, 32, 33, 43, 54, 59, 65–68, 107, 108–16, 117, 118, 119, 121, 124, 175
    translating tendencies 6
médecin 134–35
Miles, Dudley H.:
    The Influence of Molière on Restoration Comedy 7, 54
Molière:
    career:
        Illustre Théâtre 1
        Louvre performance 2
        Palais-Royal 2, 88, 98
        patronage of the prince de Conti 1
        Petit Bourbon, Théâtre du 2
        tour in the provinces 1
        Troupe de Monsieur 2
        and rivalry with the Troupe royale at the Hôtel de Bourgogne 2
    death 3
    plays:
        L'Amour médecin 3, 128, 131, 132, 134, 138, 139, 140, 141–42, 151, 152
        Amphitryon 3, 6, 20, 31–33, 55, 59, 69–76, 79, 176
        L'Avare 11, 34, 79, 172
        Le Bourgeois gentilhomme 3, 5, 9, 53, 76–78, 157, 158, 159–60, 161–64, 165, 166, 167, 168, 172–73, 179
        La Comtesse d'Escarbagnas 91
        La Critique de l'École des femmes 2, 85, 98–100
        Le Dépit amoureux 2
        Le Docteur amoureux 2
        Dom Juan, ou Le Festin de pierre 3, 107, 119–24
        L'École des femmes 2, 4, 5, 21–23, 25, 76, 85, 87, 88, 90, 91, 94, 97–98, 100
        L'École des maris 21–26, 49, 76, 179
        L'Étourdi ou les Contretemps 2, 5, 27, 76, 79
        Les Fâcheux 5, 28, 50, 76
        farces 11
        Les Femmes savantes 3, 72, 91, 151
        Les Fourberies de Scapin 91
        George Dandin, ou le Mari confondu 5, 76–77, 85, 92–93, 96–97, 103
        L'Impromptu de Versailles 2
        Le Malade imaginaire 3, 11, 91, 127–28, 131, 132–34, 135, 139–40, 142, 143–48, 150, 151, 176
        Le Mariage forcé 32
        Le Médecin malgré lui 3, 11, 34, 128–30, 132, 134, 136, 137, 140, 141, 142, 148–51, 153, 176
        Le Misanthrope 3, 5, 11, 28, 99, 176
        Monsieur de Pourceaugnac 3, 5, 35, 43, 51, 76, 157, 158, 163, 164, 165–73, 179, 180
        Les Précieuses ridicules 2, 22–25, 49, 151, 179
        La Princesse d'Élide 79
        Psyché 79

Sganarelle ou le Cocu imaginaire 2, 3, 21, 22, 44, 59, 60–65, 85, 86–90, 93–94, 95, 97, 100
Le Tartuffe, ou l'Imposteur 2–3, 4, 9, 20, 29–31, 36, 43, 54, 65–68, 107–19, 120, 121, 124, 146, 175, 178
mountebank 141–43

Newcastle, 1st Duke of (William Cavendish):
    translation of *L'Étourdi* 27–28

Ozell, John:
    biography 39 n. 39
    Monsieur de Pourceaugnac; or, Squire Trelooby 35, 43, 51, 157, 167–68, 169–72, 180
    Works of Monsieur de Molière 35, 51, 52, 79, 176
        Don John; or, The Libertine 107, 120–24; *The Forced Physician* 134; *The Gentleman Cit* 157, 159, 162, 163; *George Dandin; or The Wanton Wife* 93; *The Hypocondriack* 127, 132–33, 134; *The Imaginary Cuckold* 87, 89, 95, 97; *Love's the Physician* 134; *The Princess of Elis* 79–80; *A School for Women* 87, 90, 91–92; *The School for Women Criticised* 98–99; *Tartuffe: or, The Hypocrite* 107, 113, 117, 118, 119

Payne Fisk, Deborah:
    Four Restoration Libertine Plays 122
Peacock, Noël:
    'Molière' in *The Encyclopedia of Literary Translation into English* 8
Pepys, Samuel 38n. 14, 59, 81 n. 1, 125 n. 14
Philips, Katherine 4
Pitel, Henri:
    and French acting troupe in London 144
Les Plaisirs de L'Île enchantée 2, 79
Plautus 42, 53
    Amphitruo 31, 51, 55, 176
Popish Plot 9, 108
Porter, Roy:
    Health for Sale: Quackery in England, 1660–1850: 128
Prest, Julia:
    Controversy in French Drama 107, 108, 117
Purcell, Henry 79
Pure, abbé de:
    La Prétieuse 93
Puritanism:
    anti-Puritan satire 30, 43, 106, 108, 111, 113–16, 117, 118, 124, 131, 175

quackery 127–28, 139–43, 152–53, 179
Quinault, Philippe:
    L'Amant indiscret 27–28, 79
    Psyché 79

Racine, Jean 4, 20
Ravenscroft, Edward 6

biography 81 n. 10
The Careless Lovers 5
The *Citizen Turn'd Gentleman* 5, 76–78, 157, 159, 162–63, 164, 166–67, 169, 172, 175
The London Cuckolds 87
Scaramouch a Philosopher, Harlequin a School-Boy, Bravo, Merchand and Magician 5
Rawlins, Thomas:
biography 81 n. 3
Sir Tom Essence; or, The Modish Wife 60–65, 80, 86
Restoration Comedy 6–8, 13 n. 11
rhyme:
alternance des rimes 71–74
masculine and feminine rhymes 71–76, 80
rimes croisées 70, 71 74, 75
rimes embrassées 70, 71, 75
rimes plates 73, 75
Rich, Christopher 5
Roper, Alan, and Vinton Dearing:
Dryden, *Prose: History of the League* 124
Roscommon, Earl of (Wentworth Dillon):
Essay on Translated Verse 53–54
Rye House Plot 105

Scott, Clive:
The Riches of Rhyme 66–67, 68, 72
Shadwell, Thomas:
biography 38 n. 19
The Libertine 121–22
The Miser 34, 50, 79
Psyche 79
The Sullen Lovers 5, 28, 50
Shakespeare 4, 8
Salter, Denis, 'Acting Shakespeare in Postcolonial Space' 8–9
Shapiro, Barbara:
Political Culture and Political Communication in England 106
Sheridan, Thomas 180
song collections:
A Choice Collection of the Newest Songs 79
The New Academy of Complements 79
Playford, John: *Choice Songs and Ayres* 78–79
Spanish comedy 48
Spurr, John:
English Puritanism 1603–1689: 113
Swift, Jonathan:
Sentiments of a Church of England Man 123

Todd, Janet:
'Editing Aphra Behn' 144–45
Toleration Act 116

Translation Studies 8, 41–42, 44, 46
translation terms (in the early modern period) 45
Troupe du Roi 3
Turner, David:
Fashioning Adultery 86, 89, 95

Ungerer, Gustave:
'Thomas Shadwell's *The Libertine* (1675)': 122
unities 17–18, 179
unity of action 17–18
unity of interest 38 n. 20
unity of place 17
unity of time 17
urbanity 157–58, 168, 172–73

Vanbrugh, John:
The Cuckold in Conceit 87
Van Laun, Henri:
The Dramatic Works of Molière 159
Venuti, Lawrence:
domestication 42, 179
foreignization 43, 179
Viala, Alain:
La France galante 91, 95, 97
Visions of Sir Heister Ryley 177–78
Voiture, Vincent 79
Voltaire:
Lettres philosophiques 178
La Prude 176

Wadsworth, Philip S.:
Molière and the Italian Tradition 171
Walsham, Alexandra:
Providence in Early Modern England 111
Wars of Religion 105–06
Wilcox, John:
The Relation of Molière to Restoration Comedy 7, 177
William III:
and the Nonjuring schism 116
and Mary II 116
Worth-Stylianou, Valerie:
Practising Translation in Renaissance France 46
Wright, James:
biography 155 n. 30
translation of *Le Malade imaginaire* 145–47, 151, 176
Wycherley, William:
The Country Wife 87, 99, 176
and influence of Molière 8
The Plain Dealer 99, 176
time in France 3

zealotry 107–18, 179

www.ingramcontent.com/pod-product-compliance
Lightning Source LLC
Chambersburg PA
CBHW081259110426
42743CB00046B/3349